From Rebel to Rabbi

STANFORD STUDIES IN JEWISH HISTORY AND CULTURE

EDITED BY *Aron Rodrigue and Steven J. Zipperstein*

From Rebel to Rabbi

*Reclaiming Jesus and the
Making of Modern Jewish Culture*

Matthew Hoffman

STANFORD UNIVERSITY PRESS
STANFORD, CALIFORNIA
2007

Stanford University Press
Stanford, California

Published with the assistance of the Koret Foundation.

Printed in the United States of America on acid-free, archival-quality paper

Library of Congress Cataloging-in-Publication Data

Hoffman, Matthew (Matthew B.)

  From rebel to rabbi : reclaiming Jesus and the making of modern Jewish culture / Matthew Hoffman.
     p. cm. – (Stanford studies in Jewish history and culture)
  Includes bibliographical references and index.
  ISBN-13: 978-0-8047-5371-5 (cloth : alk. paper)
  ISBN-10: 0-8047-5371-7 (cloth)
  1. Jesus Christ–Jewish interpretations. 2. Jews–Identity. 3. Haskalah. 4. Jews–Historiography. 5. Yiddish literature–History and criticism. 6. Art, Jewish. 7. Judaism–Relations–Christianity. 8. Christianity and other religions–Judaism. I. Title.
BM620.H64 2007
232.9'06–dc22

                                               2006033702

Typeset by Bruce Lundquist in 10.5/14 Galliard

*This book is dedicated, with love and respect, to my first and greatest teacher:
my mother, Anita Hoffman Horan.*

Contents

Acknowledgments

This book began as a doctoral dissertation written under the guidance of my teacher, mentor, and friend, David Biale, who, from its earliest stages to its more recent incarnations, has provided me with innumerable comments and valuable insights. Also instrumental in guiding the early stages of this project was Naomi Seidman, whose ideas and editorial suggestions have helped this work immensely.

I also want to thank a number of teachers, colleagues, and friends who have provided ideas, comments, and feedback on various parts and at different stages of this project: Zachary Baker, Yael Chaver, Hannah Berliner Fischtal, Bluma Goldstein, Sheila Jelen, Eli Katz, Chana Kronfeld, Harriet Murav, Anita Norich, Avraham Noversztern, Irina Paperno, Benjamin Pollock, Stephen Prothero, Michael Weingrad, Seth Wolitz, and Steve Zipperstein. I am especially indebted to my friend and colleague David Shneer, who, from this project's inception, has read numerous different versions of it, and has provided me with incredibly helpful and insightful suggestions, often on short notice.

I owe special thanks to the students who have taken my Jewish Perspectives on Jesus seminar at the Graduate Theological Union, Berkeley, the University of California, Davis, and Franklin and Marshall College; those seminars allowed me to develop my thoughts and share my research, and my students provided me with multiple perspectives that have enriched my own understanding and strengthened my interpretation of certain texts and pieces of art.

I would like to thank Eliyah Arnon and Kevin Bryant for their valuable technical support; and the librarians and archivists at the National and Hebrew University Archive in Jerusalem for their assistance in the early stages of my research. I am also grateful to all of my editors at Stanford University Press, who have helped shepherd this book along through its various stages.

The dissertation that forms the basis of this book was written with the aid of a University of California Chancellor's Dissertation-Year Fellowship, and the Koret Jewish Studies Publication Program has awarded me a generous grant to assist with the publication of this book.

Finally, I would like to express my deepest gratitude to my wife, Tama, for the continual love and support she has given me since the outset of this project, without which I could not have done it.

From Rebel to Rabbi

Introduction

Jesus and the Jewish Question

> No, they ain't makin' Jews like Jesus anymore,
> We don't turn the other cheek the way they done before.
> They ain't makin' Jews like Jesus anymore,
> They ain't makin' carpenters who know what nails are for.
> Well, the whole damn place was singin' as I strolled right out the door
> "Lord, they ain't makin' Jews like Jesus anymore!"
> —Kinky Friedman (1974)

From the end of the eighteenth century, Jewish proponents of modernization, enlightenment (Haskalah), and reform began to reject the traditionally negative Jewish views of Jesus in favor of increasingly sympathetic appraisals of him. This complex and intriguing trend in modern Jewish history has come to be known by scholars as the Jewish reclamation of Jesus. Typically, definitions of this reclamation are limited to Jewish scholarship on Jesus and Christian origins, ignoring the ubiquity of this trend within modern Jewish culture as a whole. However, since its origins in the Berlin Haskalah circle of Moses Mendelssohn in the 1780s, countless rabbis and theologians, philosophers and historians, intellectuals and activists, poets and artists, have attempted to reclaim Jesus as a Jew in a profusion of different ways. Throughout the modern era Jews have appropriated Jesus as a malleable cultural symbol—a figure who can serve as the paradigm for a variety of religious, political, and cultural ideologies and positions. In fact, Jesus became a central symbol in virtually *all* forms Jews created in striving for a modern Jewish culture.

Most Jewish movements and many Jewish intellectuals refigured Jesus to fit into their own creation of a modern Jewish culture and identity. This means that for different thinkers Jesus reflected the particular ideology of their movements, often serving as a model for such a vision of Jewishness; he could be viewed variously as a Reform rabbi, a fallen prophet, a suffering martyr, a tormented artist, a Jewish socialist

1

revolutionary, or a Jewish nationalist. Jesus became a mirror through which Jewish thinkers could reflect their own particular ideological or spiritual vision; they could relate to Jesus on some level as a kindred spirit, proud or persecuted, nationalist or universalist, reformer or redeemer. As Jewish notions of self-understanding and self-definition changed and evolved, so too did Jewish perceptions of Jesus evolve to correspond to these new identities. In its essence, Jewish writing on Jesus tells us more about Jews than about Jesus. Thus, closely scrutinizing these multiple Jewish reclamations of Jesus provides us with a window onto how Jews have represented themselves in the modern world. By bringing together a variety of cultural sources this book seeks to explore the pervasiveness and centrality of the figure of Jesus to modern Jewish movements as diverse as Reform Judaism and Yiddish modernism.

Reclaiming the figure of Jesus functioned as an important part of modern Jews' attempts to secure a prominent place in Western civilization, to gain normalcy and even centrality in that civilization. Representing Jesus in a positive light served as a bridge between things Jewish and things Christian-Western and as a means of breaking down boundaries between the two. Embracing Jesus as a legitimate subject of Jewish discourse and cultural expression was a way of embracing the culture and civilization that had worshiped him as their Lord and Savior and at the same time persecuted Jews in his name. In this sense, Jewish intellectuals who were forging a new Jewish culture used the image of Jesus to simultaneously claim Western culture as their own and to show that Jesus was "just like they were." Differing images of Jesus often clashed with one another as these intellectuals seemed to be doing contradictory things—asserting their Jewishness while bringing themselves into Western culture. From the outset this process was beset with seemingly conflicting motives as the reclamation of Jesus has always involved Jews asserting his Jewishness and thus implicitly rejecting the Christian Jesus of Western culture. The Jesus that these Jews wrote about and portrayed was not the Christian Lord and Savior, but their ancient Jewish brother. Jewish writers have always disassociated the Jewish man, Jesus, from the Christian god, Christ, as they consistently tried to demonstrate the Jewish qualities of his life and teachings. This move effectively transferred ownership of the figure of Jesus, and all of the cultural patrimony that flowed from him, to the Jews. Furthermore, this re-Judaization of Jesus also equipped these modern Jews with a potent weapon for critiquing a still predominantly intolerant Christian world as they asserted that the Christians had misunderstood Jesus' intrinsically Jewish teachings and "kidnapped" their ancient Jewish brother, who now had to be returned home.

By focusing on changing Jewish approaches to the figure of Jesus we can lay bare the process by which Jews created modern alternatives to traditional modes of Jewish identity, thought, and culture. In this sense, I argue that the "Jesus question"—how do modern Jews relate to the figure of Jesus?—is really a microcosm of the "Jewish question"—how do modern Jews define themselves in relation to the general non-Jewish environment? If we understand the "Jewish question" to encompass the difficult challenges posed by the Enlightenment and the emancipation of the Jews in Europe, such as their integration into modern European society and culture, and the search for new forms of Jewish identity, then we can look at the various stands on the "Jesus question" as strategies for negotiating these challenges. Thus, traditionalist Jews who rejected the changes wrought by modernity and chose to remain apart from non-Jewish culture typically maintained deeply entrenched negative views of Jesus and all symbols of Christian culture. On the other hand, those Jews who accepted the basic premise of participating in non-Jewish society and culture while forging new forms of Judaism and Jewishness often reenvisioned Jesus in more sympathetic terms as part of this process. The "Jesus question" is so entangled in the larger "Jewish question" precisely because of Jesus' dual status as a figure who simultaneously embodies the West and is associated with all that is not Jewish, while historically originating as a Jewish figure, a product of the first-century Palestinian Jewish world. This essential duality of Jesus makes him an ideal border figure whom Jews can embrace as part of their move toward things Christian, while rendering him meaningful only within a Jewish interpretive framework.

The phenomenon of Jews reclaiming Jesus as one of their own presents us with a another way of understanding the process of Jewish modernization and integration into non-Jewish society. This modernization process has frequently been understood in terms of assimilation—the notion that the Jews transformed themselves and emulated their Christian neighbors in order to belong to "the West."[1] Indeed, many of the thinkers and writers I will discuss in this book were accused by their more traditional opponents of "Christianizing" or "currying favor with the Gentiles" when they embraced aspects of Western ("Christian") thought or culture. However, the Jewish reclamation of Jesus in all its various manifestations reveals a much more assertive and complex model of modernization and integration into non-Jewish culture, one best described as "transformative integration."[2] Rather than simply adopting Western culture and its core narratives as their own, modern Jewish theologians, historians, and writers revised certain master narratives of European civilization, such as the story of Jesus and the origins of Christianity, in order to create their own counternarratives and competing interpretations.

These modern Jews also significantly revamped premodern Jewish perceptions of Jesus as part of this process. Traditionally, Jews had depicted Jesus in disparaging and unfavorable terms. From the early years of Christianity, when the religio-cultural conflict between Jews and Christians commenced and quickly expanded, Jews saw Jesus as a Jewish heretic and rebel who had incited the antagonism that now raged between the two communities. Although references to Jesus in the Talmud are scarce, those that exist unanimously portray him as a rebellious and deviant figure, a sorcerer and enticer (*mesit*) who is rightfully executed by the Jewish Sanhedrin (Sanhedrin 43a). The Talmud envisions Jesus as a clever rabbinic disciple who strays from the proper path, initiates an idolatrous religion, and ultimately pays for his transgressions against his people by suffering eternal punishment in a seething pit of excrement (Sanhedrin 107b, Gittin 56b–57a).[3]

In the Middle Ages, as relations between Jews and Christians worsened, and Jews increasingly became victims of anti-Jewish discrimination and persecution at the hands of Christians, the figure of Jesus became etched in the Jewish collective consciousness as the primary emblem of Christian antipathy. Popular texts such as the *Toldot Yeshu* (Life of Jesus), which presents a carnivalesque parody of the Christian gospels, circulated widely from as early as the fifth century, and helped to establish such negative images of Jesus in the Jewish folk imagination. These narratives portrayed Jesus as a *mamzer* (illegitimate child), a wily trickster and magician, who impudently challenged his rabbis and led an insurrection against the Jewish establishment before being ultimately vanquished by the Jewish sages, led by Yehudah Ish Kariot (Judas Iscariot).[4]

As polemics and disputations between Christians and Jews continued to escalate throughout the Middle Ages, derisive images of Jesus proliferated in Jewish cultural discourse, by far outnumbering the few relatively tolerant portrayals that existed. Popular polemical anthologies such as the thirteenth-century *Nizzahon Yashan* (Old Polemic) systematically impugned Jesus' moral character in vulgar terms.[5] A "semantics of hatred"[6] developed in which Jews used puns and wordplay to express their disdain for Christianity's sacred figures and terms. Motivated by a combination of fear and contempt, Jews commonly refused to utter Jesus' name and he became known instead by such facetious designations and titles as *oto ha-ish* ("that man"), *ha-talui* ("the hanged one"), and *Yeshu ben Pandera* (which combines a corruption of the Hebrew name Yeshua with the surname Pandera and may have been an allusion to Jesus' illegitimate birth) and its Yiddish variant, *Yoyzl Pandrek* (a combination of the diminutive Yiddish name for Jesus—*Yoyzl*—with the surname *Pandrek*, a distortion of Pandera, meaning "Mr. Shit"). Legends and folk tales spread, depicting Jesus as a demonic bogeyman who was feared by Jewish children and mocked and despised by adults.[7] By the close of the Middle Ages, Jesus and the religious symbols associated with him—the cross, the crucifixion, the Madonna, etc.—had become emblems of fear and repulsion in the minds and hearts of most traditional Jews; he represented all that was other, alien, and dangerous.

In light of this premodern tradition, we can see that with the onset of modernity in the Jewish world, such tremendous changes took place in Jewish cultural discourse that, by the end of the nineteenth century, numerous Jews viewed Jesus proudly as a devout rabbi and paragon of moral piety. There developed a widespread fascination with the figure of Jesus among European Jewish intellectuals, as the Jewish process of modernization involved a reevaluation—indeed a reclamation—of Jesus of Nazareth. In an ironic sense, this sort of positive appropriation of Jesus was more challenging to Christians' cultural claims on him than all of the premodern Jewish polemics disparaging Jesus. Thus, the Jewish reclamation of Jesus reflects a more aggressive approach by Jews to participating in Western thought and culture than is usually acknowledged, and a far more complex engagement with non-Jewish cultural forms. If Roger Chartier's assertion that "the most pressing question inherent in cultural history today . . . is that of the different ways in which groups or individuals make use of, interpret and appropriate the intellectual motifs or cultural forms that they share with others,"[8] is true, then to understand modern Jewish identity and culture, we need to examine Jewish appropriations of Jesus.

Throughout this book, I present examples of Jewish thinkers, historians, writers, and artists who share in the civilization of the West, not by mocking or mimicking it, but by appropriating, and thereby transforming, some of its key intellectual motifs and cultural forms. What this amounted to was, on the one hand, an attempt to insert Jews into the heart of modern Western civilization by claiming the West as Jewish, rather than merely assimilating into the West by erasing all signs of Jewishness. On the other hand, this process also played a central role in the creation of a uniquely modern and predominantly secular Jewish culture by generating revised images of Jesus that came to symbolize contemporary Jewish movements and ideologies. It is a subtle distinction between "insertion" and assimilation, and the line between the two is often blurred beyond recognition. However, I believe that it is crucial for a richer and more nuanced understanding of Jewish cultural history in the modern period that we attempt to uncover the tension between these two paths toward modernization.

Some of Homi Bhabha's ideas about minority cultural construction can be helpful in theorizing about the role of the Jewish reclamation of Jesus as part of the Jewish process of modernization and integration within (secularized) Christian culture in Europe and America in the nineteenth and twentieth centuries. His notions of cultural hybridity and the importance of "in-between spaces" in carrying the burden of the "meaning of culture" are relevant and applicable to this trend. For Bhabha "in-between spaces" refer to a sort of no-man's-land of cultural space, which cannot be exclusively claimed by either the majority or the minority culture. He argues that "these in-between spaces provide the terrain for elaborating strategies of selfhood—singular or communal—that initiate new signs of identity, and innovative sites of collaboration, and contestation, in the act of defining the idea of society itself."[9] For Jews in search of a new place—a redefined cultural space—within

Western-Christian culture, the creation of a Jewish Jesus represents such an "in-between space" that allowed them to elaborate a new strategy of communal selfhood, a new site of identity as part of this transformation and realignment of Jews and Jewish culture. Bhabha suggests that "the social articulation of difference, from the minority perspective, is a complex, on-going negotiation that seeks to authorize cultural hybridities that emerge in moments of historical transformation."[10] For Jews, the Jewish reclamation of Jesus operated as an "articulation of difference"—a way to show how Jews are different than Christians while claiming not to be *too* different—that was simultaneously a product of cultural hybridity, while also legitimating the very process of cultural hybridity. Seeing the Jewish reclamation of Jesus as a practice of cultural hybridity and a new "strategy of selfhood" entails a more complicated understanding of modern Jewish identity, in which old models of "Jewish" and "Western" are transcended in order to create distinctly hybrid modern forms of identity and culture. In the following chapters I will uncover the myriad forms of this cultural hybrid: the Jewish Jesus.

In chapter 1, I begin with an overview of the "quest for the Jewish Jesus" in Western Europe and America from its origins with Moses Mendelssohn and the Berlin Haskalah to the "Jesus the Jew" trends in Jewish historiography and Reform theology, chiefly pioneered by Heinrich Graetz and Abraham Geiger. Whether they saw him as a rabbi, an Essene, or a prophet, these writers unanimously rejected the traditional Jewish view of Jesus as a rebellious heretic, and saw him as integrally related to Jews and Judaism. I attempt to contextualize these trends against the background of the "historical Jesus" movement in European Christian historiography in the eighteenth and nineteenth centuries. In addition I see them as part of the process of the Enlightenment and the emancipation of European Jewry and the beginnings of modern Jewish historiography and the *Wissenschaft des Judentums* (science of Judaism) movement. The assertion of the Jewishness of Jesus, which is the crux of Jewish historical writing on Jesus, functioned as an innovative form of anti-Christian polemics and criticism, as well as an important tool in the overall process of creating a modern Jewish identity, both individual and collective. As the Jews of the Haskalah, *Wissenschaft des Judentums*, and Reform movements redefined the essence and meaning of Judaism, Jewishness, and Jewish history for the modern age, they also reconceptualized the place of Jesus within the world of Judaism in ways that conformed to and even bolstered such new definitions. The figure of Jesus thereby played an important role in their ideological reconstruction of the Jewish past. This chapter helps to establish the widespread nature of this modern Jewish appropriation of Jesus and examines the deeper cultural significance it possesses.

Against this background, I proceed to investigate the Jewish reclamation of Jesus undertaken by East European Jewish intellectuals, writers, and artists, as it is only within the context of the trend of reclaiming Jesus in Western Europe that we can understand the unfolding of the "Jesus question" in modern Yiddish and Hebrew literary and intellectual circles in the first few decades of the twentieth century. In chapter 2, I look at two raging debates within the Jewish intellectual community between 1909 and 1913, one in the Yiddish socialist press, and one primarily in the Hebrew Zionist press, which illustrate how profoundly the issue of Jesus was bound up with ideological self-definition for various circles of Jewish intellectuals. Both controversies involved some of the leading figures in the Russian-Jewish intelligentsia and literary world, Chaim Zhitlovsky and S. Ansky in the first instance, and Ahad Ha-Am and Yosef Chaim Brenner in the latter. The question of how far modern Jewish intellectuals could or should go in embracing Jesus and Christianity as part of the Jewish cultural renaissance they were seeking was at the center of both of these debates, as testing the boundaries of Jewishness often involved taking a stand on Jesus and Christianity.

In chapters 3, 4, and 5, I focus on images of Jesus, Christ-like figures, and Christian symbolism in modernist Yiddish literature and the visual arts by employing close readings of Yiddish texts and works of art. I situate this phenomenon within the broader context of the creation of a secular Jewish culture as these images serve as lenses through which to view some of the central tensions within modern secular Jewish culture and identity. The works I analyze here reflect the dichotomous conflicts that confronted Jewish modernists, such as the struggles between universal and particular, Jewish and Christian, traditional and modern, and religious and secular. The creation of Jewish literature and art with Jesus at its center was simultaneously an explicit act of cultural appropriation and a bold declaration of Jewish cultural autonomy. Embracing Jesus provided these writers and artists with a means of entering into the Western canon and sharing the fruits of its creative treasures. Yet, it also allowed them to rebel against that canon by reclaiming Jesus in a way that separated him from Christianity and reinscribed him into Jewish history and culture. Using the figure of Jesus in such a manner also allowed these Jews to rebel against traditional elements within Jewish society in their attempt to imagine modern alternatives. The clusters of literary symbols and emblematic images that I explore represent important intellectual paradigms at the heart of modern, secular Jewish culture.

For such writers and artists as Sholem Asch, Uri Tsvi Grinberg, and Marc Chagall, refiguring Jesus as intrinsically Jewish and using Christological themes to express aspects of the modern Jewish experience were an integral part of creating a new and distinctive secular Jewish culture. Their rebellion against the theological-religious essence of Judaism included the creation of a Jewish Jesus that unhinged the figure of Jesus from his Christian theological moorings and allowed him to be part of an emerging secular Jewish cultural discourse. The Jewish writers and artists I examine in these three chapters were no longer solely interested in Jesus as a historical or theological figure; they became primarily fascinated with the image of the crucified Jesus for the symbolic meaning it could bring to their work as an emblem of martyrdom, failed redemption, tragedy, and suffering, both Jewish and universal. It was part of the modernist penchant for cultural hybridity and symbolic syncretism that was at the center of creating secular Jewish culture. However, in many ways, the central components of the reclamation of Jesus in the German Haskalah and Reform movements also permeated the portrayals of Jesus in Yiddish literature and the visual arts. For many Jewish writers and artists, the Jewish Jesus they created was a weapon against Christian anti-Semitism and cultural dominance; it served as a polemical thrust against Western-Christian culture by depicting Jesus as an inherently Jewish cultural symbol, and the Jews as the quintessential Christ-like victims of Christian violence and persecution.

I focus at length on the genres of literature and visual art because I am concerned with the creation of culture, and how the clusters of images, symbols, motifs, and themes employed in the creation of a modern, secular Jewish culture reflect the underlying ethos of that culture and mirror or convey its fundamental intellectual paradigms.

Since my focus is largely on the attraction to Jesus and Christian imagery among secular Jewish writers and artists, it is important to examine the modernist self-understanding and culture that they created. As part of explaining the appropriation of Christ-figures and Christian motifs, I will also examine the underlying poetics and cultural contours of Jewish modernism: the interest in cultural hybridity, in symbolic syncretism, and in blurring the boundaries between self and world, individual and community, Jew and Christian, traditional and modern, religious and secular, that formed such a large part of the Jewish modernists' identity and ideology. These Jewish writers and artists were constantly looking for new literary and visual symbols to represent the various crises and suffering that befell modern Jewry; they broke from explicitly theological responses to Jewish suffering, yet still utilized theological symbols, although these were totally divorced from their original religious context and framework. Poets and artists like Itzik Manger and Marc Chagall drew from rich storehouses of traditional symbols and images, tapping into the cultural consciousness of both Jews and Christians, in creating secular art and poetry that responded to uniquely modern problems.

My switch in focus from mainly German Jewish theologians and historians in the nineteenth century to Russian-Polish Jewish writers and artists in the twentieth century also reflects the shift away from theology as the defining essence of Jewish identity for East European Jewish intellectuals in favor of a cultural or secular nationalist self-definition. In particular, the literary and artistic concern with history and theology rests primarily in the realm of symbols, and, typically, the significational context of various traditional images and concepts is radically transformed by the modern artist and writer. For East European Jews at the beginning of the twentieth century especially, their relationship to traditional Jewish sources and theology was one of familiarity and rebellion; they were in a constant state of creative tension with these symbols and ideas, and frequently set out to subvert them. Subsequently, there often existed a strongly transgressive element in the use of Christ-figures and Christian themes among these Jewish literati and intellectuals. It has to be seen as part of their maverick stance as the avant-garde of the new Jewish culture; they dared to knock down boundaries and overturn taboos. Crossing borders and breaking down boundaries was an integral part of the Jewish intellectual's quest for a modern Jewish identity and culture, especially in literature and the arts, and embracing the figure of Jesus was part of this radical transformation of Jewish culture.

I also explore how modern Jews have adopted the crucifixion as an appropriate archetype—theological, historical, literary, and visual—for representing Jewish suffering, both ancient and contemporary, culminating with the Holocaust. In chapter 4, I bring together significant trends in modern Jewish historiography, theology, literature, poetry, and art in an effort to demonstrate the evolution and widespread permutations of such Christological notions of the Jewish historical experience, what I call the "passion of Jewish History." I elucidate how in these works Jesus' Christian identity as a vicarious sacrifice is inverted and he is portrayed as being essentially a Jewish martyr, meaningful only within a Jewish context, and paradigmatic of Jewish experience. Whether by identifying the suffering Christ with the entire nation, or with the individual Jew, all of the profound meaning and significance traditionally associated by Christians with Christ and his passion became rendered as uniquely Jewish. The works I consider in this chapter often combine a palpable anti-Christian polemic, if not rage, with a desire to recognize Jesus as the emblematic Jewish martyr, and thereby frame Jewish suffering in traditionally Christian terms. These authors and artists saw the Jews as a "people of Christs" whose history embodies the passion typically associated with Jesus' crucifixion. This chapter also explores some of the controversies elicited by this trend, as there were many Jews who reacted negatively to such an appropriation of the crucifixion as an emblem of Jewish martyrdom, especially during and after the Holocaust.

It must be stressed that the writers, artists, and intellectuals considered in this book often formed an avant-garde or constituted an intelligentsia; they typically removed themselves from popular Jewish attitudes and beliefs, as these were what they were rebelling against and often trying to transform. They formed an elite group within Jewish society to a certain extent, and consequentially, their ideals and ideas were not always adopted by the Jewish "masses." This is especially the case with the Jewish modernist embrace of Jesus, as this phenomenon did not spread widely in the popular Jewish imagination where, particularly among East European Jews, negative views of Jesus and Christianity still persisted well into the twentieth century. In this respect, the phenomenon of Jews reclaiming Jesus was for the most part limited to the progressive, intellectual, religious, and literary elite segments of Jewish society. However, it must be added that much of the cultural fruit of this trend trickled down, as it were, to the general segments of Jewish society, for, it must be remembered, the dividing lines between elite and popular, and between high and low culture in Jewish society were not too firmly drawn. Many of the modernist artists and writers I examine, as well as public intellectuals like Chaim Zhitlovsky and S. Ansky, had wide followings, as their work frequently appeared in the popular Yiddish press. Therefore, I attempt to trace the reactions that these works provoked in intellectual circles, as well as the broader historical and cultural issues that are reflected in them, in an effort to establish both the ubiquity and the limitations of the Jewish reclamation of Jesus in modern Jewish culture.

From Rebel To Rabbi

In his classic book chronicling the origins and development of European critical scholarship on Jesus, *The Quest of the Historical Jesus*, Albert Schweitzer makes the claim that "there is no historical task which so reveals a man's true self as the writing of a Life of Jesus . . . each individual created Him in accordance with his own character."[1] While the distinction between the Jesus of history and the Christ of dogma was at the heart of this quest for the historical Jesus among European scholars, Schweitzer observes that "each successive epoch of theology found its own thoughts in Jesus."[2] In other words, the "historical" Jesus served contemporary needs as theologians and historians tended to craft an image of him that was in their own likeness; various theories as to who Jesus was and what he taught helped to legitimate modern theologies and movements. Jesus functioned as a valuable device in the creation of modern religious identities and ideologies that reflected the ideals of the European Enlightenment with its emphasis on scientific inquiry and rational religion over against irrational Church dogmas and faith in the supernatural. By means of critical scientific scholarship, European theologians began to search for an image of Jesus that could be meaningful for enlightened Christians, that could serve them as a model of moral piety and religious perfection suitable for their own age.

Christians were not alone in this quest for the historical Jesus. For European Jews of the Enlightenment era and beyond, scholarly writing about the historical Jesus also became an important part of their own accommodations to modernity. Just like their Christian contemporaries, enlightened Jewish scholars and theologians began to craft an image of Jesus "in their own likeness," which for them meant, almost

13

without exception, depicting Jesus unequivocally as a faithful Jew. In response to the changing intellectual climate brought by the European Enlightenment—and its Jewish offshoot, the Haskalah—and the shifting socio-political realities resulting in their gradual Emancipation, European Jews began to confront a series of profoundly momentous questions about their changing place in the world: What is the new position of Jews and Judaism in modern European society? How are Jewishness and Judaism now defined? How can one be both Jewish and Western at the same time? How is the relationship between Jews and Christians and Judaism and Christianity to be redefined? Accordingly, as Arnold Eisen has observed, "Jewish culture in all its forms in the modern period has been devoted to describing a place for Jews in the new social, political, and economic orders and to imagining forms of Judaism (religious or not) suitable to that place."[3]

One of the significant ways in which modernizing Jews have attempted to "describe a place" for Jews and Judaism in the modern world has been by reclaiming Jesus as a Jew; their new approach to Jesus transformed him from a figure who had been associated with Jewish marginalization and oppression in European Christian society into a vehicle for their own self-transformation and integration into that very society. Indeed, the Jewish reclamation of Jesus aided in the process of redefining Judaism and in the repositioning of Jews and Judaism vis-à-vis Christians and Christianity in a plethora of ways. For one, stressing Jesus' Jewishness was a way for Jewish scholars to promote Jewish integration into Christian society since they were essentially saying "we're not as other as you think, since your founder was—one of us."[4] Moreover, claiming Jesus as Jewish helped combat Christian anti-Semitism by defusing much of the Christian basis for anti-Semitism, which traditionally drew on the opposition of Jesus to Judaism.

However, Jewish writers who wrote about Jesus as a historical Jew did more than simply strive for acceptance within Christian society, they also tried to improve the status of Judaism in the eyes of both Christians and Jews. Perhaps above all, their scholarly views promoted Jewish cultural dominance within Christian European society by asserting that Jesus' teachings came from Judaism, thereby implying that "they got everything from us" and that "Christian history is back-

ground to Jewish history, not the other way around."[5] Thus, reinterpreting the figure of Jesus as a Jew, and viewing him in a sympathetic
manner, became a way for modernizing Jews to try to acquire for themselves a more rooted place in modern European society. It provided
them with a means of integrating both Jews and Judaism more reso-
lutely into the culture of the West by illustrating that culture's Jewish
roots. The reclamation of Jesus as a Jew, and his teachings as inherently
Jewish, helped to locate Judaism as central to Western civilization, and
many even claimed that Judaism was the foundation of that civilization
along with, or in place of, Christianity. In this way, "the negative Jesus
of medieval Jewish polemics, created in self-defense, now became the
positive Jesus of modern apologetics, created in an act of Jewish self-
assertion."[6] The creation of a Jewish Jesus allowed Jewish advocates of
Emancipation and integration to elaborate new "strategies of selfhood"
both outwardly and internally.

Schweitzer's claim that "each successive epoch of theology found its
own thoughts in Jesus" applies equally to modern Jewish writing on
Jesus. Reinterpreting the past as a way of asserting modern alternatives
to tradition was a dominant feature of the Haskalah movement, and the
turn to modernity in general within the Jewish world, and Jesus played
an important role in this ideological reconstruction of the Jewish past.
As Jews of the Haskalah and its successor movements redefined the
essence and meaning of Judaism, Jewishness, and Jewish history for
the modern age, they also reconceptualized the place of Jesus within
the world of Judaism in ways that conformed to and even embodied
such new definitions. Their new assessments of Jesus became an integral part of their various programs for transformation of Jewish life. In
the many different works written by modern Jewish intellectuals incorporating Jesus in a positive way, we see this strategy at play. For Moses
Mendelssohn (1729–86), the leading figure of the Berlin Haskalah,
arguing the Jewishness of Jesus functioned as an apologetic for continued Jewish religious observance—in a slightly modified guise—and
was part of his argument for the inclusion of Jews in European civil
society. The leading scholars of Reform Judaism in nineteenth-century
Germany, Abraham Geiger and Samuel Hirsch, fashioned an image of
Jesus that could serve as a model for the contemporary Reform Jew in

a number of ways. Geiger's historical conception both of Jesus, and of the Pharisaic school to which he claims Jesus belonged is highly revisionist. For him, the Pharisees were not the rigid legalists whom Christian scholars had portrayed so negatively for centuries. They were also not the progenitors of the legally stringent, narrow-minded Orthodox rabbis with whom Geiger quarreled. Rather, the Pharisees, and by extension Jesus, were liberal, open-minded interpreters of the law, true precursors of the Reform rabbis of Geiger's own day. For Geiger and the majority of his Reform contemporaries and disciples, Jesus was the prototypical Reform Jew. Invariably, these Reform writers stressed Jesus' emphasis on ethical doctrines and social action and his flexibility in observing the *halakha* (Jewish law); like the Reform rabbis of their day, they depicted Jesus as expressing an ethical and prophetic type of Judaism rather than a cultic and legalistic one.

The exact image of Jesus that emerges from these various works depends on the precise religious/ideological orientation of the writer creating that image. In effect, as Jonathan Brumberg-Kraus has claimed, "there is nothing else but ideology in the Jewish study of Christian origins."[7] This formulation applies not only to writers within the Reform movement of the nineteenth century, but also to representatives of varying Jewish movements in the modern period, each relating to Jesus in a way that is relevant and meaningful within the particular ideological context of the movement concerned. In historical studies from the nineteenth and early twentieth centuries by I. M. Jost, Joseph Salvador, Heinrich Graetz, Simon Dubnow, Joseph Klausner, and many others, asserting the Jewishness of Jesus and the Jewish roots of Christianity is both part of the process of (re)claiming the writing of history as a legitimate Jewish pursuit, and of declaring Jewish history as central to the history of the West in general. Moreover, Zionist thinkers like Klausner (as well as other Zionist/Israeli historians) presented Jesus as an ardent Jewish nationalist, and sought to reclaim him as a "native son" of Israel, part of a great Jewish national legacy that belonged to Jesus' own people—the Jews. For Jewish socialists like Moses Hess in Germany, and a whole generation of Jewish revolutionary socialists in Russia in the 1860s, 1870s, and 1880s, Jesus was seen as a proto-socialist whose teachings, the Socialist Gospel, provided them as Jews with a natural link to the socialist movement of their day. Also as cosmopolitans who espoused a more universal way of looking at the world and often worked side by side with Christians, embracing Jesus, even their own particular Judaized conception of him, was a means of attaining common ground with their Christian comrades. These diverse Jewish reclamations of Jesus became a constitutive feature of the larger process of carving out a new self-definition, a new identity, and a new essence, for the modern Jew.

As Alan Mittelman has astutely observed, the reclamation of Jesus that formed part of this process of modern Jewish self-definition has been fundamentally linked to the emergence of historical consciousness that inspired modern Jewish historiography: "[T]he Jewish rediscovery of Jesus . . . is rooted in a new appreciation of Jewish history. . . . The 'homecoming of Jesus,' therefore, is an aspect of the modern Jew's act of historically oriented self-discovery, or of self-recovery. It is an aspect of the modern Jew's search for essence and definition."[8]

Indeed, the earliest Jewish authors who began to focus on Jesus in the modern period did so in the context of a nascent Jewish historiography, which was influenced both by developments in general European historiography and by the new atmosphere of Enlightenment and Emancipation. In the nineteenth century, I. M. Jost, Abraham Geiger, and Heinrich Graetz (and, to a lesser extent, Joseph Salvador) included assessments of Jesus within larger projects of writing comprehensive histories of the Jewish people. They were all affected by the general German cultural environment in which the writing of history was gaining a new importance, namely historicism—the movement to chronicle past events "as they actually happened" ("wie es eigentlich gewesen ist"); specifically, the scholarly impulse to reconstruct the "historical Jesus" that arose in Western Europe at the end of the eighteenth century had a powerful and lasting impact on the Jewish historical recovery of Jesus. As Samuel Sandmel suggests, the focus of Protestant scholarship on the Jesus of history "made some Jews feel compelled to give serious attention to him, and, indeed, there arose in some of them the tendency which has properly been called the 'Jewish reclamation' of Jesus."[9]

The primary Jewish manifestation of these new developments in European scholarship and historiography coalesced in the *Wissenschaft des Judentums* (science of Judaism) movement—a major by-product of both historicism and the Haskalah—which originated in Berlin in 1819 at the inception of a long period of reaction against Jewish emancipation within German/Prussian society. This movement's desire to treat Judaism as a legitimate academic subject worthy of historical exploration must be seen as part of an overall plan of integrating Judaism into general Western culture and history, and making Judaism seem less foreign to Christian scholars. Indeed, this "new historiography—based on the respectable and objective methodology of *Wissenschaft*—would be their [the *maskilim*'s] principal weapon to battle the venomous calumny against Judaism . . . *Wissenschaft des Judentums*, in other words, would facilitate Jewry's integration and honorable assimilation into Europe."[10] Furthermore, this turn toward the scientific exposition of Jewish history can be viewed as "a collective act of translation, a sustained effort to cast the history, literature, and institutions of Judaism in Western categories," and render "the Jewish experience in terms comprehensible to the Western mind."[11] As such, the link between the Jewish turn to history and the Jewish recovery of Jesus allows us to situate the trend of the Jewish reclamation of Jesus within this broader attempt to integrate and assimilate Jews within the culture of Western Europe.

However, besides facilitating a new mode of integration into Western civilization, the burgeoning historical awareness expressed in the Haskalah in general, and in the *Wissenschaft des Judentums* movement in particular, also effectively served to increase Jewish pride—part of the "historically oriented self-discovery" that Mittelman speaks of. As Ismar Schorsch notes, "the heady recovery of the Jewish past filled Jews with pride and self-confidence. Their growing appreciation for the pathos of Jewish history, for the power of Jewish values and ideas, and for the persistence of the Jewish people countered the blandishments of assimilation."[12] This assertion not only reveals the importance of writing Jewish history as a means of creating Jewish self-esteem and a sense of belonging in modern Western civilization, but it also suggests that this process worked as a countermeasure to assimilation, functioning as a justification for continued Jewish existence in modern European society. However, somewhat ironically, this type of Jewish scholarship was also intended to promote acceptance of Jews by Christian society in order to accelerate assimilation. Proponents of Jewish *Wissenschaft* believed that the academic study of Judaism by Jews would serve as a corrective to previous Christian scholarship on Judaism, which had propagated anti-Jewish sentiments in Christian society, and would thereby help to secure Jewish emancipation and civil rights.

The presence of chapters on Jesus and the origins of Christianity within works of Jewish history emerging from *Wissenschaft* circles, especially the generally positive treatment accorded Jesus in comparison to premodern Jewish accounts of him, affirms the paradoxical nature of the *Wissenschaft des Judentums* movement. On the one hand, it bespeaks an attempt to "integrate and assimilate" Jewish history into the canon of the West. However, as is the case with most manifestations of modern Jewish writing on Jesus, the direction of this assimilation and integration is ironically inverted. Despite vastly different theories as to the precise nature and position of the historical Jesus, these Jewish historians all situate Jesus firmly within the context of Jewish history. His story is part of the Jewish story, and his life and teachings can only be explained within the context of the various Jewish sects and schools of thought extant in first-century Palestine. This assumption seems to contradict the primary goal of assimilation and acculturation by the *Wissenschaft des Judentums* and Haskalah in general, since, in effect, the history of Christianity is portrayed as flowing out of Judaism. Reclaiming Jesus as part of Jewish history, not as a traitor or a rebel, and asserting the Jewishness of his life and teachings were a way of Judaizing Christianity and, by extension, Western civilization. Jews could integrate into the culture of the West not by grafting themselves on to the fully grown tree of Western civilization, but by showing Judaism to be the seed from which this civilization sprang. In many ways this historiographic trend was strongly permeated with a modern form of anti-Christian polemics, which was part and parcel of the Jewish reclaiming of Jesus from the outset. This polemical subtext reflected the ongoing religio-cultural conflict that persisted between Christianity and Judaism, even in the age of Enlightenment and Reason.

Despite the nascent mood of tolerance that existed in Europe, in the writings of various Jewish historians, philosophers, and rabbis from this period, the assertion of the Jewishness of Jesus is often accompanied with the implication that Christians, from Paul on, have misinterpreted and misappropriated Jesus' intrinsically Jewish teachings. Most of them claim that Jesus' teachings, while noteworthy, were neither unique nor radically deviant from the normative Jewish teachings of his day. According to this view, all Christian teachings and doctrines that can be authentically traced to Jesus were part of one or another normative strand of Judaism, and the remaining Christian teachings were mere inventions of Paul and the founders of the early Christian Church. This implied that those who truly followed the teachings of Jesus would be closer in spirit to contemporary Jews than Christians, and that the remainder of Christians adhered to a religion that was drastically different than the one adhered to by their own "Lord and Savior." These writers further posited that the historical legacy of Christian persecution and violence against Jews was the work of these inauthentic Christians, who were merely "baptized pagans" and not true followers of Jesus. Jesus himself, a loyal and observant Jew, would never condone such behavior against his brothers and sisters, and if he were alive today, he would throw his lot in with the Jews, and not their Christian persecutors.[13] This stridently polemical tone was not the only component of the Jewish reclamation of Jesus, but it existed in all of the various genres and media this reclamation entailed, from the writings of Moses Mendelssohn in the eighteenth century through the middle of the twentieth century in the fiction of Sholem Asch and the paintings of Marc Chagall.

However, this component cannot be regarded as separate from the assimilationist-integrationist aspect of the Haskalah, as the whole project of integrating Jews and Jewish culture into the West involved a continual negotiation of the age-old Jewish-Christian conflict that existed on many different levels: religious, political, economic, social, and so on. In its earliest form, this negotiation, which can be best observed in the writings of Mendelssohn, involved Jews justifying the continued existence of a slightly modified and modernized traditional Judaism within the context of full Jewish civil participation in all walks of Christian society. As part of this process, Mendelssohn and others began advancing sympathetic views of Jesus, whom they conceived of in wholly Jewish terms. Later writers advanced considerably bolder and occasionally more radical evaluations of Jesus than Mendelssohn and the early *maskilim*, yet the nature of their project remained essentially akin.

Moses Mendelssohn's writings concerning the figure of Jesus are consistently informed by his desire to vindicate the Jews against what he saw as specious Christian assertions regarding Jewish attitudes toward Jesus and Christianity; he himself had often been charged with harboring contemptuous views of Jesus. A few years after Mendelssohn's Christian friend and fellow supporter of the Enlightenment, Gotthold Ephraim Lessing, published a radical critique of the New Testament (*Fragments*, 1778) by the Dutch scholar Hermann Samuel Reimarus, Mendelssohn was accused of being the author. Christian scholars critical of Lessing's anonymously published *Fragments* implied that Jews would enjoy the central arguments of the *Fragments* as they would "be more useful to them than even their *Toledot Yeshu*" [14] in bolstering their rejection of Jesus and Christianity. Others maintained that even if Mendelssohn himself was not the author, Jews must have been responsible for authoring the *Fragments*, or that possibly it was a revised version of an older Jewish book blaspheming Jesus. In his correspondence with the Swiss theologian Johann Caspar Lavater, Mendelssohn was forced to defend and explain his position on Jesus and Christianity, and felt compelled to rebut Lavater's and other Christians' claims that "the vilification of Jesus was an essential part of the Jewish tradition." [15] In asserting his positive assessment of Jesus in a letter to Lavater, Mendelssohn makes it clear that he, as well as other Jews, cannot accept the divine Christ of Christian doctrine. While demonstrating to Lavater that some Jews go even farther than refraining from blasphemies concerning Jesus, he writes: "I also know many a Jew who, like me, go a step further and, basing themselves upon the statements of Christian testimonies (for, I repeat, we have no reliable Jewish ones), acknowledge the innocence and moral goodness of that founder's [Jesus'] character." [16] This type of warm praise of Jesus' character typifies the approach of Mendelssohn and many of his peers in the Haskalah. Above all, for Mendelssohn the historical Jesus, divested of Christian dogma about him, could be embraced by Jews of the Enlightenment as proof to their Christian contemporaries that even as practicing Jews they maintained no inherent enmity toward Jesus or Christianity, and thus they should not be barred from full participation in Christian society.

As part of his rejection of the notion that Jews must abandon, or at least seriously alter, their religion, or be forever estranged from Christians and Christian society, Mendelssohn argued that Jesus himself was just as Jewish as the Jews of eighteenth-century Germany. In his magnum opus, *Jerusalem* (1783), in which he sets out to prove that traditional Judaism need not contradict modern European intellectual or societal and legal norms, Mendelssohn depicts Jesus as a model rabbinic Jew as part of his justification for continued Jewish observance of the rabbinic law:

> Jesus of Nazareth was never heard to say that he had come to release the House of Jacob from the law. Indeed, he said, in express words, rather the opposite; and what is still more, he himself did the opposite. Jesus of Nazareth himself observed not only the law of Moses but also the ordinances of the rabbis; and whatever seems to contradict this in his speeches and acts ascribed to him appears to do so only at first glance . . . the rabbinic principle evidently shines forth from his entire conduct as well as the conduct of his disciples in the early period.[17]

Mendelssohn's claim that Jesus was an observant rabbinic Jew was a bold departure from both established Jewish and Christian conceptions of Jesus.[18] For Mendelssohn, envisioning Jesus as a loyal rabbi fit squarely within the context of his argument for the acceptance of Jews qua Jews in Christian society; it rested on the assumption that if like-minded Christians could also view Jesus in his "true" historical setting as a Jewish rabbi, they would have no basis for discriminating against Jesus' descendants, the Jews of their own time. This illustrates just how much pressing social concerns affected Jewish characterizations of Jesus. Mendelssohn's socio-political agenda of Emancipation is made even clearer in the subsequent paragraph of *Jerusalem*:

> And you, dear brothers and fellow men, who follow the teaching of Jesus, should you find fault with us for doing what the founder of your religion did himself, and confirmed by his authority? Should you believe that you cannot love us in return as brothers and unite with us as citizens as long as we are outwardly distinguished from you by the

ceremonial law, do not eat with you, do not marry you, which, as far as we can see, the founder of your religion would neither have done himself nor permitted us to do?[19]

This was not the first time Mendelssohn explicitly linked positive Jewish views of Jesus with the issues of Emancipation and Jewish-Christian reconciliation. In a letter to the Crown Prince of Brunswick-Wolfenbüttel in 1770 Mendelssohn proposed that Jews and Christians could join together under a religion that would embrace both faiths. He believed that this could only happen "if Christianity would divest itself of its irrational dogmas and would agree that its founder had never freed the Jews from the Mosaic law, [and] Judaism in turn would recognize Jesus as a 'prophet and a messenger of God,' sent 'to preach the holy doctrine of virtue and its rewards in another life to a depraved human race.'"[20] Here, Mendelssohn implies that a positive Jewish assessment of Jesus would be part of a quid pro quo agreement in which Christians would similarly modify their views of Judaism as well as rendering Christian dogma more rational, and hence acceptable, in (enlightened) Jewish eyes. Thus, Mendelssohn began to free Jesus from the realm of taboo and stigmatization that had dominated how premodern Jews conceived of and related to him; he even envisioned Jesus as a harbinger of Enlightenment who preached "the holy doctrine of virtue," one of the central tenets of Enlightenment thought. His position on Jesus set the stage for later generations of enlightened Jewish intellectuals to claim Jesus as part of their arguments for the integration of Jews into European society, and, moreover, for asserting the centrality of Jews, Judaism, and Jewish history in Western civilization.

The Reclamation Begins: Pioneering Jewish Accounts of Jesus

Mendelssohn's sympathetic appraisal of Jesus caught on as the floodgates of Western learning and secular knowledge that opened to European (especially German and French) Jews in the early decades of the nineteenth century spurred the coalescence of the *Wissenschaft des Judentums* movement, which attempted to reconcile "Jewish" and "Western" categories of knowledge. The Verein für Cultur und Wissenschaft der Juden (Society for the Culture and Science of the Jews) was founded in Berlin in 1819 in the aftermath of the anti-Semitic "Hep! Hep!" riots in Prussia with the goal of holding up Jewish history to the penetrating light of objective scientific scholarship and thereby exonerating Jews and Judaism from further spurious attacks. Shortly thereafter, Isaak Markus Jost (1793–1860) composed and published his nine-volume history *Geschichte der Israeliten* (*History of the Israelites*, 1820–28), spanning from the Maccabean era to 1815, as the first major historical work to emerge from the new *Wissenschaft* movement, and the first comprehensive work on Jewish history written by a Jew in a European language. Jost was a Jewish teacher in Berlin and a former member of the *Culturverein* who had become a harsh critic. Jost, as Schorsch claims, had "a strong desire to free Jewish history from its bondage to Christian theology."[21] Yet he was also motivated in his scholarship by a strong antipathy to rabbinic Judaism that pervaded his historical writing. He conceived of the history of rabbinic Judaism as one of decline and depicted it in a wholly negative manner. It is important to note that Jews such as Jost, Geiger, and others who took part in the revolution of *Wissenschaft des Judentums* often set out to criticize rabbinic Judaism from an insider's perspective while simultaneously refuting negative Christian scholarly treatments of rabbinic Judaism. The polemical and the apologetic thrusts of the Haskalah/*Wissenschaft* project effectively worked side by side.

Jost's comprehensive history of the Jews was significant in a number of ways, and was notable for its extensive use of non-Jewish sources and its reliance on Josephus. Jost's programmatic critique of rabbinic Judaism comes closest to the charge leveled by Gershom Scholem against the *Wissenschaft* movement that its aim was to give Judaism a "decent burial."[22] Jost was supported by many of Mendelssohn's radical disciples in Berlin, and espoused a strongly assimilationist agenda, often doubting the validity of a continued Jewish existence in enlightened Europe. He saw pristine Christianity as a "pure and purged Judaism" while he claimed that contemporary Judaism was only a "debased Christianity."[23] In his history, Jost "dwelt at length on what he regarded as the flaws and defects of Judaism . . . he had internalized much of the secular critique of Judaism . . . his history amounted to a pedantic and passionless plea for the interment of rabbinic Judaism."[24] His presentation of Jesus and the origins of Christianity in his *Geschichte der Israeliten* tended to glorify Jesus in contradistinction to the surrounding "degenerate rabbinic culture."[25] Unlike later Jewish scholars, Jost adhered more closely to Christian accounts of Jesus' character and teachings and depicted the corrupt state of the Judaism of Jesus' lifetime, especially perpetuating Christian-engendered negative stereotypes of the Pharisees in his account of first-century Judaism.[26] In volumes 1 and 3 of Jost's history, in which he deals with the Pharisees and the rise of Christianity, he trenchantly denounces the Pharisees, holding them responsible for the death of Jesus and indicting rabbinism in general as the major harmful influence on postbiblical Judaism. The first product of Jewish *Wissenschaft*'s attempt to treat Jesus as part of Jewish history failed to depart significantly from prevailing Christian conceptions of Jesus. Yet, Jost's very inclusion of Jesus in his comprehensive history of the Jews must be seen as a radical first step.

Unlike Jost, Joseph Salvador (1796–1873) presented Jesus as a Jew firmly planted in the context of first-century Judaism, who was in no way superior to the Pharisees. Salvador was a French Jew of Sephardic ancestry with a Catholic mother who nonetheless remained loyal to Judaism. Although Salvador identified himself as a Jew he received no traditional Jewish education, and considered the Bible as the essence of Judaism. Salvador was a physician, and never trained formally as a historian. His interest in Jewish history in general and Jesus in particular must be understood as part of his affinity for French liberalism and rationalism, which informed much of his thought and scholarship. Like the proponents of *Wissenschaft des Judentums* in Germany, Salvador was infected by the scientific/scholarly zeitgeist and "devoted himself to interpreting Judaism and Jewish history in the spirit of nineteenth-century rationalism."[27] An even more important force driving Salvador's historical impulse was his desire to use history as a vehicle for promoting Jews and Judaism as belonging, and even integral, to French/European society. His historiography epitomized modern Jewish apologetics par excellence, and thereby reflected the program of the *Wissenschaft des Judentums*.

Salvador's early historical works, also inspired by the same anti-Semitic outbreaks in Germany in 1819 that galvanized the formation of the original *Wissenschaft des Judentums* movement there, were motivated by the desire to secure equal rights for Jews. He set out to accomplish this in his first book in which he explored the Mosaic system of law in 1822,[28] by demonstrating that Moses had founded the first republic and that a perfect social order had existed in ancient Israel. Salvador argued that the "Mosaic state was a paradigm of the ideal, rational modern state,"[29] positing that the essence of pure "Mosaism" was represented by the "quaternity" of principles that corresponded to the modern values of liberty, equality, universalism, and the alliance of peoples. In this respect, Salvador boldly suggested that Jews and Judaism (or Mosaism) provided the founding principles for the modern universalist era, a theory that ran counter to the dominant notion in Christian scholarship (traditional and modern) that Judaism was obsolete and anachronistic. He claimed that this entitled modern Jews to equal rights, and even to "a place of honor in democratic societies."[30] Paula Hyman observes that Salvador's interest in Jewish history was thus motivated by "a fascination with the religious-national ideas of Judaism and with the Jewish contribution to civilization, which he elaborated as a basis for Jewish self-esteem."[31] In fact, Salvador himself freely admitted that one of the primary aims of his research on ancient Jewish history was to "render them [the Jews, and thus himself] honor."[32]

Salvador, along with many contemporaneous and subsequent Jewish scholars, believed that the way to secure for Jews "a place of honor in democratic societies" was to prove through scholarly research that all of the noble and glorious elements of modern Western society and civilization, including Jesus and Christianity, stem from Judaism. Nahum Glatzer maintains that such inflated ideas about the role of Judaism in world history "helped the modern Jew to overcome his feeling of isolation in the new world."[33] In this respect, Salvador, more than Mendelssohn, was the first modern Jewish scholar to incorporate Jesus in his attempt to assert the primacy and centrality of Jewish history, Judaism, and the "Jewish idea" in the structure of Western civilization. Salvador's historical study of ancient Judaism and the origins of Christianity was informed by the desire to redraw the map of Western civilization with Judaism at the center rather than the margins.

In 1838 Salvador set out to offer a scholarly interpretation of the life and teachings of Jesus with his book *Jésus-Christ et sa doctrine* (*Jesus and His Teachings*), which is considered to be the first modern history of Jesus written by a Jew (not to be seriously followed until Joseph Klausner in 1922). Salvador's study came just three years after D. F. Strauss's groundbreaking work of New Testament scholarship, *The Life of Jesus* (1835), and must be considered as Salvador's attempt to offer a Jewish counterview to Strauss's book, as well as to the plethora of popular, liberal Christian accounts of Jesus' life that were being produced at the time. Salvador portrays Jesus essentially as a loyal Jew who never intended to start a new religion, and depicts Christianity as a confluence of Jewish and pagan influences. Salvador employed the method—soon to become a trend among nineteenth- and twentieth-century Jewish scholars—of finding the origins of Jesus' teachings solely in contemporaneous Jewish sources, and emphasizing the Jewish historical context of the gospels. Also, like so many Jewish historians writing about Jesus in the years that followed, Salvador "traced the ethical elements [of Jesus' teaching] to Judaism and the impurities to pagan sources."[34] Salvador was essentially arguing that everything that was admirable about Jesus' teachings was adopted from the normative Jewish concepts of the time, while the less admirable aspects of his teaching were the product of his embrace of various sectarian and pagan beliefs. In opposition to Christian scholars, as well as to Jost, Salvador depicted the normative Judaism of Jesus' lifetime (Pharisaism) as superior to the religious teachings of Jesus, and as encompassing them. In this way we can see how "in his presentation of the early development of Christianity, Salvador was able to swell Jewish pride by reinterpreting the role of the Jews in the story of Jesus and by reasserting the superiority of their social and religious morality."[35]

Unlike most later scholars, Salvador asserted that Jesus himself was responsible for the break between Christianity and Judaism, as his teachings and actions went beyond the pale of normative acceptability; his attempt to blend Jewish and pagan doctrines went too far. Salvador posited that Jesus was an Essene, which served to explain some of his "otherworldly," nonlegalistic concerns, as portrayed in the New Testament (which Salvador basically accepted as a historical source for Jesus' life and teachings). Salvador claims that Jesus' Essene beliefs in individual morality and the insignificance of the Law, his emphasis on resurrection, and his identification of himself with God alienated him from the Pharisees and the majority of the Jews.[36] He maintains that Jesus did indeed challenge the Pharisees, and that the Jewish trial and subsequent execution of Jesus were totally justified.[37] Salvador's stance is atypical compared to the preponderance of subsequent liberal Jewish views on the trial of Jesus and on the opposition to Jesus among contemporaneous Jewish groups like the Pharisees. Yet, despite his criticism of certain aspects of Jesus' ministry, Salvador argues that "hardly a single commandment has been attributed to the individual inspiration of Jesus which does not stem from Jewish ethical teachings; this is true both in idea and form."[38] In the final analysis, for all of his failings Jesus was still to be thought of as a son of the Hebrew people—Salvador preferred the term Hebrew to Jewish—whose teachings (at least the positive ones) sprang from Jewish soil. His was an act of reclaiming Jesus as a Jew without fully exonerating him, an important early step in what was to be an ongoing process throughout the century.

As part of his attempt to demonstrate the fundamental Jewishness of Jesus and his teachings, Salvador argued that the "Hebrew people played an important role as a symbol of suffering humanity, as a Christ people" and that "the evangelists themselves wanted to realize on a new level in the passion of Jesus the long and terrible passion of the Hebrew people."[39] This implies that not only was Jesus' doctrine a product of Jewish tradition, but the writers of the gospels drew their inspiration in constructing the passion narrative of Jesus from the passion history of the Jews. (It seems likely that Salvador's theory was anachronistic in that he was reading the history of Jewish suffering in medieval Europe back into the time of the writing of the gospels.) With this theory, Salvador became the first modern Jewish thinker to explicitly appropriate the symbolism of Christ's passion in order to elucidate the meaning of Jewish history, a salient example of the assertive type of assimilation that was often part of the strategy of integration advocated by modernizing Jews like Salvador, Geiger, and even Mendelssohn himself.

With the argument that the Jews were the original "Christ people," the Christians of history are supplanted by the Jews. Jesus, along with the core symbols of Christianity, are proven to be intrinsically Jewish. In this spirit, Salvador maintained that the Jews have made the most significant contribution to the foundation of Western civilization, and that Christianity was, in fact, "an inferior deviation from Mosaism."[40]

Furthermore, Salvador contended that the "continued passion of the Jews throughout history bore witness before the world, not to the triumph of Christianity, but to the fact that 'there was reason to await an entirely new era,' a new messianic age."[41] Salvador's understanding of the Jews as a suffering Christ people responsible for establishing the fundamental principles of Western civilization became linked to his utopian vision of the future. He asserted that a messianic transformation would occur that would usher in a new, universal religious order in the world predicated on core Jewish/Mosaic ideals. Salvador "thus attempted to prove that Christianity, the religion of the established order, had to be supplanted by the liberal faith of an eternal Mosaism, which would restore nationalism and concern for social justice."[42] Salvador's new utopian messianic vision was informed by what I call "enlightened Jewish triumphalism," a phenomenon that subsequently pervaded the majority of Jewish works on Jesus and Christianity. As liberal Jews like Salvador and his peers sought to "describe a place" for Jews and Judaism in the new social order, they often did so at the expense of Christianity. In this vein, Ismar Schorsch observes that "the tragedy of the Jewish predicament was that to make a case for continued group survival inevitably entailed denigrating the faith of the very society into which Jews sought to integrate. Judaism's right to survive could only be established at the expense of Christianity."[43]

Moreover, this type of enlightened Jewish triumphalism was a device used by modernizing Jews to justify—both to Christians and to themselves—their programs of reform, assimilation, integration, and abandonment of traditional Judaism. In response to strong criticism of such sweeping transformations of traditional Jewish life, they made the claim that they were not making Judaism more Christian, but reclaiming Judaism's proper place at the heart of Christianity and, by extension, Western civilization. The whole enterprise of "redrawing the map of Western civilization" with the Jews at the center was a means of carving out a niche for modern Jews in a world that seemed foreign and, at times, hostile. It was a new myth of Jewish history, although not entirely fabricated, that supported the modern Jew's attempt to integrate into the non-Jewish world all around. The alien was made familiar, the West was rendered Jewish.

In the writings of Samuel Hirsch (1815–89) on Jesus and Christianity we encounter another striking example of such "enlightened Jewish triumphalism" in support of the budding Reform movement in Germany and the attainment of civil rights for the Jews. Hirsch was a pioneering figure in both the German and American Reform communities, serving as rabbi in several cities in both countries. He participated in the rabbinic conferences of 1844–46 at Brunswick, Frankfurt, and Breslau, and also played a major role in the "Pittsburgh Platform" of 1885, which helped to shape the Reform movement in America. Besides his clerical and institutional role, Hirsch was a philosopher of Judaism, strongly influenced by Hegel, and wrote a major systematic work of philosophy, *Die Religionsphilosophie der Juden* (*The Jewish Philosophy of Religion*, 1842), in which he tried to lend a philosophical basis to the ideology of Reform Judaism. Hirsch conceived of his work as a "philosophical exposition of the system of Jewish theology" whose purpose was "to draw sharply the boundaries between Judaism, Christianity, and paganism."[44] Despite his immersion in the philosophical thought of the time, Hirsch's *Religionsphilosophie* "yields very little to its intellectual milieu" and it "seems apparent that Hirsch was not seeking to cut and shape Judaism to fit the dominant philosophy of the day,"[45] as critics of such attempts frequently maintained. Like many of his contemporaries, especially Geiger, Hirsch wanted to illustrate the vitality and original genius of Judaism by fully articulating it in modern terms in a way that would assert its centrality to the current intellectual environment. On this note, the contemporary historian of Jewish thought, Eliezer Schweid, has claimed that Hirsch "succeeded in moving from the measurement of his Judaism by the criterion of his environment to the measurement of his environment by the criterion of his Judaism."[46]

Michael Meyer highlights the tightrope that thinkers like Hirsch and Salvador had to walk between assimilationist acquiescence and polemical stridency (universalism and particularism) in their interpretation of Judaism, noting that Hirsch attempted to reassert the particularity of Judaism, "but to be respectable that reassertion had to be made within the context of contemporary philosophical thought."[47] Hirsch's desire to render the genius of Judaism into modern Western categories reveals the underlying socio-political motivation of his scholarship. Hirsch's intellectual impulses and understanding of Judaism were strongly informed by the principles of the *Wissenschaft des Judentums* movement and the hope of civil equality for the Jews. For Hirsch, as well as for countless other Jewish Reformers of his day, *Wissenschaft des Judentums* was "the major instrument for altering the structure and image of Judaism so as to accord with the legal status eagerly sought by certain sectors of the Jewish community and grudgingly held out by a deeply ambivalent Christian society."[48] It was entirely within this context that Hirsch argued that Judaism and Christianity, especially Protestant Christianity, need not exist in enmity, and that "because of the similarities between Jewish and Protestant conceptions of the state, it was not possible on theological grounds to deny Jews the right to participate in the modern state."[49] Thus, Hirsch offered a revised historical assessment of the relationship between Jews and Christians, attempting to show that Judaism and Christianity have not always been antagonistic, oppositional cultures.[50] In this spirit, he provided an apologetic explanation for the historically negative attitudes of Jews toward Jesus, and cited the *Toldot Yeshu* as a product of the medieval ghetto outlook, claiming, moreover, that it was composed by a baptized Jew! Hirsch alleged that more often Judaism conceived of Christianity as "its beloved child, its beautiful fruit."[51] So, on the one hand, Hirsch attempted to mute the differences between Judaism and Christianity in order to facilitate tolerance and acceptance for Jews within Christian society. Yet, on the other hand, he strongly asserted in philosophical, ethical, and theological terms the superiority of (his conception of) Judaism.

Hirsch's version of enlightened Jewish triumphalism, however, did not emerge in a vacuum. The philosophies of Kant, Schelling, and Hegel all, to a certain extent, accord Christianity a central place, seeing it as far superior to Judaism. It was against this contemporary philosophical expression of Christian triumphalism that Hirsch was working. His philosophical analysis of Judaism, Christianity, and paganism, then, should be seen as an attempt to invert this modern Christian triumphalist position by illustrating "how much Judaism towered over Christianity."[52] Hirsch attempted to prove that Judaism—the religion of the spirit—and paganism—the religion of nature—were the two basic forms of religion, and that Christianity was a synthesis of the two; an attempt to "elevat[e] Paganism to Judaism."[53] He argued that Christianity was a corrupt form of Judaism that had little merit on its own except for the fact "that Christianity had played a positive role in world history. It had brought ethics and monotheism to the pagan world."[54] Hirsch felt that Christians would be better off (following his own example) by focusing on the historical Jesus, best found depicted in the synoptic gospels, especially Matthew, as opposed to the "abstract Jesus" found in the Gospel of John. He sees the historical Jesus, as portrayed by Matthew, as a Jew "who attempted in his own life to exemplify the ideals by which every Jewish life should be guided."[55] More than Salvador, or, for that matter, any modern Jewish writer before him, Hirsch conceived of Jesus not just as a Jew, but as *the* Jew: the perfect embodiment of the ideals of Judaism.

Carving out a middle ground between Jost and Salvador, Hirsch constructed an image of Jesus that presented him as a champion of true biblical Judaism over against the corruptions of the Sadducees and Pharisees. For Hirsch, "Jesus and true Judaism are synonymous," as he claimed that "the pure teaching of Judaism is the pure teaching of Christ."[56] Asserting that Jesus represented a "pure" expression of Judaism was an important point for Hirsch in that part of his larger Reform ideology focused on distilling the essence of Judaism from unnecessary accretions. In Jesus, Hirsch saw a Jew who was able to shunt aside the artificial modes of religious expression introduced by the Sadducees and the Pharisees and recapture the essence of biblical-prophetic Judaism. This two-pronged approach allowed Hirsch to champion the essential Jewishness of Jesus while maintaining a critical stance toward Pharisaic Judaism. According to Hirsch, Jesus accomplished what he did because "he was born a Jew, studied the Law and the Prophets, and strove to be what a Jew should be, in order that every Jew might attain the level of Jesus."[57] Hirsch posits that Jesus attained the ethical-religious perfection of Judaism by becoming a "son of God," as all Israel was intended to do, and thus fully realized the divine mission of the Jews. Thereby removing the Christological component from the notion that Jesus is the son of God, Hirsch asserts that Jesus "did not think that he would be the only person to reach such wholeness, but calls upon every man to follow him and be sons of God, and to accept the sufferings of the servant of the Lord."[58] Moreover, he proclaims that "every Jew, for that matter every man, should be what Jesus was; that was the summons of every prophet. Every Jew and every man will become so; that is the promise of the messianic hope."[59] Hirsch's conception of Jesus as the paradigm of religious perfection, whom all Jews, and all mankind for that matter, should emulate, was a radical departure from previous modern Jewish notions of Jesus.

Despite his extremely complimentary appraisal of Jesus' religious greatness, Hirsch is unwilling to attribute anything radically new to the teachings of Jesus. Hirsch contends that "all that he taught, as he himself admitted, had already been given by Moses and the prophets. He did not die for an idea; nor did he leave his disciples a legacy independent of his person."[60] Hirsch goes on to acknowledge that the uniqueness and accomplishment of Jesus lay in his extraordinary personality: "the unusual attainment of Jesus lay in something that was far more than an idea, it lay in his personality. He understood, realized, and fulfilled the idea of Judaism in its deepest truth—that was the greatness of Jesus."[61] Just like so many liberal Protestant scholars of his time, Hirsch was proposing that the genius of Jesus stemmed from his personality. Yet, Hirsch differed from his Christian contemporaries by alleging that the potency of Jesus' teachings was their intrinsic Jewishness. Even Hirsch's evaluation of Jesus' personal charisma remains within a Jewish purview as he credits him with renewing the prophetic voice at a time when "the voices of living prophets had long faded away."[62] Arguing against all possible claims of Christian triumphalism—traditional and modern—Hirsch maintains that Jesus never intended to establish a new religion, but rather "he wished to realize the total content of the old [Judaism]."[63]

Like most other Jewish scholars of the modern period, Hirsch believed that the split between Christianity and Judaism came not with Jesus, but with his disciples, especially Paul and the evangelist John. It was John's depiction of the "abstract Jesus" and, more powerfully, Paul's notions of the divinity of Jesus and the doctrine of original sin, that severed the Jesus movement from its Jewish roots and brought it closer to the pagan world. Hirsch posits that Paul had a very limited grasp of Judaism, and therefore his critiques of Judaism are based on his own ignorance of its true essence. Moreover, Paul's fiery polemics against Judaism, Hirsch contends, were responsible for establishing the prominent anti-Jewish sentiment that prevailed in Christianity up until Hirsch's own day. This scenario allowed Hirsch, and others who advanced it, to embrace Jesus while at the same time harshly criticizing Christianity as a religious system, and condemning the historical legacy of Christian anti-Semitism. This "pro-Jesus" and "anti-Christian" stance—essentially advanced by Salvador as well—became prevalent in Jewish writing on Jesus and Christianity throughout the nineteenth and into the twentieth century. This position reflected the ambivalence these Jewish scholars and rabbis felt as they began to depict Jesus in favorable terms. Even glowing assessments of Jesus' spiritual achievements, such as Hirsch's, had to be tempered with the assertions that Jesus embodied the pure essence of Judaism and that Christianity had utterly distorted and misunderstood the true religion of Jesus: Judaism.

Reinscribing Jesus the Jew:
The Work of Geiger and Graetz

The pioneering attempts to formulate modern views of Jesus based on the principles of Enlightenment, Emancipation, *Wissenschaft*, and Reform culminated in the writings of two of the towering figures of nineteenth-century German Jewry: Abraham Geiger (1810–74) and Heinrich Graetz (1817–91). While the contributions of Jost, Salvador, and Hirsch set the stage for modern Jewish writing on Jesus, the work of Geiger and Graetz developed and crystallized these views for later generations. Both men were thoroughly influenced by the ideals of

Haskalah and *Wissenschaft*, yet the ways in which each one applied these ideals in their respective ideological agendas differed substantially. Geiger was a fervent advocate of the Reform movement and became known as one of its leading figures during his own life, while Graetz was a much more conservative proponent of *Wissenschaft*. Aligning himself with Zacharias Frankel's positive historical school of Judaism (later known as Conservative Judaism), Graetz turned to Jewish history as a means of fortifying traditional Judaism with only subtle modifications. In this respect, Geiger and Graetz were representative of two distinct trends that were emerging among enlightened German Jews in the middle of the nineteenth century. While both camps sought to thoroughly integrate Judaism into general European culture, Geiger's school of more radical reformers was willing to drastically revamp the edifice of traditional Judaism and Jewish culture, while Graetz and the conservative camp attempted to preserve as much of the old edifice as possible while implementing only moderate changes. At the root of many of the differences between these two schools of thought was the question of to what extent general European cultural norms and the prevailing zeitgeist would dictate the reform of traditional Jewish society. Despite offering contrasting solutions to such quandaries, each group availed itself of the ideal of *Wissenschaft* and turned to the Jewish past as a means of constructing its ideology for the future. In this light, history served both extreme reformers like Geiger, as well as conservative advocates of change like Graetz, as a vehicle for progress.

The conservatives within the realm of Jewish *Wissenschaft*, such as Frankel, the older Leopold Zunz, and Graetz, were very critical of the Reform movement's uses of *Wissenschaft*, which they believed to be shoddy and superficial, merely part of an attempt to "barter Judaism for emancipation." They also felt that the Reformers were overly critical of rabbinic Judaism and that many of their ideas and programs "smacked of Christianity."[64] Writing against Reform historians like Samuel Holdheim, Geiger, and Jost, Graetz (as well as Frankel and Zunz) depicted rabbinic Judaism in a more sympathetic light in his historical writings. Indeed, Graetz "defended talmudic literature as a great national achievement of untold importance to the subsequent survival of the Jews."[65] Graetz and his conservative colleagues were clearly not

comfortable with the critiques leveled at rabbinic literature by many
Reform writers, as they took this to be a sort of betrayal of Judaism
inspired by disparaging Christian conceptions of rabbinic Judaism. Indeed, Graetz's entire scholarly career was informed by a strong antipathy to the reform of Judaism. He declared that "I will fight against the
Christianization of Judaism, which is entailed in the reform of Judaism, to my last breath and with all the weapons at my command."[66]
Graetz's scholarly research into the Jewish past was meant as a countermeasure to the historical studies of the Reformers, and served as part
of his effort to buttress traditional Judaism. Graetz's basic theory of
Jewish history was constructed largely in opposition to the prevailing
theories propagated by these Reformers as part of their program to
amend Jewish law and practice. The basic Reform concept, articulated
best by Geiger, was that Judaism changed and developed historically,
maintaining an essence that remained constant, but otherwise adapting
itself to the changing spirit of the times with all of its various outward
guises and dominant idioms. The "essence" of Judaism and Jewish history for these Reformers was monotheism, or, more specifically, "ethical, prophetic monotheism." In his foundational essay of 1846, "The
Structure of Jewish History," Graetz challenged the Reform notion of
the essence of Judaism by asserting that there has always been a political as well as a religious component to Judaism. The socio-political
structure of Judaism, based on the Torah, was the vehicle for connect-
ing a transcendent God to his people, and Graetz advocated preserving
many ritualistic and nationalistic components of Judaism that Reformers such as Geiger strongly opposed.

The allegations put forth by Graetz and his peers that the proponents
of Reform exploited Jewish history as a means of "bartering Judaism
for emancipation" and that their program for transforming Jewish life
amounted to a "Christianization of Judaism" indicate the heated nature
of the clash that raged between the two camps. These charges also effectively propagated the widespread assumption among later generations
that Jewish historiography served Reformers as a vehicle for assimilation
and acculturation, a way to make Judaism more palatable for Christians
and appropriate for a de-ghettoized Jewish society. Despite possessing
some kernels of truth, these claims fail to recognize the sharp polemical

components in the historical writings of Geiger and others (like Hirsch), who often scathingly criticized Christianity while reinterpreting Judaism as the fountainhead of Western civilization. While Geiger did attempt to reinterpret rabbinic literature in a critical light, it was often intended as a way of sifting the past for that which was essential in order to discard that which was not; historical precedents were sought in order to legitimize contemporary religious reforms. Yet, on the whole, Geiger's interest in ancient Jewish history, especially the Second Temple period and the origins of Christianity, must be seen as part of his attempt to bolster Jewish pride by reclaiming the Jews' place as the true progenitors of Western civilization. Susannah Heschel argues persuasively that a close reading of Geiger's historical scholarship "overturns the prevailing image of the *Wissenschaft des Judentums* as advancing an apologetic and assimilationist agenda."[67] Graetz's charge that Geiger and his associates were attempting to "Christianize Judaism" needs to be inverted; they were trying to Judaize Christianity.

In many ways Heschel's analysis of Geiger's historical writings on the life of Jesus and the origins of Christianity effectively captures the true nature and import of his work. Rather than currying favor with contemporary Christian scholars, or even the populace at large, by treating Jesus in glowing terms, Geiger was radically challenging the fundamental assumptions of these scholars regarding the nature of Judaism, Jesus, and Christianity. Heschel suggests that Geiger's scholarship was a means of "reversing the gaze" that had previously dominated the mode of Christian-Jewish relations, seeing Geiger as "the first Jew to subject Christian texts to detailed historical analysis from an explicitly Jewish perspective"[68] as he "redefined Jesus as a Pharisee and early Christianity as a paganization and ultimate betrayal of Jesus' Jewish message."[69] Like Salvador and Hirsch before him, Geiger was subverting the long-standing position of Christian triumphalism by asserting an explicitly Jewish understanding of Jesus and Christian history. For Geiger, "telling the story of Christian origins from a Jewish perspective was an act of Jewish self-empowerment."[70]

If Geiger's historical works can be considered as a polemical assertion of Jewish pride, especially in regard to the origins of Christianity, then we see that Graetz's historical writing shares many of Geiger's objectives. Schorsch notes that "as a proud, assertive Jew, Graetz also was eager to show the Jewish impact on general history"; he then cites several examples, including Graetz's use of rabbinic sources for illuminating the origins of Christianity, concluding that "these attempts to explain significant aspects of general history in terms of Jewish history implied a confidence in the continued centrality and uniqueness of the Jews. Graetz had recast the religious concept of chosenness in secular terms."[71] While both Graetz and Geiger ostensibly saw their historical scholarship as part of an attempt to facilitate Jewish integration within Christian society, such bold assertions of Jewish self-esteem and uniqueness, especially at the expense of Christianity, often resulted in hostile Christian reactions, and both liberal and conservative Christian scholars frequently condemned their work. Graetz was accused of hating Christianity, promoting Jewish nationalism, and discouraging Jewish integration within the German nation. Even some German Jews with a stronger assimilationist agenda than Graetz rejected the nationalist sentiment of much of his history. In Geiger's case, his work was even more widely read by liberal Protestant theologians in Germany, most of whom found it very controversial and typically rejected his theories about the Pharisees and Jesus' connection to them. Liberal Protestant theology and scholarship, well into the 1860s, continued to propagate long-held negative conceptions of first-century Judaism in contradistinction to Jesus and his followers, which was precisely what Geiger was trying to overturn. Heschel details how Christian theologians, liberal and conservative, often reacted very negatively to liberal Jewish depictions of Jesus such as Geiger's, which they saw as deprecations of his character and stature, accompanied by portraits of Christianity as a degenerate, paganized Judaism.[72] These Christian scholars were appalled at seeing scholarly work by Jews who championed Judaism above Christianity or the rabbis over Jesus in any way, and located Jesus firmly in the general Jewish environment of his day. They consistently maintained Jesus' superiority over the rabbis of his time.

Like many of his Jewish *Wissenschaft* forebears, Geiger included in his attempt to vindicate Judaism a vigorous critique of this type of conception of Judaism and Jewish history among Christian scholars. He set out to show that these scholars had "got it wrong," and that this perpetuated negative attitudes toward Jews in general. By setting the record straight and presenting Jewish (and early Christian) history in a different light, Geiger sought to overturn these biases and change the negative mood regarding Jewish Emancipation in Germany. Part of this task was the vindication of rabbinic literature as an important source for understanding Islam and Christianity.[73] Here we see that despite Geiger's critical scrutiny of rabbinic literature for the purposes of Reform, he held it aloft, much like Graetz, as an example of Jewish brilliance and continued relevance. Despite the apologetic motives of such an undertaking, a polemical stridency rings through Geiger's critique of Christianity and contemporary Christian scholarship as well. In his zeal to defend Judaism and Jewish history against spurious claims that made full Jewish equality in Christian society more difficult, Geiger assumed an assertive polemical stance that ironically hindered his emancipationist objectives. Graetz, in a similar vein, conceived of his historiographic task partly as a countermeasure to specious notions of Jewish history among Christians. In "The Structure of Jewish History" Graetz maintains that "the Christian conception of history, as is well-known, fully denies to Judaism any history . . . it scarcely grants Judaism a few lines and believes to have discharged its obligations as soon as it refers, in a meager footnote, to a few disparate facts of Jewish history in the margin of the annals of world history."[74] Thus, both Graetz and Geiger sought to reposition Jewish history from the margins to the center of world (read Western) history. Moreover, for each of them, reclaiming Jesus as an important part of this distinguished history helped them to that end.

Geiger most succinctly articulated his historical vision of Second Temple Jewish history and the origins of Christianity in his book *Judaism and Its History* (*Das Judentum und seine Geschichte*), which was first delivered as a series of popular lectures in Frankfurt in 1863 and 1864. Geiger reinterpreted many aspects of this period in sometimes radical ways that challenged many standard Christian (and Jewish) assumptions. He attempted to offer an interpretation of Jewish history that supported the contemporary tenets of Reform ideology and theology, as well as turning modern claims of Christian triumphalism on their head. In the preface to the first volume of the book, Geiger acknowledges that many of his views will arouse controversy, especially those concerning Christianity, yet he feels that "it is undoubtedly high time that Jews, also, should openly declare how they understand events, the very consideration of which involves the difference of the two Religions."[75]

In the chapters preceding Geiger's treatment of Jesus and early Christianity, he attempts to rethink certain cultural and religious trends, as well as important religio-political factions, from the Second Temple period, in order to establish historical precedents for Reform Judaism. For example, in his chapter on Hellenistic Judaism Geiger argues that Jews living in various Diaspora communities, especially Alexandria, were deeply influenced by Greek culture, yet they remained Jewish. He writes that "the professors of Judaism though remaining faithfully attached to their religion, nevertheless, identified themselves with the manners and the language of the country in which they lived" (150). Thus, Geiger attempted to legitimate the kind of hybrid Jewish-German identity he advocated in his own time. Geiger speaks of the synthesis, or compromise, that constituted Hellenistic Judaism, in much the same way as he elsewhere lauds the synthesis of (Reform) Judaism and modern Western ideals.

After briefly mentioning the Hasmonean revolt against Hellenism, Geiger introduces the Sadducees and the Pharisees, the two groups so vital to his historical revisions. He traces the origins of the Sadducee and Pharisee schools to the end of the Babylonian exile, seeing the Sadducees as the priestly/princely party (the "ancient nobility") and the Pharisees as the popular party who separated themselves from those "mongrel Jews" who had remained in Palestine during the exile and were estranged from Jewish customs and practices. He proposes that after the Hasmonean uprising these two groups became more distinct and well defined. Geiger goes to great lengths to flesh out the dynamics of the conflict between the Sadducees and the Pharisees, with one of his motives obviously being a desire to overturn New Testament/Christian conceptions of these two parties with all of their attendant negative connotations. He declares that "it is high time that all fable and fiction about Sadducees and Pharisees should cease" (171). Geiger assertively contradicts the prevalent Christian image of the Pharisees, calling them the "very body of the people" who struggled "toward the establishment of equal rights for all classes" (172). It is important to note that Geiger was also concerned with revamping prevalent Jewish perceptions of the Pharisees in a way that would present them as the forerunners of liberal-minded Reformers like himself, and not of the religiously stringent Orthodox rabbis of his day.

To this end, Geiger presents the Talmudic rabbi Hillel as the quintessential Pharisee. He portrays him as a man who reflects "the very soul of the nation" and whose name is identified with "Regenerated Judaism" (182–83). Geiger attempts to depict Hillel as the genius of first-century Judaism who invigorated a "paralyzed" Judaism with real spirit and life. Geiger wonders whether or not Hillel's "Golden Rule" could have been an appropriation of Jesus' teaching, then rules this out, implying that the opposite is true (190). Most importantly for Geiger, "Hillel presents the picture of a true *Reformer*," and he emphatically declares that "this word will not profane him, it will be his nobility" (192). Even more than to Jesus, Geiger turns to Hillel as a historical precedent for his own conception of a Reform rabbi, stressing the strength of Hillel's character as well as his flexibility and compassion in interpreting the law over against the rigidity of his rabbinic opponent, Shammai. Geiger cites many legendary tales that emphasize Hillel's humility, meekness, compassion, and the like. He also cites cases of Hillel adapting the written Torah, such as the laws of the sabbatical year, to show that he was indeed a "Restorer or Reformer of Judaism" (196). In this manner, Geiger constructs an image of Hillel that portrays him as a model for modern Reformers, who also possesses all of the positive qualities that are typically associated with Jesus. In this way, Geiger establishes the central premise of his historical revision: Hillel and the Pharisees are the true heroes of Jewish history, and Jesus is simply one manifestation of this authentic Pharisaic Jewish culture.

In the introductory section of his chapter on Jesus and the origins of Christianity, Geiger further lays out the terrain of Jewish life and the basic "sects" of Judaism in first-century Palestine, elaborating on the Sadducees and Pharisees, and introducing the Zealots and Essenes. For Geiger, as well as for the majority of Jewish scholars before and after, it was crucial to prove that Jesus could only be understood as having emerged from this dynamic Jewish environment. Moreover, it became common, starting with Salvador, to attempt to determine Jesus' place among these various Jewish groups. Salvador himself had identified Jesus as loosely associating with the Essenes, and several later Jewish scholars, including Graetz, followed suit. Geiger depicts the Essenes as hermetic miracle workers who secluded themselves from the events transpiring within the Jewish commonwealth. He claims that the Essenes did not differ greatly from the Pharisees, and that they exerted no influence upon the developments at the center of Judea (210). Geiger perpetuates the notion that Galilee was an ignorant outpost of bumpkins and half-breeds, with many foreign influences on such matters as language, customs, and beliefs (212). He also implies that the rebellious nature of many Galileans helped promote an apocalyptic spirit, expressed by John the Baptist's cry: "Repent, for the Kingdom of Heaven is near at hand." It is within this context of popular Galilean apocalypticism, Geiger proposes, that Jesus appeared claiming that the Kingdom of Heaven was here and that he was its messenger, the Son of Man. Geiger allows that Jesus was invested with messianic enthusiasm and aspiration, thus conceiving of himself as the redeemer. Without going as far as Salvador, who argues that Jesus succumbed to pagan (oriental) mystical influences, Geiger attempted to explain Jesus' messianic aura as emanating from indigenous Jewish religious currents, which, although exceptional, were not necessarily deviant.

However, Geiger's central and most revolutionary claim about Jesus asserts that "he was a Jew, a Pharisean Jew with Galilean coloring—a man who joined in the hopes of his time, and who believed that these hopes were fulfilled in him. He did by no means utter a new thought; nor did he break down the barriers of nationality. . . . He did not repeal the smallest tittle of Judaism; he was a Pharisee who walked in the way of Hillel" (215–16). By identifying Jesus as a Pharisee who taught nothing unique or original Geiger was effectively rejecting traditional Christian beliefs that maintained that the Pharisees were flawed and corrupt, and that Jesus' message was a radical departure from theirs. Indeed, even liberal Protestant scholars affiliated with the historical Jesus movement typically promulgated these negative images of the Pharisees and associated them with all that was inferior and negative about Judaism. They often chose to obfuscate Jesus' Jewishness by portraying him as a unique religious consciousness over against the various streams of Judaism of his day. Acting against this paradigm, Geiger's argument functioned as a "subversion of Christian hegemony," which effectively worked to "sever the connection between Christianity and Jesus."[76] Geiger reconstructed a usable past in a way that served multiple objectives; he formulated a bold new path for the propagation of a modern Jewish alternative to traditional religious and cultural norms (particularly by means of his revised view of the Pharisees), while simultaneously subverting long-standing Christian claims of superiority and dominance over Judaism. His reinterpretation of Jewish and early Christian history also challenged the dominant mode of contemporary (Christian) scholarly discourse in a way that established a place for a strong Jewish voice in a realm where none had previously been heard. Moreover, Geiger's revision of Jewish history and his theories concerning the Jewishness of Jesus contained the apologetic ambition of exonerating Jews and Judaism from common anti-Semitic accusations in a way that would further facilitate their integration into mainstream German society.

To support his central argument Geiger turned to the gospels, selectively citing examples—especially from Mark's gospel, which he felt to be most reliable—in order to show that Jesus' teachings were essentially Pharisaic and completely unoriginal: Jesus said and taught nothing new! He alleges that all of the authentic teachings of Jesus are either Pharisaic (if Geiger views them positively) or they are "diseased" deviations from Pharisaism that stem from the dire conditions of the day (218). Here, Geiger critiques the "otherworldly" or ascetic qualities of Jesus' teachings. He theorizes that Jesus' new (non-Jewish) doctrines, such as "turn the other cheek," "love your enemy," and so on, are the product of apocalyptic modes of thought affecting Jesus. In order to account for the stark differences between the apocalyptic brand of Pharisaic Judaism practiced and preached by Jesus during his lifetime and the forms of Christianity that existed after his death, Geiger presents the history of early Christianity as a gradual betrayal of Jesus' Jewish message. He refers to early Christianity as a sect of Judaism that "arose on the very soil of Pharisean Judaism: *that of the fulfilled Messiahship*" (225), yet he specifies that the majority of Pharisaic Jews did not believe the early Christians' claims that the "new world" had already arrived. Geiger posits that the lower classes of Palestinian Jews were among the first (and only) followers of the Christian sect in Palestine in its earliest years, and that they were responsible for covering the new doctrine with "the most luxuriant weeds" of superstition (228). He also contends that it was among the Jews of the Diaspora, especially the Hellenistic, or "Grecian," Jews (including Paul), that the "Messianic Judaism" of the Christian sect caught on. He understands early Christian doctrine to have been informed by Greco-Jewish philosophy, especially the idea of the logos, and sees such concepts as the virgin birth and the divine sonship of Jesus as resulting from the contact of "incipient Christianity with Grecian Judaism" (234). For Geiger, the doctrine of original sin and the depictions of Christ in the Gospel of John represented the second phase of Christianity, and drove a wedge between Judaism and nascent Christianity. He sees the third phase of Christianity, in which it breaks away decisively from Judaism, as being initiated and created by Paul, who "made the religious and moral idea of Judaism the common property of mankind, but without their distinct forms as expressed in clear and emphatic laws" (239). Thus, the succumbing of Jewish-Christianity to heathen (Gentile) Christianity under the leadership of Paul was the culmination of this third phase of Christianity.

In general, Geiger's evaluation of Jesus is somewhat positive, yet it is consistently tempered with the assertion that Jesus was unoriginal, and did or said nothing truly new. Even regarding his role in the founding of Christianity as a breakaway sect from Judaism, Geiger contends that Jesus was not a strong enough leader to establish a new religion, even if this had been his aim. He states, "We cannot deny him a deep introspective nature, but there is no trace of a decisive stand that promised lasting results . . . there was no great work of reform nor any new thoughts that left the usual paths. He did oppose abuses, perhaps occasionally more forcefully than the Pharisees, yet on the whole it was done in their manner."[77] This statement reiterates Geiger's central apologetic premise that all that is admirable in Jesus' teachings was borrowed or adapted from contemporary Jewish teachings, which were fundamentally superior to Jesus' adaptations. Geiger argues that "the noble religious and ethical concepts and teachings which are put into his heart and mouth, even if we only provisionally and with reservations attribute them to him, must not be taken as his own. He was not their creator nor the first to conceive or state them; rather at best he took them from those who preceded his work and then made them his own."[78] Even Geiger's praise of Jesus typically includes a certain reluctance to proclaim his individual greatness. In this respect, David Catchpole, in his discussion of Geiger's treatment of Jesus, claims that his "is an attitude both respectful and disapproving—an attitude indeed characteristic of Jewish scholars of Geiger's time, who are involved in the rescue operation of reclaiming Jesus from Christianity back into Judaism even though they are aware that Jesus cannot be totally dissociated from the birth of the daughter religion."[79] This ambivalence in reclaiming Jesus becomes evident when they portray the very "un-Jewish religion" that was established in his name. Is Jesus to blame? Or is the onus on Paul and the early Church?

Geiger's assertion of the Jewishness of Jesus does not amount to his utter glorification; rather, Geiger's main goal in reclaiming Jesus as a Jew is to extol the brilliance of Judaism at the expense of Jesus and Christianity. Therefore, it is hard to imagine that Geiger's historical writings about Jesus and Christianity could be construed as assimilationist, or seen as an attempt to curry favor with Christians in order to gain better treatment for Jews in Christian society. While Geiger no doubt believed that he was participating in the enterprise of objective, scientific scholarship, a pursuit shared by Jew and Christian alike, he seems well aware of and engaged in the persistent cultural struggle between Christians and Jews that took place on the pages of the scholarly journals of the day. Geiger's trenchant criticism of the anti-Jewish biases in the writings of Christian scholars like Strauss and Ernest Renan was a new form of polemics that continued age-old Jewish-Christian disputations in a modern guise. As Heschel puts it, "Jews such as Geiger have claimed Jesus for the glory he brings to Judaism; he is the ultimate trump card whose Jewishness makes Christianity, for all its supersessionist claims, at best a deviant branch of Judaism."[80]

Despite their pronounced ideological differences, Heinrich Graetz's conception of Jesus' relationship to the Jewish world of his day as well as his theory regarding the origins of Christianity share Geiger's polemical thrust in many significant ways. In fact, Graetz's entire project of compiling a multivolume history of the Jews cannot be divorced from such polemical motives. After all, Graetz wanted his eleven-volume *History of the Jews* to be a "Jewish history," and not simply another "history of the Jews." Graetz combined a strong Jewish "patriotic" sensibility with scientific scholarship in crafting his narrative of Jewish history. He frequently put forth highly sympathetic portraits of Jewish struggles for survival and highlighted acute periods of Jewish suffering and martyrdom at the hands of Christian persecutors. As Schorsch notes, this "vivid and charged narration of Jewish suffering was intended to intensify the attachment to Judaism, whose institutions and beliefs had been sanctified by the blood of countless martyrs."[81] Graetz did not refrain from emphatically and emotionally scolding enemies of the Jews from various times, including Jews themselves who had somehow betrayed their people or their religion. Given these tendencies then, it is very surprising that Graetz's treatment of Jesus is, for the most part, highly sympathetic. One might have expected that Graetz would have embraced premodern Jewish views of Jesus that typically vilified him as a rebel and betrayer of his people. Instead, he saves his rebuke for Paul and the Church rather than Jesus himself, whom he conceives of as a loyal Jew. Like Geiger, Graetz depicts Jesus in a way that attributes his strengths to his Jewish background and completely dissociates him from "pagan" Christianity.

Graetz's chapter dealing with Jesus and the origins of Christianity was omitted from the first edition of the third volume of his *Geschichte* and first published in 1862 as an epilogue to his close friend Moses Hess's *Rome and Jerusalem*.[82] Heschel argues that for Graetz and Hess (as for many other Jews of the modern period) "the assertions of Jesus' Jewishness and the derivation of Christianity from Judaism served . . . as an affirmation of Jewish pride, and as an effort to combat Jewish conversions to Christianity in their own day."[83] Yet, against these apologetic considerations, we see in Hess's introduction to the epilogue a glowing endorsement of the accomplishments of Jewish *Wissenschaft*, which seems to suggest quite a different impetus for Graetz's endeavor. He writes:

> From Judaism permeated with the scientific spirit, Christianity will receive full justice and its importance will be properly estimated. The

Jewish historian no longer finds it necessary to assume an attitude of fanaticism toward it. Graetz, in the third volume of his history, has shown how one can be a loyal Jew and at the same time an objective judge of that phenomenon which has been a source of persecution to the Jews for the last eighteen hundred years. A few quotations from that writer will show with what freedom of spirit and objectivity a Jewish historian, not a reformer, has characterized Christianity and its founder.[84]

Hess's claims of objectivity and fairness in Graetz's account of Jesus and Christianity are predicated on the basic Haskalah-*Wissenschaft* assumption that his "scientific spirit" allows him to be both a loyal Jew and an "objective judge" of Christianity. Could it be that Hess, and possibly Graetz himself, did not recognize the triumphalist nature of Graetz's work? Was it simply self-delusion for Jews such as Hess, Graetz, and Geiger to claim a stance of scholarly objectivity while simultaneously assailing the religious origins of their Christian neighbors? Or did they explicitly embrace the enterprise of *Wissenschaft* in order to conceal the polemical function that writing Jewish history from a Jewish perspective inherently served? Indeed, it is clear that both integrationist and polemical inclinations coexisted, often discordantly, in their writing.

Graetz's characterization of Jesus diverges from Geiger's in several key ways. He, too, sketches out the religious landscape of first-century Palestine in order to establish Jesus' integral link to core Jewish practices and beliefs, especially Jesus' participation in the "messianic hope" that Graetz portrays as a perpetual and central concern for Jews of that time. Like Geiger, Graetz also stresses the unique religious and social climate of the Galilee where Jesus lived and taught. However, unlike Geiger, Graetz asserts that both Jesus and John the Baptist were more closely identified with the Essenes than with the Pharisees. Graetz conceived of the Essenes as an apocalyptic sect of ascetics who engaged in magic and popular healing. Graetz posits that the Essenes did not come into conflict with the school of the Pharisees. In fact, they basically upheld Pharisaic laws even though their main concern was the imminent coming of the Messiah—the Kingdom of Heaven. It is within this environment that Graetz situates Jesus, claiming that he "must . . . have been powerfully attracted by the Essenes, who led a contemplative life apart from the world and its vanities."[85] In this way Graetz is able to account for many of the qualities of Jesus—his otherworldliness, his contempt for wealth and support of the poor and disenfranchised, and his magical healing—which were often cited as illustrating his opposition to normative Judaism, by attributing them to his Galilean origin and affiliation with the Essenes. Thereby Graetz depicts Jesus as being both normative in his religious outlook, and heterodox in his affinity with Essene thought and practice.

In his description of Jesus' ministry and teachings Graetz portrays Jesus as a simple, extremely pious preacher who is concerned with bringing repentance to the poor and unlettered. He claims that Jesus "animated them with his own piety and fervor."[86] Indeed, Graetz alleges that Jesus himself was not especially learned and therefore his greatness was to be attributed to his unique moral character and personal piety. In many ways, Graetz followed Hirsch in praising Jesus' personality rather than the originality of his teaching as his strong suit. Thus, Graetz proclaims:

> On account of his Galilean origin, Jesus could not have stood high in th[e] knowledge of the Law . . . His deficiency in knowledge, however, was fully compensated for by his intensely sympathetic character. High-minded earnestness and spotless moral purity were his undeniable attributes; they stand out in all the authentic accounts of his life that have reached us, and appear even in those garbled teachings which his followers placed in his mouth. The gentle disposition and the humility of Jesus remind one of Hillel, whom he seems, indeed, to have taken as his particular model.[87]

In this manner, Graetz constructs an image of Jesus as a saintly teacher of Judaism for the masses who imparted the core principles of the religion to those who were alienated and uneducated. Again, we see that Graetz was concerned with explaining Jesus' apparent idiosyncrasies as being well within mainstream Judaism. This attempt was important in Graetz's effort to combat Christian claims, traditional and modern, that Jesus stood apart from Judaism, superseding it with his own superior religious expression. To emphasize this point, Graetz declares that "Jesus made no attack upon Judaism itself, he had no idea of becoming the reformer of Jewish doctrine or the propounder of a new law."[88]

With this claim Graetz also seems to be refuting the incipient Reform view, as expressed by Geiger and others, that Jesus was a model reformer of Jewish tradition. To this end, Graetz cites Talmudic sources to bolster his argument that Jesus maintained compliance with Jewish law, especially Sabbath observance, which the gospels underscore as being a major point of conflict between Jesus and the Pharisees. To be sure, Reformers such as Geiger and his disciples also stressed Jesus' loyalty to the Pharisaic/rabbinic laws as part of their effort to assert his Jewishness. However, Geiger ambiguously depicted Jesus as both a full Pharisee and simultaneously as a deviant from the Pharisaic norm in some ways. Graetz, too, goes to great lengths in order to demonstrate Jesus' fidelity to the legal norms of the day, but readily acknowledges that his unique personality and religious mission set him apart in a significant way. Graetz and Geiger, as well as those who followed in their footsteps, were consciously rebutting Christian perceptions of Jesus and his relationship to the Jewish world around him. By presenting a more complicated picture of first-century Jewish life in Palestine, where boundaries between sects were not hard and fast, and groups like the Pharisees were actually diverse and not monolithic, these Jewish scholars were overturning the dominant Christian master narrative originating in the New Testament. They were asserting their ownership, as Jews, over the narration of their own history, and by extension, over the narration of Jesus' life, which they now viewed as an integral part of that history. Therefore, it was possible for scholars such as Graetz to claim Jesus as fully belonging to the Jewish world of his day even when his beliefs and actions were deemed repugnant by the Jewish leadership of the time. Thus, Graetz is able to assert that Jesus "wore on his garments the fringes ordered by the Law, and he belonged so thoroughly to Judaism that he shared the narrow views held by the Judeans at that period, and thoroughly despised the heathen world,"[89] while at the same time he presented Jesus as believing himself to be the Messiah and the son of God. Graetz is willing to concede that Jesus may have voiced blasphemous views, but unlike Christian interpreters, Graetz sees this as a confirmation of Jesus' Jewishness rather than a rejection of it.

The writings of Geiger and Graetz on Jesus and early Christianity had a profound impact on both contemporaneous and later Jewish scholars, and, as we shall see in the following chapters, on the ways in which numerous Jewish writers and artists would come to depict Jesus. The Russian Jewish historian Simon Dubnow (1860–1941), as well as the leading American Reform rabbi and scholar, Kaufman Kohler (1843–1926), and several others, followed Graetz's lead in depicting Jesus as an Essene. A far greater number in Reform and *Wissenschaft* circles were influenced by Geiger's writings, often echoing his assertion that Jesus must be understood within a Pharisaic/rabbinic orbit.[90] Joseph Derenbourg (1811–95), a German Jew and close friend of Geiger's who held a chair in rabbinic Hebrew language and literature at the Ecole Pratique des Hautes Etudes in France, wrote about Jesus that "his teaching can be explained in rabbinic terms, his methods were Pharisaic, and he respected temple and Sabbath."[91] One of the founding figures of the American Reform movement, Isaac Mayer Wise (1819–1900), held that "Jesus of Nazareth . . . was a Pharisaic scribe and a Jewish patriot" who died as a martyr in defense of his homeland.[92] Another Jewish scholar, Tobias Tal of Holland, based his comparison of the Talmud with the Sermon on the Mount on Geiger's work, concluding, "The ethics of the gospel are no other than appear in the Talmud . . . the same that are held as law to this day by the Talmud-Jews."[93] In a similar manner, the Italian Orthodox rabbi and philosopher Elijah Benamozegh (1823–1900) showed the resemblance between parables and ethical imperatives in the gospels and the Talmud, concluding that "when Jesus spoke these words he was in no way abandoning Judaism. He preaches no strange or unfamiliar doctrine but aligns himself squarely with the two leading Pharisaic schools."[94] Benamozegh "found little in the practical ethics of Christianity that was not rooted in Judaism."[95]

It must be noted that most of these reform-minded Jews distinguished themselves from "Talmud-Jews" and no longer held the Talmud to be an authoritative, normative text. (Benamozegh was an exception, as he was an Orthodox Jew and opponent of the liberal streams of Judaism.) Nonetheless, by recognizing the significance of the Talmud, and rabbinic literature in general, as sources of Jesus' teaching, and by extension basic Christian doctrines, these Jews were able to assert the prominence of Judaism over against Christianity. Although rabbinic literature was no longer binding for the modern Jew, it was part of the

Jewish cultural patrimony, and by asserting its importance for under-standing the teachings of Jesus and early Christianity, they affirmed the Jewish purview of both. Indeed, modern Jewish scholars from Gei-ger and Graetz on have typically asserted that one must be thoroughly acquainted with rabbinic literature in order to truly comprehend the life and teachings of Jesus.

The True Christians:
American Reformers Assume the Mantle of Christianity

Just as the ideological programs of the Haskalah, *Wissenschaft des Judentums*, and Reform movements in Europe were substantially driven by the desire for Jews to become integrated into mainstream society and culture, so, too, were the Reformers in America in the last few decades of the nineteenth century motivated by such concerns. More than ever, they attempted to formulate an effective synthesis of Jewish and "universal" (which typically meant Western-Christian) ideas and tenets and to create a worldview that would bridge the gap between Jewish ideals and core American ideals, including Christianity. Jonathan Sarna argues that "the belief that Judaism and Americanism reinforce one another, the two traditions converging in a common path, encapsulates a central theme in American Jewish culture that may be termed 'the cult of synthesis.' . . . It reflects an ongoing effort on the part of American Jews to interweave their 'Judaism' with their 'Americanism' in an attempt to fashion for themselves some unified, 'synthetic' whole."[96] Sarna further contends that this synthesis was often used "both to legitimate [the] Jews' place in America and to demonstrate their patrio-tism and sense of belonging," and that it often involved "siez[ing] upon and Judaiz[ing] America's founding myths, placing 'Jews' . . . at their center."[97] In other words, this "cult of synthesis" involved the construc-tion of Jewish counterhistories in order to secure a rooted place for Jews in American society (and in the West more generally). This attempt by Jews to Judaize the Christian/Western world they were trying to enter highlights the profound paradox of modern Jewish existence: Jews were forced to radically alter their understanding of "Jew," "Christian," and

"West" in order to construct a niche for themselves in this new world. Formulating Jewish counterhistories of Jesus played an integral role in this process, in that Jews could try to become more American by asserting the essential Jewishness of Jesus and Christianity.

As was the case with Hirsch, Geiger, and other earlier Reformers, these attempts to redefine the relationship between Judaism and Christianity, and between Jews and Christians, frequently incorporated strong polemical elements. This unique blend of assimilationist acquiescence and polemical self-assertion seems to pervade Jewish efforts aimed at describing a place for Jews and Judaism in the modern world, including the Jewish recovery of Jesus. Along these lines, George Berlin explains American Reform writings on Jesus and Christianity as a "paradoxical attempt on the part of the Jewish writers to mute the differences between Judaism and Christianity and emphasize their commonalities, and at the same time to condemn Christianity on theological and ethical grounds."[98] Like Susannah Heschel, Berlin argues that it was precisely the closeness, the blurring of boundaries between liberal Protestants and Reform Jews, that gave rise to this new form of polemics as each group tried to justify its own religious system's continued existence as a separate, distinct, and worthwhile religious group.[99] Reclaiming Jesus helped affirm the superiority of Judaism over Christianity at a time when the two religions were shedding many of their age-old differences. By identifying "pure Christianity" with Reform (nonlegalistic) Judaism, these Reformers sought to equate Judaism with Americanism, and show the justification for the continuation of Judaism as separate from Christianity.

As we have noted above, part of this ongoing attempt to carve out a new Jewish identity also involved turning to Jesus as a model for religious ideals, which the Reformers championed as essential for modern Jews. Even more than Geiger and his contemporaries, the American (and British) Reformers of the late nineteenth and early twentieth centuries sought to depict Jesus and his religious orientation in a way that harmonized with their own theological agendas: he was conceived of as the prototypical Reform rabbi. Beyond the unanimity of this basic premise, there existed a wide range of theories that attempted to classify and define Jesus' particular form of religious expression. Many saw

Jesus as belonging to the Jewish prophetic tradition, which they held to be the most relevant form of biblical religion. The British Liberal (Reform) scholar C. G. Montefiore (1858–1938), especially, advanced the notion that, above all, Jesus was a prophet, "spiritually and religiously akin" to Isaiah, Jeremiah, Ezekiel, and the other great prophets of Israel.[100] Montefiore saw Jesus as a harbinger of his own version of a universalized, prophetic type of Liberal Judaism. Many contemporary scholars have noted the extent to which Montefiore portrayed Jesus as "an idealized Montefiore in miniature,"[101] seeing in Jesus' ministry the "very same attributes . . . characteristic of his [Montefiore's] own Liberal Jewish struggle."[102]

Other rabbis represented Jesus chiefly as an ethical teacher of social justice and a reformer who opposed the rigid legalism and Orthodoxy of his day. The assertion of the leading American Reform ideologue and scholar, Kaufman Kohler, that Jesus was a "bold religious and social reformer, eager to regenerate Judaism" as well as a "paragon of piety, humility, and self-surrender"[103] epitomizes this Reform point of view. In this spirit, a distinguished American Reform rabbi of the early twentieth century, H. G. Enelow (1877–1934), proclaimed that "the modern Jew realizes the ethical power and spiritual beauty of Jesus. In this regard Jesus takes his place among the noble teachers of morality and heroes of faith Israel has produced."[104] Countless Reform writers from this period (1880s–1920s) portrayed Jesus as a loyal, normative Jew, many even ascribing to him a unique greatness and special standing. This must be viewed as part of their attempt to cast Jesus in their own likeness, seeing him as a proto–Reform Jew who modeled a prophetic, ethical Judaism for their own day. All the spiritual power and religious greatness Jesus represented was harnessed for the cause of crafting a potent form of Reform Judaism. Noting the anachronistic approach of these Reform scholars, Samuel Sandmel claimed about I. M. Wise and H. G. Enelow that they "wrote about Jesus as if Jesus were a nineteenth-century American rabbi."[105]

As we have seen above, however, viewing Jesus positively did not always entail viewing Christianity positively, as oftentimes this was part of a new, modern anti-Christian polemic meant to prove Judaism superior. In this context, the issue of ethics was at the fore of Jewish-Christian discourse among the Reform rabbis and their liberal Protestant contemporaries. The Reformers tried to show that Jesus' ethical teachings were primarily based on Jewish teachings, and that the ethics of Judaism are superior to those of Christianity. In this context, Jewish authors went to great pains to show that the ethical teachings attributed to Jesus in the New Testament had parallels in the rabbinic literature stemming from this time. Any divergence of Jesus' teachings from the ethical concepts of Judaism was usually explained by the Reformers as a feature of Jesus' messianic consciousness and apocalypticism. This insistence on the ethical superiority of Judaism must be understood as part of the larger trend of enlightened Jewish triumphalism which, above all, served to justify the continuation of a separate Jewish identity and religion while the boundaries between Judaism and Christianity were being constantly weakened. Because Reform Jewish thinkers unanimously stressed the ethical component of Judaism as part of its unchanging essence, asserting that Christian ethics were actually Jewish to begin with became an important part of demonstrating the ongoing vitality and viability of Reform Judaism as *the* religion for the modern age.

As part of their concerted effort to combat Christian anti-Semitism and reconcile Jews and Christians, American Reform scholars frequently reinterpreted the crucifixion story in order to exonerate the Jews from any kind of ongoing guilt for their alleged complicity in the death of Jesus. I. M. Wise's *The Martyrdom of Jesus of Nazareth* (1874), Emil Hirsch's essay "The Crucifixion Viewed from a Jewish Standpoint" (1892), and Joseph Krauskopf's *A Rabbi's Impressions of the Oberammergau Passion Play* (1901) were three of the main treatises created to deal exclusively with this issue. Each author, to varying degrees, questions the authenticity of the gospel accounts of Jesus' arrest, trial, and crucifixion, and in place of the gospel versions offers his own hypothesis as to the events in the last week of Jesus' life. This concern with proving that the Jews as a whole had no reason to see Jesus dead was part of the general aspiration, shared by these writers and many of their contemporaries, to uproot New Testament–based Christian anti-Semitism, as well as to illustrate how thoroughly Jesus belonged to the mainstream Jewish world of his day.

Perhaps the most vehement articulation of these related concerns comes from Krauskopf, who offered a detailed critique of the traditional Christian interpretation of the passion of Jesus and its role in fomenting anti-Semitic persecution. Krauskopf's book chronicles his experience of attending the Passion Play in Oberammergau, Austria, and his reactions to this Christian tradition. From the outset he conveys a tone of bitter resentment at the way Christians have maltreated Jews for eighteen hundred years—an attitude he sees embodied in the Passion Play itself. He claims that this condition is ironic, considering Judaism is responsible for sculpting both the person of Jesus as well as the basic tenets of Christianity itself: "He it was, the Jew, who was the mighty sculptor of Christianity; his creative genius it was that gave it its colossal dimensions; it was his mallet and chisel that sculptured the towering grandeur of Jesus . . ."[106] Like his predecessors and contemporaries, Krauskopf claims that Jesus was a "Hebrew of Hebrews" and that his authentic teachings were completely Jewish in form and content. In this sense, Krauskopf boldly asserted Jewish ownership and authorship of the figure of Jesus and the religious truths found in Christianity, a radical form of reclamation. His response to the Passion Play itself is infused with a strong denunciation of the Christian historical legacy of persecution against the Jews and a biting criticism of the chasm between expressed Christian doctrines of love in the face of a historical legacy of hatred. Krauskopf believes that once the Christian world—at least the intelligent sector of it—hears the Jewish perspective on the New Testament narrative, their attitude toward the Jews will radically improve. Krauskopf diplomatically but firmly asserts the need to defend Judaism from Christian misinterpretation, mistranslation, misunderstanding, and outright lies, not to attack Christian belief, but to defend those aspects of Judaism that Christianity assails a priori. He admits his admiration and respect for Jesus as one who "made humanity divine," yet not at the expense of seeing his deification negatively affect the Jews.[107]

In addition to advancing such scenarios that absolved Jews of any guilt for the death of Jesus, Krauskopf, as well as Wise and Hirsch, often adopted the crucifixion as a meaningful emblem for Jewish martyrdom throughout the ages. Reviving a popular strand of medieval Jewish theology that understood Israel to embody the "suffering servant" mentioned in Isaiah 53, these Reformers advanced a more potent brand of Jewish martyrology that explicitly appropriated traditional Christological symbolism. In this connection, Kaufman Kohler claimed that not Jesus but the Jewish nation as a whole was "the man of sorrows from whose wounds flow the balm of healing for the nations. . . . The Jews are a people of Christs. Not A Jew but THE Jew is the God-chosen mediator between the nations and creeds and classes of men whose life blood has so often [flowed] to atone for the sins of the world. This is the solution of the Jewish problem, this is the explanation of the perplexing puzzle concerning the Wandering Jew."[108]

In a similar manner, Krauskopf concludes his book on the Passion Play at Oberammergau by proclaiming that throughout history it has been the Jews who have suffered as a Christ among the peoples. After mentioning a storm that filled the sky during the performance of the Passion Play, he writes:

> To me that seeming protest of nature against the defamation of the Jews on the stage of Oberammergau, was a prophecy, a prophecy that the storm that has raged over the Jew eighteen centuries long, and that has deluged him with torrents of expatriation, expulsion, massacre, torture, degradation, prejudice, ostracism, will cease, that the sun of justice will burst forth at last, and, in the radiance of light, and in the beauty of truth, reveal the Jew to the world as having, eighteen centuries long, walked *the way of the cross*, as having been the real *Suffering Messiah*, as having been the real *Saviour of Man*.[109]

This utilization of the notion of vicarious atonement and the symbolism of Christ's passion for Jewish purposes was a way of rendering the Jewish experience fully comprehensible in terms meaningful to the Western-Christian mind. These Jews were providing a new vocabulary—drawn from the Western canon—that could eloquently express Jewish anguish to their Christian neighbors in powerful and familiar ways. Ironically, however, they were also reasserting the intrinsic Jewishness of the Isaianic concept of the suffering servant that Christians had previously appropriated from Hebrew Scriptures. Moreover, by seeing the Jews as a people of Christs, they challenged traditional Christian explanations of Jewish suffering, which were based on the Jewish rejection of Jesus. This new Christological understanding of

Jewish suffering said, in effect: "We do not suffer because we rejected Christ, but because we are the real Christ."

Explaining Jewish history by means of such Christological symbolism also served these Reformers in their desire to relocate the place of the Jew in American society. Not only could they now narrate Jewish history in terms understandable to Christians, but they could also effectively displace Christians as the bearers of the rich symbols so integral to Western-Christian culture, an example of the model of Jewish integration most appropriately called "insertion" rather than assimilation. Along these lines, Emil Hirsch (1851–1923), a leading rabbi and scholar on the Reform scene (and son of Samuel Hirsch), explicitly identified the core texts and symbols of Christianity as essentially Jewish. In his frequent interactions with Christians, he stressed that Christianity was Jewish in origin, that Jesus was a practicing Jew, and that most of the New Testament was Jewish literature reflecting reworkings of Talmud and Midrash. He argued in *The Doctrine of Jesus* (1894) that not only are Jesus' ethical teachings Jewish in origin, but the New Testament "is flesh of our flesh and bone of our bone."[110] Later in the same treatise Hirsch adamantly expresses his desire to see Jesus returned to his proper place among the Jewish people:

> In his doctrines, Jesus is the best exponent of the thoughts, the moral ideas and the religious aspirations of the Judaism of his time. . . . He was of us; he is of us. We quote the rabbis of the Talmud; shall we then, not also quote the rabbi of Bethlehem? Shall not he in whom there burned, if it burned in any one, the spirit and the light of Judaism, be reclaimed by the synagogue? Yea, he hath been reclaimed; the old mother clasps him today to her bosom as he lays at her feet the fruitage of his work in the world, and old mother Judaism lifts her hand and blesses him who was her child, and blesses also those who though they thought they had accepted him, had heaped injury upon the old mother. Happy this day when Judaism finds again her son . . ."[111]

Hirsch takes this notion of reclamation one step further by arguing that the symbol of Jesus' passion and martyrdom, the cross, has become the symbol of the Jewish people themselves. In Hirsch's formulation of this Christological interpretation of Jewish history he claims that "the Jew for fifteen centuries has often had to toil up Golgotha's steep and heavy ascent. We bore a cross the weight of which was a thousandfold heavier than that which Jesus carried to the place of execution. The thorny crown; who wears it? The Jew today; the Jew yesterday. He will wear it tomorrow."[112] Hirsch continues on in this vein, invoking all of the symbols of Jesus' passion and proclaiming that they best characterize the Jewish historical experience of suffering and persecution. For Hirsch, just as Jesus "belongs to us," so too does all of the rich symbolism associated with his suffering and martyrdom; the Jews truly are a people of Christs.

Another component in Hirsch's program to return Jesus and Christianity to their Jewish roots was his assertion that it has been the Jews who have best practiced Jesus' doctrines of love and forgiveness, not those who call themselves Christians. The Christians have neglected Jesus' call to love one's enemy and instead have persecuted the Jews for centuries, while the Jews, according to Hirsch, have refrained from hating their enemies. In this and many other ways, the Jews have been the true champions of Jesus' teaching of love (which, Hirsch argues, conforms to Jewish teachings predating Jesus in the first place). The claim that the Jews are indeed the "true Christians" and sole bearers of "Christian" morality recurs frequently in the writings of Reform leaders from this period. The Reform rabbi Bernhard Felsenthal advanced similar views in proclaiming that "the religion of Christ is essentially identical with the religion of Israel. Paradoxical as it may sound, it is nevertheless true that *the Jews are the true Christians*, and the so-called Christians are not Christians, inasmuch as they profess a number of doctrines totally foreign to the religion of Christ."[113] This stance is an extension of the notion that Christians have repeatedly misunderstood, or perhaps purposely exploited the doctrines of Jesus, while Jews have been the ones best equipped to comprehend his teachings and embody his ethical code.

The tendency to identify Jews as the "true Christians" and as a "people of Christs" once again reveals the complex nature of modern Jewish identity. These Jewish thinkers imagined that the outsider status of the Jew in American (or European) society could be overcome by assuming the mantle of Christianity for themselves. At the same time, they formulated new conceptions of Judaism and Jewishness in order to secure the survival of modern Jews qua Jews. This process of identity transformation is complicated even further when we consider the strong universalizing impulse that informed these thinkers. For them, eradicating the chauvinistic particularism often identified with traditional Judaism and replacing it with a more inclusive, universal vision of Judaism and Jewish culture was at the center of the Reform agenda. The culmination of this mode of thought was the desire to see traditional demarcations between Jews and Christians completely dissolved. In this light, Hirsch and his fellow Reform leaders all advanced utopian visions of a merger between Jew and Christian that would result in some sort of universal brotherhood of faith in which old boundaries would no longer apply. Hirsch claimed that "the time will come when better Christians than now reject, will welcome the better Jews, yea, better than they who would now desert the post of danger, though of duty and honor. The walls then will fall. But in the new temple of humanity, a niche will also be consecrated to the lowly Jew of Nazareth, one of that people called to the hero's, the martyr's crown."[114]

Kaufman Kohler also spoke of a time when "Jew and Gentile, synagog [*sic*] and church, will merge into the church universal, into the great city of humanity whose name is 'God is there.'"[115] Likewise, I. M. Wise envisions a "gorgeous temple of humanity, one universal republic, one universal religion of intelligence, and one great universal brotherhood," which he identifies as "the new covenant, the gospel of humanity and reason."[116] If the main challenge facing the Jew in the modern world was the struggle between competing modes of existence—old and new, traditional and modern, Jewish and Gentile, universal and particular—then these utopian visions may be seen as part of an attempt to blur these boundaries and escape the need to choose between what appeared to be distinct, polar opposites. Yet, was this desire for "one great universal brotherhood" to be a synthesis of the two cultures, or a total erasure of one in favor of the other? The challenge of creating a Jewish-Christian synthesis as opposed to erasing Jewish identity altogether became endemic to the process of finding a place for Judaism and Jewishness in modernity.

As we have seen throughout this chapter, the process of Jews reclaiming the figure of Jesus has always involved these tensions between the particular and the universal, between assimilation and Jewish self-affirmation, between cultural synthesis and bold appropriation, that have continually informed the Jewish negotiation with modernity. As Jews have attempted to integrate themselves into Western culture they have stressed both their sameness and their difference with that culture. They have claimed Jesus as one of their own to stress that they are at home in Western culture, but this has often involved the displacement of Christians and Christianity as the primary authors of that culture. Modern Jewish appraisals of Jesus, while influenced by new principles of scientific scholarship, cannot be understood without considering the ideological component that such appraisals have always included. The struggles modernizing Jews faced in their attempts to redefine Jewish life for a new age were inextricably linked to their quest for the Jewish Jesus. As we will see in the following chapters, in the first decades of the twentieth century this quest extended beyond the realm of *Wissenschaft des Judentums* and Reform Judaism in Western Europe and America, as East European Jewish intellectuals, writers, and artists in search of new forms of Jewish culture and identity continued and broadened the reclamation of Jesus the Jew. The fundamental reevaluation of the historical Jesus begun by foundational figures like Mendelssohn, Geiger, and Graetz had a profound and lasting impact on subsequent generations of modernizing Jews coming from Eastern Europe, despite diverse ideological affiliations and markedly different cultural forms and contexts.

Two   The Crucifix Question

"Us and the Cross":
Russian Jewish Intellectuals Take a Stand

In 1909 an impassioned debate erupted on the pages of the socialist Yiddish periodical *Dos naye lebn* (*The New Life,* published in New
York) between two Russian Jews, the writer and folklorist S. Ansky
(1863–1920) and the journal's founder and editor, the radical intellectual and cultural activist Chaim Zhitlovsky (1865–1943). The debate
was sparked by the inclusion earlier that year in the journal of two
stories with explicitly Christian images: "Der tseylem" ("The Cross")
by Lamed Shapiro and "In a karnival nakht" ("In a Carnival Night")
by Sholem Asch. The stories represented a pioneering development
in modern Yiddish literature in their use of the symbol of the cross
and the figure of Jesus respectively as their central images. However,
perhaps more significant than the stories themselves was the heated
exchange they inspired between Zhitlovsky and Ansky (and others)
regarding both the dangers and the merits of embracing Christian
themes and symbols in Jewish thought and literature. The protracted
debate between these two writers, both leading figures of the progressive Russian Jewish intelligentsia at the time, reveals just how serious
and controversial these issues were. The controversy—which came to
be known as *di tseylem frage* (the Crucifix Question) based on the title
of Ansky's article—stemmed from the central theme of both works,
which Zhitlovsky identified as: "us and the cross! The Jewish world
and the Gentile world. The movement of the Gentile world to us, and
of us to it."[1] The heart of the ensuing discussion between these Jewish
intellectuals consisted of a reassessment of the position of enlightened
secular Jews toward Jesus and the entire Christian world, as well as the

61

place of Jewish culture in the context of modern Western civilization. Above all, the issues of Jewish assimilation, integration, and acculturation within Western culture dominated the discussion. Just like the *maskilim* of Western Europe discussed in the preceding chapter, these East European Jewish intellectuals were grappling with the fundamental questions facing modern Jews who sought to carve out a niche for a new Jewish culture and identity: On what basis does Jewishness now rest? How can one be both Jewish and Western at the same time? What elements of Jewish tradition are still valid? What must one accept of Christian-Western culture and what must one reject? It is within these larger, pressing concerns that the *tseylem frage* was situated.

At about the same time, between 1910 and 1913, leading figures in the secular Zionist movement in Eastern Europe, Palestine, and beyond also took part in a fierce, lengthy debate, known as the Brenner Affair. The debate was sparked by two articles appearing in the Hebrew press in 1910, one by the Cultural Zionist ideologue Ahad Ha-Am (Asher Ginsburg, 1856–1927), and the other by the young Hebrew writer and firebrand of the Second Aliya generation,[2] Yosef Chaim Brenner (1881–1921). Numerous prominent East European intellectuals—most writing in Hebrew, but some in Yiddish and Russian as well—engaged in an often acrimonious exchange over the issues raised by Ahad Ha-Am and Brenner in their original articles, chief among them the phenomenon of Jewish apostasy, the role of religion in secular Jewish nationalism, and the place of Jesus and Christianity in the worldview of the modern secular Jew. Even more than the Crucifix Question debate in the Yiddish press in the previous year, the Brenner Affair became a defining and divisive issue within Zionist circles, fomenting major ideological rifts, political battles, and intergenerational conflicts involving both major and minor figures in the Zionist movement such as Ahad Ha-Am, Brenner, Joseph Klausner, Shai Ish Hurwitz, M. Y. Berdichevsky, A. D. Gordon, David Ben-Gurion, and others. As with the Crucifix Question, the Brenner Affair controversy touched on the deeper, underlying questions that these Zionist intellectuals were grappling with: What is the basis and what are the limits of the new Zionist Hebrew culture? What are the limits of Jewishness for the "New Hebrew" man? What role, if any, will Jewish religion play in formulating a Hebraic culture and identity?

In this chapter I utilize these two controversies as a lens through which to view some of the major tensions that defined the quest for a secular Jewish identity and culture among modern East European Jews. For the various intellectuals involved in these debates, defining the progressive Jewish intelligentsia's position on Jesus and Christianity was an important part of their own ideological self-definition; it should be seen as part of their attempt to construct a cultural locus of meaning that would constitute modern Jewish identity. For them, the Crucifix Question was a microcosm of the Jewish Question: how enlightened modern Jews related to the figure of Jesus became representative of their approach to the general non-Jewish environment, especially in regard to what role it should play in informing Jewish identity and culture. Thus, Zhitlovsky's warm embrace of Jesus as a Jewish revolutionary and martyr, and Ansky's adamant rebuff of him as the emblem of Christian anti-Semitism, correlate to their distinct views on how to integrate Jews into mainstream Western culture. Likewise, Ahad Ha-Am's harsh rejection of Jewish attempts to reclaim Jesus and view Christianity in sympathetic terms, as well as Brenner's claim that for Jews the New Testament is "bone of our bone, and flesh of our flesh," comparable to the Hebrew Bible, must be seen as part of their conflicting visions of the new Zionist culture that they were each striving to create.

The question these Jewish intellectuals ultimately grappled with—must Jews enter the Western world on Christian terms ("through Nazareth"),[3] or could they do so on purely Jewish terms?—has reverberated time and again since the origins of the Haskalah at the end of the eighteenth century. In many ways, the East European Jewish intellectuals considered in this chapter are intellectual heirs of the Haskalah and *Wissenschaft des Judentums* movements discussed above. The changes in Jewish discourse on Jesus and Christianity that started with Mendelssohn and developed through the nineteenth century also profoundly affected their own perspectives on this subject. As we shall see, they were all familiar with, and often influenced by, the writings of Geiger and Graetz on the origins of Christianity, and the historians among them, such as Simon Dubnov, Joseph Klausner, and Yehezkel Kaufmann, contributed their own research to this growing field of Jewish historical accounts of the life of Jesus and the rise of Christianity. Like their nineteenth-century, mostly German, predecessors, many of these Russian Jewish intellectuals also sought to reclaim Jesus in some way as a powerful tool in the process of rebuilding conceptions of Jewish history, Jewish culture, and Jewish identity; their writing on Jesus often shared the polemical anti-Christian undercurrents, the repudiation of Christian anti-Semitism, and the proud assertions of Jesus' Jewishness that the earlier works possessed.

Despite these similarities, there were several regional factors, political, social, and otherwise, that affected both the process of Enlightenment and the ideological orientations of the Jews from tsarist Russia especially. The fact that certain East European Jewish intellectuals, like Zhitlovsky and Sholem Asch for instance, subscribed to such a positive conception of Jesus while others like Ansky and Ahad Ha-Am maintained entrenched, negative perceptions of Christ and Christianity reflects the complicated predicament facing enlightened Jews of Eastern Europe. Unlike Reform rabbis and modern scholars living in liberal democracies such as England and America (or even in Germany for that matter) at the turn of the twentieth century, freethinking Russian Jews, even those living abroad, had to constantly contend with the exigencies of vehement political anti-Semitism (in the form of repressive tsarist legislation) and popular anti-Semitic violence (in the form of recurring pogroms). This resulted in a tension between the attraction of liberal, intellectual trends of tolerance, social justice, universal brotherhood, and so on, and the strongly particularistic needs of the Jewish people in Russia in its struggle for national survival and equal rights. These tensions were especially evident among those Jews, like Ansky and Zhitlovsky, who zealously participated in Russian revolutionary circles, an issue that Zhitlovsky addresses at the beginning of his review of Shapiro's story. The ambivalent response to the wave of pogroms beginning in 1881 on the part of Russian revolutionary leaders, as well as to the reactionary forces that exploded after the 1905 revolution, proved problematic and, at times, alienating for Jewish members of revolutionary movements, often causing them to reassess their revolutionary, cosmopolitan ideals and identify more strongly with the Jewish nation.

Moreover, the Russian Jewish embrace of nationalism of various stripes, and Zionism most specifically, set these East European Jewish intellectuals apart from the majority of their West European (and

American) predecessors and contemporaries in enlightened Jewish circles and movements. Differences with the Reform Jews of the West were the most stark, as their Jewish identity rested on a liberal religious outlook that completely rejected the national component of Judaism and Jewish identity, often leading to zealous patriotism within their respective countries and staunch opposition to Zionism. To the contrary, Russian Jewish intellectuals tended to stress both the national and the secular components of Jewishness and Jewish identity, sometimes rejecting the religious component altogether. While secularization played a major part in formulating the ideology of the Haskalah and all of its intellectual descendants, East European Jewish intellectuals in the twentieth century represented a culmination of this secularization process in their attempts to create secular forms of modern Jewish identity and culture that were completely removed from Judaism as a religion.

Another factor that distinguishes the writings of the East European Jews on Jesus and Christianity is language. These debates took place almost exclusively in Jewish languages—Hebrew and Yiddish—and therefore should be viewed as part of an internal conversation, issues to be engaged by fellow Jews having limited interaction with non-Jewish audiences (although there were some participants in these debates who wrote in the Russian-language Jewish press). In contrast, West European and American writers in the Haskalah, *Wissenschaft des Judentums*, and Reform circles wrote in the language of the land, making their work accessible to Jewish and non-Jewish audiences alike. This factor lends a certain irony to the writing of the East European Jews not found in that of their West European counterparts: Zhitlovsky and countless others preached secular humanism and universalism in a particularistic national language that could only be read by fellow Jews. Conversely, writers like Geiger in the nineteenth century and C. G. Montefiore in the twentieth century aimed their German and English writings on Jesus and Christianity at a mixed audience, while also attempting to make those "Gentile" languages "Jewish" languages in which Jews could create literature and philosophy.

Despite these numerous differences, even in the twentieth century Russian Jewish intellectuals remained in conversation with their Western European counterparts on various common Jewish issues, including Jewish perspectives on Jesus and Christianity. In this context, it is significant to note that Ahad Ha-Am wrote his initial article on Judaism and Christianity in 1910 in response to a book (in English) on Jesus and the Gospels by C. G. Montefiore that appeared earlier that same year. In this sense, the debate over these issues within Hebrew circles was firmly connected to the contemporaneous Jewish scholarship on Jesus and Christianity developing in English and other "non-Jewish" languages. While certain clear distinctions exist between the context and content of these discussions among East European and West European Jewish intellectuals, there also exist many common or universal themes and issues among these writers in their treatment of Jesus and Christianity. In both cases, Jewish approaches to the subjects of Jesus and Christianity are closely linked to questions of Jewish self-definition and the nature of Jewish interaction with the wider non-Jewish environment.

Between Two Worlds:
Zhitlovsky and Ansky on *di tseylem frage*

In the case of Zhitlovsky and Ansky—two pivotal figures in the creation of a secular, Yiddish-oriented, Jewish culture—their attempt to find a balance between things Jewish and things "goyish" reflects the inherent tensions of that nascent culture. In fact, we can look to the intellectual biographies of Zhitlovsky and Ansky in order to get a sense of the cultural moment during which this controversy took place, and to frame the debate that constituted the Crucifix Question. The cultural mood of Russian Jewry in the first decade of the twentieth century can best be described with one word: revolution. The failed Russian Revolution of 1905 was a watershed of political, cultural, and societal change for Russia's Jews, especially for the members of the Jewish intelligentsia who either played an active role in effecting the revolution (e.g., Ansky and Zhitlovsky) or were powerfully affected by its immediate aftermath and ramifications. A new generation of Jewish literati and cultural activists came of age in the years immediately following the 1905 Revolution, translating many of the aspirations of the revolution into various forms of Jewish cultural discourse; they were inspired by the desire to expand horizons, break down boundaries, and challenge established traditions as they charted new realms of Jewish culture. In many ways the 1905 Revolution also marked a juncture in Jewish intellectual life, a pivotal moment in which Jews found themselves free to pursue divergent political and ideological solutions to both Jewish and universal problems. A mood of optimism for a future with limitless possibilities competed with a profound sense of disappointment and a postrevolution malaise, largely provoked by outbreaks of pogroms and tsarist counterrevolutionary measures, such as the abolition of the newly elected Duma. In this way, both the successes and the failures of the revolution served as catalysts for the crystallization of various paths that Jewish intellectuals chose to follow. They were faced with such options as choosing between ardently supporting the revolution or seeking alternatives, advocating various stripes of Jewish nationalism or supporting international socialism (choices that profoundly affected both Ansky and Zhitlovsky), and choosing between Hebrew and Yiddish (or Russian and other non-Jewish European languages) as languages of artistic and political expression. Essentially, these Jewish intellectuals were faced with the task of completely redefining Jewishness and Jewish culture in an age of revolution, and, in some cases, eradicating such particularistic, restrictive categories altogether.

There are, perhaps, no two better examples of the entire range of ideological choices that faced modernizing Russian Jewry than the intellectual journeys of S. Ansky and Chaim Zhitlovsky. These two childhood friends from Vitebsk, both reared in fairly traditional Jewish educational and family settings, rebelled against that tradition and pursued numerous, often radically opposed alternatives. In many ways, each one's intellectual development and changing ideological affiliations mirrored the other's, yet regarding certain key issues, they eventually differed. As young men, both Ansky and Zhitlovsky found themselves alienated from Jewish shtetl life and became increasingly intoxicated with the Hebrew literature of the Haskalah, and eventually Russian radical literature as well. Subsequently, both men drifted far from the Jewish world, becoming involved in Russian Populist and socialist revolutionary causes. Yet, after years of estrangement, both Ansky and Zhitlovsky eventually returned to actively participate in (nonreligious) Jewish life, each in his own particular manner. Their stories of alienation, abandonment, and return are, to a large degree, paradigmatic of the modern Jewish narrative.

For Ansky, the Dreyfus Affair in Paris began to reawaken his identification with the Jewish people, yet he remained committed to the cosmopolitan ethos of the Socialist International and continued writing almost exclusively in Russian until 1902, when he composed "Di shvue" ("The Oath"), the Yiddish anthem of the Jewish Labor party, the Bund. He gradually became more involved in Jewish issues, writing in Yiddish and Russian, and returned to Russia in 1905, where he played an active role in the leadership of the Social Revolutionary party. After the revolution he dedicated himself to various Jewish causes, especially the desire to recover the treasures of the Jewish people through the fields of folklore and ethnography. Ansky was deeply influenced by Zhitlovsky in his decision to return to active participation in Jewish life. Indeed, Ansky's childhood friend had long struggled to find a vision of Jewish cultural and political life that did not compromise his newfound socialist ideals. From the early 1880s onward, Zhitlovsky's main ideological linchpin was his attempt to wed revolutionary socialism with Jewish nationalism. Instead of choosing between these seemingly opposing worlds, Zhitlovsky attempted to merge them, staunchly advocating a "synthesis of international socialism and [Jewish] national culture, of political radicalism and Yiddish culturism."[4] He spent years trying to find the right formula to balance and reconcile these divergent streams.

At first, Ansky completely rejected Zhitlovsky's undertaking, for he maintained that one must choose between the old and the new, between revolution and Jewish nationalism.[5] Eventually, Ansky joined his old friend in attempting to synthesize the old and the new, things revolutionary and things Jewish. After 1905, he, too, struggled to restructure Jewish life according to the radical models he had learned as a member of the Russian Populist and socialist camps. In 1912–14 Ansky traveled through the Jewish provinces conducting ethnographic and folkloric research in an effort to extol the Jewish folk; this was his second experience of "going to the people," yet this time, they were the Jews of the remote *shtetlach* throughout the Pale, and not the Russian Orthodox peasants. The original title of Ansky's famous play *Der dibuk* (*The Dybbuk*) was *Tvishn tsvey veltn* (*Between Two Worlds*), which aptly describes the challenge both he and Zhitlovsky had to negotiate: how to carve out a Jewish space that was between two worlds, part neither of the traditional Jewish world nor of the dominant Christian world, but occupying a liminal space on the margins of both, or creating a new space that drew on both but in essence was something radically different and new. The *tseylem frage* debate between these two thinkers touches at the heart of these issues and reveals each one's distinct vision of the Jewish cultural renaissance they both worked so hard to realize.

It is against this backdrop that we must now briefly sketch the two pivotal stories at the root of the *tseylem frage* (a more detailed analysis will be given in the following chapter). Sholem Asch's "In a Carnival Night" presents a legendary tale set in medieval Rome, in which Jesus descends from the cross to show solidarity with his fellow Jewish martyrs who are persecuted by the local Christians. Asch depicts his Jewish protagonists as noble martyrs, constantly suffering at the hands of the barbaric Catholic Church and the local Christian population. Into this scene, Asch inserts Jesus, miraculously released from his place on the cross in the Church of St. Peter. He depicts him as a powerful, mystical, though human figure, who deeply empathizes with the plight of his fellow Jews. Jesus rejects the Christians' worship of him, and begs forgiveness from the Jewish Messiah (who according to a Jewish legend is chained to the gates of Rome) for all of the atrocities that Christians have committed against Jews in his name. In the story's climax Jesus is shown walking the martyr's path with the elders of the Jewish community, while in a mysterious epilogue, the matriarch Rachel and the Virgin Mary are portrayed sewing shrouds for all of the fallen martyrs. Clearly, Asch related to Jesus and Mary in a positive light while remaining very critical in his treatment of the story's Christian characters.

Although Asch's story of 1909 was not the first attempt to recover Jesus as a Jewish martyr and tragic hero, it was the first serious articulation to date of such sentiments in the realm of Yiddish literature. Yet, published one month before Asch's sensational work, Lamed Shapiro's even more startling story "Der tseylem" uses the cross in a very different way. It is a graphically violent and nightmarish tale that features murder and mayhem at its core, and offers no promise of Christian-Jewish reconciliation. Shapiro paints a gruesome picture of apocalyptic chaos in the form of a violent pogrom in Russia in which the pogromists carve the sign of the cross on their Jewish victim's forehead in an attempt to "save his Yid soul from hell." Instead of symbolizing Christian brotherly love, Shapiro's cross stands for a world of violence and anarchy, as the Jewish pogrom victim—himself an ardent revolutionary—branded with the cross becomes transformed into an "iron man," a brutal rapist and murderer. Shapiro's iconoclastic story, centered around the symbol of the cross (although it is depicted in a negative light), proved to be a very important catalyst in the process of East European Jews freely adopting Christian symbols and themes and inscribing them into the emerging secular canon of modern Jewish culture.

Themselves two of the most prominent architects of this emerging secular canon, Zhitlovsky and Ansky quickly engaged each other regarding the crucial issues these provocative stories raised. In a sense, Zhitlovsky forced the issue by choosing to publish the two stories in the journal he edited and then offering his review of them in the same issue in which the Asch story appeared. Ansky's contribution to the discussion, a two-part article entitled "Di tseylem frage," was primarily a response to Zhitlovsky's initial review, and not so much concerned with the stories themselves. As *Dos naye lebn* was essentially a mouthpiece for Zhitlovsky, it served as a vehicle for him to articulate his views on socialism, Jewish nationalism, secularism, Yiddishism, and a host of other progressive ideologies. As is apparent from his review, Zhitlovsky saw these two stories, especially Asch's, as sharing many facets of his own "enlightened" (*gebildete*) views regarding Jesus and Christianity. Furthermore, he exclaims that the stories "beg to be compared to each other" as they share a vitally important theme that, according to Zhitlovsky, reflects the great "stirring in the modern Jewish soul" (413). He asserts that both authors are courageous to deal with the subjects that they do, since they are grappling with the crucial question of how Jews and Christians could reconcile their bitter history and coexist in one universal "humanist culture."

This concept of the Jewish and Christian worlds coming together in one universal culture was a dominant facet in the ideology of the Haskalah dating back to the end of the eighteenth century, and the notion of rapprochement or even "merger" (*tsunoyfgissen*) between Jew and Christian, in a somewhat modified form, remained central in Zhitlovsky's worldview. In fact, he believed that such a merger even required Jews and Christians to fuse together their collective memories of the past as well as to forge a shared vision of the future. He recognized that the enduring problem of Jewish-Christian antagonism still presented a major obstacle for the realization of this harmonious vision, and he believed that each of the stories attempted to solve this problem in drastically different ways. Zhitlovsky viewed Shapiro's position as "purely nationalistic, dictated by a boundless hatred of the cross" while seeing Asch's solution as a "universal humanist one . . . full of forgiveness and sorrow for the persecuted [Jews] as well as the persecutors [Christians]" (414). Throughout his essay Zhitlovsky elucidates these two conflicting visions while advancing his own solution to the Crucifix Question, which explicitly embraces the universalist, humanist point of view expressed by Asch.

In analyzing Asch's story Zhitlovsky spends a great deal of time framing the story itself within the larger issues of the day. He focuses especially on establishing his notion of universal humanist culture (a central concern throughout Zhitlovsky's writings), as both his and Asch's understanding of Jesus and Christianity rest upon this notion. He begins this task by sketching out the history of Western civilization, which he sees as an aggregate of cultural contributions from different nations, starting with the Greco-Romans and including the Jewish people—until Christianity separated from Judaism—and the Germanic peoples. Here, we have a prime example of a modern Jewish thinker placing Jews and Judaism at the very foundation of Western civilization, a key ingredient in justifying the full participation of modern Jews in the civilization of the West. Yet, Zhitlovsky posits that this civilization came to be embodied by Christianity, as its religious stories, symbols, customs, and meanings became the very pillar of this civilization: the "spiritual treasure of the modern civilized world . . . even for atheists and freethinkers" (414). The Jews, he explains, have lived in this world permeated with these cultural influences (Greco-Roman, biblical, and Christian) for over a thousand years, yet have remained largely estranged from it. In detailing how the Jews have remained culturally distinct and isolated from these various cultural worlds that together make up Western civilization, Zhitlovsky presents an image of the Jews as outsiders, alien to modern civilized culture, cut off from their own ancestral patrimony by centuries of prejudice and isolation.

In stark contradiction to this history of Jewish cultural alienation, Zhitlovsky depicts the period of the Enlightenment movement (in the late eighteenth and early nineteenth centuries) as a time when both Jews and Christians began to create a new secular civilization free of religious dogmas and traditions, where science and reason prevailed, and common ground between Jews and Christians existed. Yet, despite his attraction to such utopian Enlightenment visions, Zhitlovsky homes in on one of the main dilemmas that had plagued this process from its inception, asking "on whose terms" this merger will be carried out. He tacitly acknowledges that pithy Enlightenment mottoes like "common ground" and "universal culture" really imply "Western" and "Christian," and posits that until now Jews who have "passed" in Western European civilization have typically used that civilization as the standard for evaluating Jewish culture and history. In other words, the Jewish past is reevaluated, put through a crucible that is provided by Christian civilization. However, at times Zhitlovsky himself blurs this distinction between "universal humanist ideals" and "West-European Christian" ideals, occasionally identifying them as one and the same (416). Zhitlovsky therefore, driven by his desire to "reintegrate the Jewish people into the mainstream of progressive human history,"[6] proposes that Jewish history and culture can only be made meaningful when reinterpreted by means of these "universal humanist ideals." Accordingly, he suggests that "we [Jews] can be elated by the richness that we find in our old treasure, we can be sure in our belief that these rediscovered riches will enrich all (human) culture with new values,—the 'value-criterion' being that which we took from modern Christian civilization" (417).

For Zhitlovsky then, it is necessary for the Jew to assimilate universal humanist values and ideals, born of Western-Christian civilization, in order to reinterpret Jewish culture and history and render it meaningful for the present. In essence, the Jew can only enter the Western world on its terms, no matter what role the Jew had in laying the foundations of this world. As we shall see, this subject became the major bone of contention for many of Zhitlovsky's critics, including Ansky, who criticized his ideology as overly assimilationist, ceding too much ground to European cultural norms and values. In any case, it is Zhitlovsky's conception of the centrality of Christian-Western culture in modern civilization that deeply informs his position on Jesus and Christianity.[7]

Zhitlovsky makes it abundantly clear that part and parcel of the integration of Jews into the dominant Christian culture is a thorough reevaluation of traditional Jewish contempt and hatred for the figure of Jesus and things Christian. In fact, he contends it is this ingrained hatred and animosity that often serves as a stumbling block for modern Jews trying to navigate mainstream Western culture. He admits that even educated Jews often maintain a negative attitude toward Christianity, and that he is himself uncomfortable at times when reading European literature in which sacred Christian themes are evoked. However, Zhitlovsky claims that for today's Jewish youth, and for the older Jews who have "taught their heart respect for Christianity," these age-old feelings of contempt and disparagement of Christianity are long gone. He states that "our youth is surrounded from all sides with the atmosphere of Christian tradition" (417), and that they absorb Christian influences in all aspects of their life: education, literature, recreation, and the like, because the dominant culture in which they live is Christian. Zhitlovsky argues that the more European education begins to influence the Jewish masses, the more Christian-friendly attitudes take hold among them. To illustrate this he claims that Jewish writers in European languages, who were typically more assimilated than Yiddish and Hebrew writers, have lost the traditional Jewish hatred for things Christian. In this light Zhitlovsky maintains that the time has come for East European Jewish intellectuals to critically reevaluate this anti-Christian tradition, and he alleges that Asch's story is the first in Yiddish literature to attempt such a reevaluation.

Illustrating his own repudiation of the anti-Christian tradition that so long pervaded Jewish culture, Zhitlovsky symbolically apologizes to the Virgin Mary, whom he refers to as his "sister Miriam," for the mocking way Jews have traditionally treated her. He alludes to the last scene in Asch's story in which Mary and the matriarch Rachel are depicted sewing shrouds together for the fallen Jewish martyrs, saying that when he was younger such a scene would have struck him as worse than apostasy. Zhitlovsky next turns his attention to Jesus himself, making the boldly provocative claim that Asch's story attempts to "revise the 'Dreyfus trial' in which our innocent brother from Nazareth is tried and crucified daily" (418). He thereby implies that Jesus is unfairly tried—as Dreyfus was by the French military—by Jews who continued to reject and disparage him, to "judge and crucify him daily." Furthermore, Zhitlovsky reiterates Asch's fictional portrayal of Jesus as "our brother," a fellow Jew who deserves his people's sympathy instead of their hatred and contempt. Especially in his second article on this theme—his response to Ansky, which I will discuss below—Zhitlovsky continually emphasizes the Jewishness (*yiddishkayt*) of Jesus, stressing that historically and culturally, Jesus must be viewed as part of the national legacy of the Jewish people.

At first glance, this stance, with its spirit of nationalistic Jewish pride, seems to contradict Zhitlovsky's aforementioned program of Jewish acculturation. However, it is precisely this sort of paradoxical tension that infuses the complex process of constructing new forms of Jewish identity and culture. Jewish thinkers like Zhitlovsky attempted to offset the intense assimilation that was often necessary for Jews to integrate themselves into Western society and culture by Judaizing certain foundational symbols of that culture—in this case, Jesus. So on the one hand, Zhitlovsky could argue that Jews had to rethink their attitudes toward Jesus as part of a larger acceptance of and attraction to the dominant Christian culture, while on the other hand, he could bolster Jewish national pride by maintaining that Jesus had to be understood within a Jewish purview to begin with.

Zhitlovsky concludes his discussion of Asch's work by contrasting the mood of tolerance and reconciliation that prevails in his story with the virulent protest against such a humane and optimistic position that is found in Shapiro's "iron man" with the cross on his forehead. He claims that many "young, pogrom-wounded" members of the Jewish intelligentsia are vehemently opposed to the merging of Jewish and Christian-European civilization into one unified "European-Jewish world" (420), a desire that clearly preoccupied both Zhitlovsky and Asch. In fact, Zhitlovsky contends that the underlying subject of Shapiro's story is actually the ambivalent position of the young Jewish revolutionary who is caught between two worlds: a traditional Jewish world he rejects, and a modern Christian world that still ultimately rejects him for being a Jew. Zhitlovsky specifically alludes to the type of Jewish intellectual whom he calls the "revolutionary penitent" (*ba'al teshuvah*)—one who renounces his new life in the revolutionary movement and returns wholeheartedly to the Jewish people—claiming that this also applies to Shapiro's protagonist, the *tseylem mahn*. (This scenario also seems to aptly describe both Zhitlovsky and Ansky, themselves revolutionary penitents of sorts.) The protagonist's repudiation of the revolution is symbolically enacted when, once branded by the sign of the cross, he rapes and strangles his Russian girlfriend and fellow revolutionary activist. Zhitlovsky asserts that Shapiro's story is a true reflection of his times, and especially the rape scene should be interpreted as showing nothing more than "the longing for power felt by a generation that in reality feels oppressed, sickly, and small" (476). Shapiro's story, according to Zhitlovsky's highly politicized reading, thereby gives voice to the pogrom-wounded and embittered Jewish intelligentsia who want to strike back violently at the revolutionary movement that betrayed them.

Zhitlovsky understands the main thrust of Shapiro's story to be a repudiation of the Jewish-Christian tradition of brotherly love in favor of the "goyish-Christian" reality of brutality and rage. (His opposition of "Jewish-Christian" with "goyish-Christian" reflects his belief that contemporary Christianity has very little to do with ancient Christianity, which was strongly rooted in Judaism.) He contrasts this message with Asch's, which he sees as the exact opposite: an affirmation of the Jewish-Christian tradition of brotherly love over the "goyish-Christian" reality. He concludes that these are "two voices from life . . . two opposites from the modern Jewish sentiment . . . which one will resound? Or must there be a third voice that will encompass them both?" (479). Clearly, in his mind, anyone who fights for revolution, universal rights, human liberation, and the like must embrace the Judeo-Christian ideals of love and compassion. This implies that any Jew fighting for universal and not just Jewish causes must not only tolerate Christians and their religion, but must really embrace the common ground of their two religions and civilizations, including the powerful symbols of these ideals, such as the figure of Jesus. It is in this spirit that Zhitlovsky, at the beginning of his article, criticizes Shapiro's story for being "purely nationalist" while applauding the "universal humanism" of Asch's story.

For a Jew like Zhitlovsky, who ascribes to a revolutionary socialist ideology in which internationalism and universalism displace narrow national parochialism, a rejection of traditional religious prejudice in which Christianity is disdained is also necessary. It therefore seems that

Zhitlovsky's vision of the enlightened Jewish attitude toward Jesus and Christianity would preclude any kind of nationally defined agenda. Yet, this is contradicted by a manifestation of Zhitlovsky's own peculiar brand of nationalism. His theory of the origins of Western-Christian civilization (like Geiger's) articulates his notion that Jews and Judaism occupy a central place in that civilization and therefore there is no need to assimilate to or mimic the Gentiles in participating fully in the ideals and practices of that culture. Rather, by throwing off the corrupt accretions of rabbinic Judaism, which for years supplanted the original spirit of primitive Judaism and Israelite religion, Jews can regain their true culture and will no longer be at odds with the authentic tenets of Western civilization, which are, after all, inherently Jewish. Christians too, in this formulation, must remove the malignant layers of their religion, which have accrued over the years, distorting its authentic meanings and values. This complex negotiation between socialist internationalism, secular humanism, and Jewish national identification, so persistent throughout Zhitlovsky's life and writings, profoundly shapes his attitude toward Jesus and Christianity. He adopts a culturally assimilationist agenda, especially in the way he conceives of Jesus and the significance of his life and teachings, yet he maintains a strong sense of Jewish particularism by claiming Jesus as an "innocent Jewish brother," and Mary as his "sister Miriam." He sees them both as integral to Jewish history. They should be accepted by enlightened Jews not because of their centrality to Christians, but primarily on account of their Jewishness.

Ansky wasted little time responding to his old friend, as the first part of his rebuttal to Zhitlovsky's essay appeared three issues later in *Dos naye lebn* under the title "Di tseylem frage."[8] Ansky, generally ignoring the two stories that prompted Zhitlovsky's article,[9] vehemently attacked Zhitlovsky's two major premises, which he outlines as follows: (1) Jews must adopt the European view on Christ and Christianity because the entire European civilization that Jews now embrace as part of their entry into the family of civilized nations is a Christian one; (2) Jews must make peace with Christ and Christianity because the current relationship of Jews with both is unworthy and unjust (613). Ansky explicitly rejects both these arguments and spends the remainder of the article thoroughly rebutting Zhitlovsky's position. For him, there is no merit to Zhitlovsky's call to reverse the unfair Jewish verdict against our innocent "crucified brother." Ansky claims that because Zhitlovsky is sure Jesus will grant forgiveness to the Jews, he calls for peace and unity between the Jews and Jesus. He also astutely recognizes that Zhitlovsky's idea that this "peace process" should include Jesus reconciling with the Messiah and Mary with the matriarch Rachel stems directly from Asch's story. Moreover, Ansky alleges that Zhitlovsky expands the idea of reconciliation to include not only "the two Messiahs and the two 'mothers,'" but also peace between "the cross and the Torah scroll, between 'Christian European civilization' and the Jewish talmudic culture" (611). Ansky clearly grasps the larger issues at hand, especially regarding cultural assimilation and the question of how far Jews must go in repudiating their own traditions while simultaneously embracing European Christian culture. For Ansky then, rejecting Zhitlovsky's invitation to embrace Jesus in a sympathetic manner also entailed his refusal to abandon what he defines as "Jewish talmudic culture" in favor of the dominant Christian culture. At stake was the legitimation of a distinct, modern Jewish cultural identity.

The first issue Ansky takes up at length is Zhitlovsky's conception of civilization and culture. He challenges Zhitlovsky's definition of civilization and wonders just what he means when he speaks of the "Christian civilized world" or "Christian civilization." Ansky defines civilization as "that phenomenon and aspiration, which widens man's horizons, frees man's spirit and [clears] the ground for human progress" (613), and declares that this civilization is inevitable for all nations that strive for a historical life. In this sense, Ansky questions why Zhitlovsky terms civilization "Christian" when, he argues, the Christian Church has historically fought against civilization in every manner possible. In fact, Ansky asserts, European civilization is actually anti-Christian, and Jews can embrace it while remaining indifferent or even unfriendly to Christianity itself. Ansky effectively distinguishes between civilization in the abstract and particular national cultures. He cites examples of several non-Western nations that had recently embraced European civilization without embracing Christianity, such as Japan, China, and Turkey. Ansky claims that the Jews have their own unique culture—like the Japanese and Chinese—and therefore do not need to adopt Christian or even Greek or German culture to partake in modern civilization. In

Ansky's view, Jewish culture needs Dante, Raphael, and Bach no more than Christian culture needs the Talmud, Yehudah Ha-Levi, or Hasidism to reach spiritual greatness. Each culture has its distinct manifestations, and one is not inherently better or more civilized than the other. Therefore, Zhitlovsky is wrong in postulating that the only way Jews can join the family of nations is through the gate of Christianity, and Ansky further muses that Zhitlovsky himself is overly enamored of Christian culture. Ansky's Jewish cultural pride bespeaks an agenda of integration—full Jewish equality and participation in all walks of modern civil society—as opposed to assimilation. Ansky's celebration of the Jewish folk and their indigenous popular culture also informs his defense of Jewish cultural distinctiveness.

Regarding Zhitlovsky's call for Jews to "make peace" with Jesus, Ansky questions what Zhitlovsky means by "Christ." Is he calling for a reconciliation with the sacred legend of Christianity and the fundamental Christian idea of the divine god-man at its center, or with Christ's teachings ("torah") about love and forgiveness? Ansky makes it clear that there is no room for Jews to accept the former, as the idea of a divine god-man is antithetical to core Jewish beliefs, and any Jew who accepts this idea ceases to be a Jew and cuts himself off from Jewish culture in its entirety. (This idea was shared by Ahad Ha-Am and his supporters in the Brenner Affair controversy.) This starkly contradicts Zhitlovsky's view that a Jew who embraces Christianity can remain a part of the Jewish people simply by speaking Yiddish and maintaining Jewish national pride. Ansky allows that it is acceptable for Jews to reconcile with the Christian legend in two particular ways: incorporating aspects of this legend in such a way that they inspire Jewish artistic creations, or assimilating European artistic works and cultural manifestations, which are permeated by Christian themes.

In this vein, Ansky opens the second installment of his article with the following question: "If the 'Christian legend' must and will remain forever foreign to the Jewish spirit, will the most beautiful and precious pearls of Christian culture also remain eternally foreign to Jews?" (665). This query again powerfully illustrates that for Ansky, as well as for Zhitlovsky, the Crucifix Question is primarily a question of the limits of Jewish cultural assimilation over against the maintenance of an authentic Jewish cultural identity. Will Jews be able to embrace the works of Bach, Beethoven or Dante, invested as they are with the Christian legend, and permeated with Christian themes and imagery? Ansky conveys an intense spirit of Jewish national particularism when he proclaims that "Jews must remain Jews and will never trade in their *yiddishkayt* even for the priceless works of Raphael and Beethoven" (665). It is only by infusing these works with some universal or (even better) Jewish meaning, Ansky feels, that they can become suitable for Jews. He claims that Jewish folklore has been able to incorporate elements of general European folk traditions by reworking the mundane motifs into authentically spiritual ones, and he feels that the same kind of transformation could occur with Christian works of literature and art. According to Ansky then, Jews can only accept these Christian cultural works once they have been invested with an authentic Jewish spirit. (As we shall see below, many of the modernist Yiddish writers who depicted Christian figures and motifs frequently clothed them in a Jewish form as Ansky suggested.)

Another factor shaping Ansky's rejection of Zhitlovsky's position is his appreciation of the popular Jewish conception of Jesus as the symbol of Christian anti-Semitism. Ansky understands that in order for Jews to embrace the Christian legend so that it becomes their own, a major psychological shift is required to overturn the two-thousand-year legacy of Christian-Jewish animosity, religious conflict, and violence. Clearly, Ansky himself does not believe that such a turnabout can, or even should, occur. He asserts that "Jews have their [own] Christian legend, which is even deeper and more tragic than Zhitlovsky thinks" (615). To illustrate this point, Ansky cites certain Jewish folk beliefs that maintain that if one sticks a knife into the earth on Christmas Eve (*nitl nakht*) blood will pour out. Ansky explains this tradition as stemming from the popular Jewish sentiment that from the time of Jesus' birth, Jewish blood has been spilled in his name and has soaked the entire earth. For the most part, Ansky, despite his enlightened bearing and intellectual stature, sympathizes with this popular Jewish superstition, showing his allegiance to and empathy for the feelings of the Jewish folk.

Unlike other Jewish intellectuals both before and after him, Ansky seems to share the popular Jewish attitude that Jesus is indistinguishable from the abominable acts that Christians have committed in his name. He even attempts to justify this attitude by locating many of the roots of Christian persecution and violence in the ethical teachings of Jesus. More so than the many Jewish historians and Reformers preceding him, Ansky stresses the differences between Jewish teachings and the teaching of Jesus. He particularly criticizes Jesus' ethical philosophy—turn the other cheek, give the shirt off your back, love your enemies, etc.—as being "a little too good, too pious,"[10] suggesting that the impossibility of living up to such rigorous ethical demands left something of a moral vacuum in Christian society. Thus, Ansky makes the claim that it was precisely these ethical codes of Jesus, these quintessential Christian teachings, that produced the historical legacy of Christian violence and oppression. Ansky maintains that Jesus' personality must be closely scrutinized before Jews can "make peace" with him and "revise the verdict" against him (667).

In an attempt to evaluate Jesus' personality Ansky lays out the criteria for determining the "godly men" of history (such as Moses, Buddha, and Socrates) and then examines whether or not Jesus meets these criteria. It seems clear from the outset that Ansky thinks Jesus does not belong among these outstanding "godly men." He regards Jesus as a run-of-the-mill magician who practiced magic in his own name as a way of gaining followers (a view reminiscent of the *Toldot Yeshu*). He faults Jesus for acting in his own name and not on God's behalf and contends that Jesus did not even practice what he preached—he was not humble, self-sacrificing, gentle, meek, and so on. Everything he did was for his own mission and self-advancement. Ansky even refers to the episode in which Jesus ejects the moneylenders from the Temple as the first pogrom! He argues that Jesus put himself above his own teachings like a "superman" exempt from moral constrictions. In this manner, Ansky takes every opportunity to harshly criticize Jesus' actions in the gospels as going against the principles of his own teachings. In conclusion, Ansky rejects Zhitlovsky's call to revise the Jewish verdict against Jesus, thoroughly renouncing him on every count, as a Jew, as a teacher, as a prophet, and as a "godly man." Ansky boldly proclaims that Jesus' name will never be untainted from the rivers of Jewish blood shed on its account (667–71).

Ansky's stance is somewhat surprising for someone of his political-ideological orientation and progressive intellectual leanings. The fact that he was so intimately involved in Russian culture and especially the Russian Populist movement seemingly contradicts the unfavorable perceptions of Jesus he articulates in "Di tseylem frage." His views seem more akin to those of someone from the traditionalist camp, or maybe those of an ardent nationalist who would want to maintain strict boundaries between Jews and Christians. Yet, I suggest that it was precisely Ansky's intellectual and ideological evolution, with his early alienation from Jewish life followed by total immersion in the Russian Populist movement and a subsequent "return" to the Jewish people, that accounts for such a stance. His biting criticism of Jesus and Christian civilization as expressed in his response to Zhitlovsky's article must be seen in this light, as a part of his renunciation of his earlier ideological and cultural stance.[11] The fact that at one point Ansky even contemplated conversion to Christianity as the culmination of his embrace of the Russian *narod* or folk and that Zhitlovsky felt compelled to talk him out of it[12] suggests the possibility that once he firmly realigned himself with the Jewish people he was anxious to distance himself from the world of Christianity; overcompensation was a mechanism of Ansky's return.

Ansky's scathing criticism of Zhitlovsky (and Asch) regarding their sympathetic depictions of Jesus reveals that the divisiveness of the Crucifix Question is closely linked to the ideological discord that gripped the progressive Jewish intelligentsia regarding crucial issues like assimilation, Jewish-Christian relations, and Jewish self-definition. In general, these secular intellectuals were constantly redefining the nature of Jewish identity and redrawing the boundaries of Jewish culture. For Zhitlovsky, Asch, and many others, this process was driven by a universalized Jewish vision of a more broadly defined, inclusive Jewish culture in which the universal was stressed over the particular. The age-old quintessential emblem of otherness and Jewish-Christian animosity— Jesus—was made assimilable by reinscribing him into an enlightened Jewish framework. This move emphatically underscores the desire of these Jewish intellectuals to assimilate the dominant ("goyish") culture while maintaining a definite, albeit renewed, sense of *yiddishkayt*. However, dissenting voices, such as Ansky's—and he was by no means alone—resisted such a bold appropriation of Jesus and other Christian symbols, seeing it as a betrayal of Jewish cultural integrity.

Dr. Issur Ginsburg (1872–1947), a publicist associated with the

Yiddish daily *Forverts* (*Forward*) in New York (and a good friend of
Asch's), also contributed to the debate in *Dos naye lebn* with a two-part
article entitled "Concerning the Crucifix Question" ("Tsu der tseylem
frage").[13] Ginsburg articulated more of a middle ground than Ansky,
criticizing both Asch and Zhitlovsky for glorifying Jesus to the extent
that they did, while reasserting the historical claims made by earlier
Jewish scholars such as Geiger and Graetz that Jesus must be viewed
as a Jew within a Jewish historical framework. In fact, Ginsburg cites
a long list of Jewish thinkers, including Maimonides, Jacob Emden,
Isaac Ber Levinsohn, Graetz, Geiger, and even Kaufman Kohler, in
order to establish that enlightened Jews have already "accepted" Jesus
as a Jewish figure; this list demonstrates that, contrary to popular assumptions, East European Jewish intellectuals writing in Yiddish were
indeed often familiar with Jewish scholarship emanating from German
and American circles.

Despite Ginsburg's acknowledgment of Jesus' Jewishness, however, he rails against those, like Asch and Zhitlovsky, who he feels have
"gone too far" in characterizing Jesus as the "greatest rabbi," "freedom
fighter," etc., seeing this as unnecessary adulation not borne out by
the historical record. Ginsburg views Zhitlovsky's appeal to embrace
Christian collective memory over Jewish memory as tantamount to
national suicide, as he astutely recognizes the importance for modern
Jews of maintaining the collective recollection of their past alongside
more scholarly accounts.[14] In 1917 Ginsburg himself published a popular history in Yiddish on the origins of Christianity (*Di entshteyung fun
kristntum*) in which he fully laid out his views on the (Jewish) history
of Jesus and his teachings.[15] Again, he echoes Geiger and Graetz, reclaiming Jesus as a son of the Jewish people while firmly maintaining
that he taught nothing new or original, and should not be glorified
or romanticized. Ginsburg asserts that, ultimately, both the traditional
versions of Jesus' life, Christian and Jewish, must be revised in favor of
the objective historical truth.

Perhaps the most insightful contribution to the Crucifix Question
discussion was a letter addressed to Zhitlovsky entitled "A Letter from a
Friend about the Crucifix Question." The author reveals the complexity
of the issues at the center of this debate by proclaiming that he agrees
with both Ansky and Zhitlovsky. He acknowledges that, like Ansky,

he sees Jesus as a symbol of Christian persecution and anti-Semitic violence. However, he confesses to Zhitlovsky that he also has a more sympathetic conception of Jesus as a rebel who fought against an oppressive regime, as a champion of the poor and downtrodden, and as a pale dreamer and preacher of love who died a tragic death on the cross on account of his ideals. He concludes that for Jews, these two models of Jesus—the saintly rabbi and the villain responsible for so much Jewish suffering—must exist simultaneously. Using a clever Yiddish wordplay, the author contends that the Christian "trinity" (*drayeynikayt*) has created a Jewish "duality" (*tsveyeynikayt*).[16] In other words, the Christian deification of Jesus and the subsequent historical legacy of Christian persecution of Jews in his name resulted in a double image of Jesus etched into the Jewish cultural consciousness. There, the life of Jesus the man competes with the legacy of Jesus the god, and the author suggests that the latter often obscures the former. In conclusion, he tells Zhitlovsky that "you are right as a historian of the poetic past; Ansky is right as a sympathetic Jew of the sorrowful present."[17] This letter underscores the profound ambivalence with which modern Jews, even those among the progressive intelligentsia, often approached the figure of Jesus.

It was precisely this widespread ambivalence that Zhitlovsky attempted to erase. In his swift response to Ansky, he assailed the fact that the one thing today's freethinking Jews (*apikorsim*) like Ansky had in common with traditional Jews was an unabashed hatred and contempt for Christ and Christianity.[18] He concedes that "there are many reasons why Jewish radicals hate Christianity" (621), and he sets out to explain several of them. He posits that there is such an entrenched hatred toward Jesus in traditional Jewish culture that even Jewish radicals who remove themselves from this culture do not necessarily expunge these ingrained feelings about Jesus and things Christian. Also, Zhitlovsky reasons, as a fervent secularist and most likely a socialist, the Jewish radical hates Christianity (and Jesus) qua religion along with all of the superstition and oppression that is associated with it. Even so, Zhitlovsky feels, it is imperative to recognize that religion is part and parcel of human culture and will never be completely eradicated. Furthermore, it is possible, even for the radicals, to embrace the "poetic content" that each religion possesses. Zhitlovsky observes that Hasidism has ceased to be a subject of scorn and derision among enlightened Jews, and is now a popular subject for modern Jewish writers because its universal, human, poetic inner meaning has been distilled from its ossified outer form. He contends that enlightened Jews have only approached Judaism in this new way, and have not yet embraced the universal-human, poetic meanings of other religions. He affirms that he, too, is a secular Jew who does not believe in the "God of Abraham" but that he embraces the universal poetic meaning of Judaism as well as other religions.[19]

As to the question of what the proper stance of Jews toward Christian civilization and culture should be, Zhitlovsky rejects Ansky's argument of cultural relativism, maintaining his position that modern Christian civilization, which he defines here as "the civilization of the educated Christian nations from the European-American culture spectrum" (742), is the best and most progressive of all the civilizations. He claims, contra Ansky, that "talmudic Jewish culture" is not equal to educated Christian culture, seeing the culture of the Talmud, the Kabbalah, and rabbinic learning as inferior to that of Raphael, Dante, and Bach. He goes as far as to proclaim that the rabbinic Jewish world is not worth the "rivers of Jewish blood" that have been sacrificed in its defense. Zhitlovsky concedes that although rabbinic culture preserved Judaism in an unusually hostile world, it should not be the end goal of Jewish culture. He claims that "we no longer believe in the Jewish religion and are searching for other, nonreligious factors that will give us the possibility to live and evolve" (743). This radical rejection of traditional Jewish culture in the pursuit of distinctly new and modern cultural forms infused Zhitlovsky's thinking and shaped most of his various ideological programs. This resulted in new formulations of Jewish national distinctiveness—such as Zhitlovsky's linguistic nationalism or Yiddishism—that primarily rested on secular universal principles and ideals.

In responding to Ansky's central point rejecting Zhitlovsky's call to "revise the Jewish judgment" passed on Jesus, Zhitlovsky offers a lengthy summary of the "unrevised" Jewish narrative of Jesus' life. He presents a composite of the Jewish folk version of Jesus' life as found in the *Toldot Yeshu*, rabbinic writings, and popular legends and customs (such as playing cards on Christmas Eve)[20] in order to demonstrate how absurd and unjust the traditional Jewish view of Jesus is. These views belong only to the now obsolete Jewish spiritual ghetto, Zhitlovsky argues, and he wonders what will happen to today's Jewish youth who drink up European culture beyond the gates of the ghetto and encounter strikingly different images of Jesus. Again, it is apparent that for Zhitlovsky, enlightened Jews must come to terms with Jesus if they are to take part in Western culture. After citing a long passage from John Stuart Mill's *On Religion* as an example of an enlightened, contemporary assessment of Jesus, Zhitlovsky asks which view of Jesus is more accurate: Is he an exemplar of morality or an emblem of evil? He concludes that Jews, as they follow the path of universal human progress, must embrace the Christian story of Jesus, which reflects more of the historical truth about Jesus' life. Although this statement sounds like an affirmation of Christian faith, it seems that Zhitlovsky has a kind of secular-universal Christian view of Jesus in mind like that of Mill or the Unitarians—one that is not concerned with traditional Christian dogma. In this sense, Zhitlovsky equates "Christian" with "universal" and "progressive." To complicate his stance even further, Zhitlovsky calls the Jewish story of Jesus a "blasphemy of all that should be precious and sacred to men" and proclaims that *"every Jew should be proud of the fact that Jesus is our brother, flesh of our flesh and blood of our blood"* (631; emphasis mine). According to Zhitlovsky's paradoxical argument then, Jews must adopt an enlightened Christian view of Jesus while simultaneously celebrating the fact that he is a Jew: "flesh of our flesh." The tension between his program of acculturation and his assertion of Jewish national sentiment is quite apparent; Jewishness is to be found even at the heart of modern Christian civilization.

To be sure, this was not the first time Zhitlovsky had taken up this theme. In one of his earliest scholarly works, *Thoughts on the Historical Destiny of Judaism* (in Russian, 1885–87), he had advanced the theory that Jesus was one of the Essene sect, and an exemplar of Jewish social justice. Zhitlovsky researched and wrote his *Thoughts* in St. Petersburg as part of his attempt to offer a "scientific explanation for Jewish national survival over the centuries."[21] It articulated an ideology that sought a middle ground between assimilation and Zionism in which Zhitlovsky called for "the revival of ancient ethical ideals that would serve both to preserve Jewry and to reintegrate the Jewish people into the mainstream of progressive human history."[22] Like many other reform-minded Jewish intellectuals at the time (including Zionist thinkers), Zhitlovsky looked to the ancient Jewish past to find meaningful ideals that had been lost during the course of the Diaspora, and which had to be reclaimed for Judaism to become revitalized and vibrant. What sets Zhitlovsky's theory apart is his stress on the importance of the Essenes as a model for communal and ethical values. Unlike the majority of scholars, he believed the Essenes to have been the most progressive Jewish sect of their time. He saw them as a group of social reformers and nationalists, closely connected to the Zealots. He also believed them to be radically apocalyptic, actively campaigning for one of their members to be declared Messiah and lead the people in a national uprising against the Romans. Zhitlovsky claimed that Jesus had to be understood within this framework, not as a heretical sorcerer and ascetic, but as an ardent nationalist and revolutionary.

Although it was not widely read by many Russian Jews upon publication, the liberal Russian Jewish historian Simon Dubnov condemned Zhitlovsky's controversial essay as a "confused and dangerous tract."[23] One of Dubnov's major objections was to "Zhitlovsky's positive view of early Christianity as reflected in the teachings of the Essenes, which he claimed would lead to mass conversion, while creating the impression among Russian readers that the acceptance of Christianity by masses of Jews would obviate the need for the granting of civil rights."[24] Dubnov's reaction to Zhitlovsky's nascent views on early Christianity anticipates Ansky's reaction to Zhitlovsky's 1909 article about Jewish attitudes toward Jesus and Christianity. In each case, Zhitlovsky's detractors were concerned that his tolerant and sympathetic stance toward Jesus and Christianity implied a desire for mass conversion and an abandonment of Jewish national loyalty. They failed to see his theories as a kind of national reclamation of Jesus as a Jew, but rather, as a defection to the enemy camp. It is important to point out however, that Dubnov himself articulated a fairly positive view of Jesus. In response to a questionnaire by the American publishers Funk & Wagnalls about the historical place of Jesus (in 1899) and a subsequent inquiry about contemporary Jewish attitudes toward the figure of Jesus (in 1901), Dubnov compared Jesus to the Baal Shem Tov, and stated that "he considered Jesus a Jewish prophet who had propounded his teachings to fellow Jews." Yet Dubnov realized that such progressive Jewish views of Jesus were antithetical to the attitudes of the common Jew. He asserted that "the progressive Jewish intelligentsia . . . saw in Jesus one of the best sons of the people, a herald of love and forgiveness. But it was difficult to ask historical objectivity of the ordinary Jew, who was in no position to forget that his forefathers had for centuries been the victims of cruel reprisals perpetrated in the name of Jesus."[25] Unlike Zhitlovsky, but siding with Ansky, Dubnov seems to privilege the position of the "ordinary Jew" and reject the possibility of reclaiming Jesus on any sort of broad national level.

David Weinberg attempts to explain Zhitlovsky's interest in Jesus and Christianity in the context of his profound hatred for Jewish Orthodoxy: "It was his negative attitude toward Orthodoxy and his search for the true essence of Judaism that explained his fascination with Christianity and with the figure of Jesus in particular."[26] Zhitlovsky's interest in Jesus also stemmed from his conviction that the Essenes were an idyllic community that should be emulated by contemporary Jews, and he saw Jesus as the "clearest embodiment of the ideals of the Essenes."[27] Weinberg's conclusion on the topic reveals Zhitlovsky's thorough, very personal identification with Jesus:

> Throughout his life, Zhitlovsky continually stressed the similarities in their thought and activity. Like Jesus, he saw himself as rejected by both rabbinic Judaism and assimilationists because of his attempt to synthesize Jewish national and universal social ideals. . . . Zhitlovsky also looked to Jesus as a powerful historical and personal symbol of the embattled Jewish nationalist during a period of rupture in established Jewish life. Though denied and rejected in his own time, Zhitlovsky believed that his message, like that of the historical Jesus, would eventually gain respectability and acclaim within his own group of Jewish "disciples" and among progressive men and women everywhere.[28]

Weinberg also stresses that Zhitlovsky never considered conversion and completely rejected Christian dogma and superstition regarding Jesus, emphasizing his prophetic rather than his miraculous nature. He did consider him to be a "holy teacher," but his main significance "was as a symbolic figure whose life, like those of other metahistorical figures, embodied significant truths about the human condition."[29] Zhitlovsky once remarked, "I believe in Jesus as much as [I believe] in the Jewish Messiah and in both no more than in the Greco-Roman

Venus-Aphrodite. None is superior to the other."[30] This statement demonstrates the cosmopolitan component of Zhitlovsky's worldview in which "metahistorical" figures ranging from Jesus to Venus could be viewed as valid modern heroes once they had been reinvented in a secular universalist guise.

As Zhitlovsky elaborates on his earlier theory in his 1909 article, it becomes clear that his historical understanding of Jesus and the Essenes is bound up with his ideological reevaluation of the past. By seeing Jesus' actions and teachings as the epitome of the Essene ideals such as communalism and contempt for wealth and personal property, Zhitlovsky was constructing an image of Jesus that harmonized with his own political orientation and social philosophy. In fact, Zhitlovsky's depiction of Jesus renders him a proto-Populist in his rigorous ethical system, ideological purity and zeal, and, above all, his "going to the people." Moreover, he proclaims that he sees in the early Christian community the "most progressive point to which the Jewish national idea could have developed in the period before the Great Revolt against Rome" (730). However, Zhitlovsky concedes that when Jesus failed to achieve national liberation as the "king of the Jews," the majority of Jews (including the Essenes) rightly turned away from him, affiliating themselves with other factions like the Zealots or the Pharisees instead. Zhitlovsky muses that if he had lived at that time he would have been one of Jesus' disciples, sword in hand, joining him in the revolution against Rome. He boldly proclaims that *"Jesus was martyred as the first Jewish socialist revolutionary"* (731, emphasis mine).

Of course, Zhitlovsky was by no means the first to evaluate Jesus' life and actions through the prism of contemporary ideology, and he was following a long line of European socialists throughout the nineteenth century who had identified Jesus as the original socialist. In this respect, Zhitlovsky's portrayal of Jesus reflects his own distinctive and complex ideology: a unique synthesis of Jewish nationalism, socialist cosmopolitanism, and Christian-oriented acculturation. Zhitlovsky's unorthodox notion of Jewish identity also finds expression in his reading of Jesus and the early Christian community. He makes it clear that for him, Jesus and the early Christians are only laudable in that they were loyal to the Jewish nation, despite any religious differences that might have distinguished them. This follows from his assertion that Jewish identity was based not only on religious conviction, but also on national allegiance. Zhitlovsky continually stresses Jesus' nationalist aspirations, claiming that the Romans were solely responsible for his execution as a political threat to the Empire. He takes issue with Ansky's claim that Jesus' dispute with the moneylenders was the "first pogrom," finding it to be anachronistic and utterly absurd. He implies that this episode in the Temple was really an act of revolution, and that in calling it a pogrom, Ansky betrays the fact that he conceives of Jesus as a "goy" rather than as a Jew. Zhitlovsky contends that in actuality Jesus was a *Jewish* prophet, a *Jewish* Messiah, and a *Jewish* freedom fighter (737).

Zhitlovsky's position on Jesus is far from being a product of assimilation, but rather is an illustration of his new breed of Jewish national identity. Zhitlovsky claims that Ansky is terribly mistaken if he believes that his view of Jesus and Christianity is the Jewish, national one, and Zhitlovsky's is the "goyish," assimilated one. The truth, Zhitlovsky proclaims, is the opposite. He sees the matter completely in terms of a new, national Jewish spirit that is neither parochial and antiquated nor assimilationist and alien. He writes in response to Ansky that only one who has not been completely freed from the "assimilationist ideal" and does not see a national life-force in the Jewish people "lives in constant fear of the surrounding environment" (744). Such a person needs to remain closed off from Christian beliefs. Again, Zhitlovsky stresses that "only such a one who does not feel the growing powers of the new (Jewish) national revival cannot manage without hatred and contempt for Christ and Christianity" (744). Out of weakness he must heap scorn on this "foreign god" before he can deny him. Zhitlovsky, however, implies that Jews of this kind (including Ansky) are in the minority: "A great part of my generation, myself included, feel the powers of Jewish national regeneration . . . and are strong enough to look this once despised and alien god in the eye. We do not need to besmirch him in order to avoid succumbing to his powers. We do not want to bow to him. On the contrary, we want to return him to the yoke from which he was wrenched. We want to once again return him to his proper place: in the history of *our* people as one of *our* most magnificent heroes, as one of the first fighters for *our* social and national liberation" (745, emphasis mine). With these words Zhitlovsky explicitly reconciles his passionate embrace of the figure of Jesus with his equally ardent support for a

Jewish national renaissance. While in the eyes of Ansky and Ginsburg, Zhitlovsky's ideas about Jesus and the new approach Jews should adopt toward him were beyond the pale of even a progressive, secular Jewish agenda, they reflected an attempt at a new kind of cultural synthesis that was integral to Zhitlovsky's entire ideological vision, and in many ways characteristic of the emerging secular canon of modern Yiddish culture as a whole.

Although Zhitlovsky admittedly goes much further in his positive assessment of Jesus' ethical and spiritual teachings than his maskilic predecessors in Western Europe such as Mendelssohn, Geiger, and Graetz, he is basically in accord with the predominant representation of Jesus emanating from the Reform movement during his own lifetime. The views of such Reform thinkers as I. M. Wise, Emil Hirsch, and Kaufman Kohler also attribute to Jesus a unique spiritual and ethical power, to an extent that many of their critics considered blasphemous. Moreover, like his Reform contemporaries, Zhitlovsky also combines this exalted view of Jesus with a plea to claim him as "one of our own" and return him to the pages of Jewish history as one of its greatest heroes.[31] These similarities between Zhitlovsky and his Reform contemporaries, with whom he had very little in common politically, ideologically, or theologically, suggest that a wider phenomenon was at work regarding Jewish perceptions and representations of Jesus. It involved Jews from distinctive regional environments and disparate ideologies, working in various genres. There were no firm intellectual boundaries in the Jewish world between Eastern and Western Europe, especially when Russian Jews like Zhitlovsky and Ansky, and countless others, spent many years living in West European countries and America. Intellectual ideas and trends disseminated widely, ignoring political borders.

The Brenner Affair

The Crucifix Question was not the only debate centering on the issues of Jesus and Christianity raging among Jewish intellectuals during the first decade or so of the twentieth century. In fact, these subjects had intermittently occupied the East European Jewish intelligentsia and periodical press since the turn of the century. As assimilation became rampant, Christianity became an explosive issue among modern Russian Jews, since assimilation often entailed conversion to Christianity. In this sense, Christianity came to be viewed as a dangerous threat to modern Jewish intellectuals ever since they began challenging and testing the foundations of Judaism and Jewish identity. In fact, the phenomenon of Jews converting to Christianity from the ranks of the young intelligentsia or the assimilated Russian Jewish youth had become a fundamental concern for many leading intellectuals, like Ahad Ha-Am, who hoped to stem this tide of apostasy and conversion.[32] Indeed, the subject of apostasy supplied the background context for both Ahad Ha-Am's and Brenner's articles, as well as many of the discussions and debates constituting the whole Brenner Affair. The often heated debates and discussions of these issues in the Jewish press can be seen as indicative of this crisis of Jewish identity, part of the cultural milieu best embodied by the question "Le-an?" ("Whither?")—which served as the title of a novel, and by itself, or in some variant form, as the title of numerous articles addressing the subject of what shape modern Jewish culture and identity needed to take to alleviate the crisis in the Jewish world.

Before the Brenner Affair emerged in late 1910, there were several earlier controversies sparked by such writers as Shai Ish Hurwitz (1861–1922),[33] who took controversial stands on the issue of conversion and Christianity more generally. This had steadily become an incendiary issue for the entire Jewish intellectual world—Zionist, Autonomist, or Socialist; Hebrew-, Yiddish-, or Russian-speaking—which often forced individuals to stake out their ideological position by taking sides on this issue. In this context, when Jewish intellectuals offered positive evaluations of Christianity, often in a scholarly framework, they were commonly linked to the trend of Jewish apostasy. Writers like Zhitlovsky, Brenner, and Hurwitz (and, later, Joseph Klausner), to name just a few, who attempted to conceive of Jesus and Christianity in more neutral or even favorable terms, often found themselves accused of grave sins, such as inciting conversion and even explicit proselytizing on behalf of Christian missionaries. Since the first Zionist Congress in Basle in 1897, when a group of Jewish converts to Christianity was refused admission to the gathering, the Zionist intelligentsia had struggled with the dilemma of whether Jewish apostates could be included among the Jewish nationalist community: Could one be a Christian by religion, but a Jew by nationality? (This issue was also repeatedly raised by Zhitlovsky and others in Yiddishist and Jewish socialist circles of the same time.) As the nature of Jewish nationalism, especially its secular variety, became better defined, many from the progressive wing of the secular Zionist camp attempted to separate considerations of religion from Jewish nationalism. Of course one could reject Judaism as a religion and still be a Jewish nationalist, they maintained, as long as one worked for the revival of Hebraic culture and a political rebirth of the Jewish nation on its land. Even the more conservative secularist Ahad Ha-Am embraced this notion (though only to a point, as we shall see), since the logical premise of an inherently secular nationalism would entail removing religion as a defining factor for inclusion or as a basis for self-definition and identity.

However, many who subscribed to this basic postulate of secular Jewish identity were not willing to extend the boundaries of Jewishness far enough to include those who, more than just rejecting the religious precepts of Judaism, had formally accepted another religion. In fact, most secular Jewish nationalists held conversion in disdain, not solely on religious grounds, but as a form of national betrayal. Many of these secularists had a complicated relationship with the religion of their ancestors; they overwhelmingly rejected the traditional Jewish Orthodoxy they had grown up with, but valued many of the facets of the religion as a sort of cultural patrimony, which, in revised form, could, and indeed should, provide many of the building blocks for a secular Jewish culture. From their vantage point, one who embraced another religion, especially Christianity, even if for purely materialistic reasons, tacitly rejected the secularized Judaism they envisioned as so essential to the Jewish national renaissance. More radical thinkers, Zhitlovsky and Brenner among them, however, pushed the boundaries of secular Jewish identity even further. They maintained that a Jew could convert to Christianity for a variety of reasons and still remain a Jew in the national sense. Once religion was removed as a defining feature of Jewish identity, these radicals saw no reason not to accept such an expansive definition of Jewishness. For the most part, the issues of conversion to Christianity (and the status of Jesus and Christianity more generally), the place of religion in Jewish nationalism, and the defining features of a secular, Jewish national identity and culture were central to the ongoing debates constituting the Brenner Affair. At the heart of the debate between Brenner and Ahad Ha-Am and their respective supporters and detractors were the questions "who is a Jew?" and "how can Jewishness be defined and recognized?" In this respect, one's attitude toward Jesus and Christianity often reflected one's position on these central questions of Jewish identity.

The Brenner Affair was so named in the Hebrew press by Brenner's contemporaries as fierce reactions began to appear there (and also to a lesser extent in the Yiddish- and Russian-language Jewish press) to his article "Ba-Ittonut u-va-sifrut" ("On the Press and Literature") in *Ha-poel ha-tsair (The Young Worker)* (November 24, 1910), on apostasy and Christianity. Even though it was Ahad Ha-Am's article earlier that year that spurred Brenner and others, such as Shai Hurwitz, to formulate rebuttals to his position, and Ahad Ha-Am himself was writing in response to a book on Jesus and Christianity published by C. G. Montefiore earlier that year, it was Brenner's article, his ideological stance, and his persona that became central to the affair as it unfolded over the following three years. As a leading writer in the emerging Hebrew literary renaissance and a radical voice within the younger circles of the secular Zionist intelligentsia in Palestine, Brenner was well suited to ignite such a fury with his always provocative and frequently polemical pen.

Starting a week after the publication of Brenner's original article, and continuing for about three years, over one hundred articles appeared in the Hebrew, Yiddish, and Russian Jewish press, many of them by leading figures in the Jewish intelligentsia of the time, taking a stand on Brenner's article or other issues raised as the debate persisted.[34] The first journalistic response to Brenner's article came from the Jerusalem Sephardi paper, *He-Herut (Freedom)*, in December of 1910, accusing him of incitement to convert to Christianity and receiving money from Christian missionaries. From the outset, *He-Herut* was so militant in its campaign against Brenner that it solicited support from Jewish papers everywhere in its battle, and in many cases, particular papers or writers became aware of Brenner's original article only because *He-Herut* brought it to their attention. Soon after, numerous papers and individual authors assailed Brenner with charges of atheism, heresy, apostasy, and missionizing. By focusing on the more provocative statements in Brenner's article, especially his comments on Christianity, *He-Herut* was able to frame the issue within the well-established and controversial phenomenon of Jewish apostasy, thereby repudiating Brenner and the whole *Ha-poel ha-tsair*[35] faction of young secular, socialist Zionists as nothing more than heretics and apostates. In many ways, it was the bitter attacks by *He-Herut* that catapulted Brenner's article onto center stage in the Jewish press, effectively creating the Brenner Affair.

As the debate progressed, the issue of Ahad Ha-Am leading a drive to cut off funding for the *Ha-poel ha-tsair* newspaper, which had published Brenner's article, became central for many involved, sometimes eclipsing the importance of the original issues of conversion and Christianity. In many ways the Brenner Affair evolved into a debate over freedom of opinion, freedom of the press, and freedom of expression. Yet, the issues of apostasy and Judaism versus Christianity also remained central to the ongoing debates. To an extent, opposing sides in the affair began to take shape, as a younger Palestinian faction—ardently secular and typically socialist—formed in defense of Brenner, and an older Diaspora faction based in Odessa, but headed by Ahad Ha-Am in England—representing the old guard of cultural Zionism, moderately secular, but more conservative in bearing—emerged against Brenner. This divide between (mostly) younger Zionists in Palestine and (mostly) older Zionist leaders in the Diaspora suggests that the age-old Jewish obsessions Diaspora Jews had with the issues of apostasy and Christianity no longer figured as relevant to the young "Hebrews" like Brenner, who had physically and mentally abandoned the Diaspora for Palestine. These younger Zionist thinkers, writers, and activists seemed more at ease addressing the issues of Jesus and Christianity than their Diaspora peers, since their Jewish (or Hebrew) identities were now firmly based on the very fact of their physical presence in Palestine and their active participation in reviving Jewish national life there.

At times it was difficult to see clear divisions between different camps or factions within the debate, because as different issues rose to the fore, different sides emerged in support of or opposition to these particular issues. Some articulated support for freedom of expression and the press even though they might have differed with Brenner on the danger posed by apostasy, or the merits of Christianity vis-à-vis Judaism. Others explicitly defended Brenner's call to embrace the New

Testament as a Jewish book and view Jesus more sympathetically. Because there were so many issues and complicated factors involved in
the Brenner Affair, it remains difficult to draw firm conclusions as to
why certain individuals took the positions they did in each case. For
instance, Joseph Klausner—a leading figure in Ahad Ha-Am's circle of
Cultural Zionists and a scholar of Jewish history and literature—generally supported Ahad Ha-Am and his camp, but he himself wrote exten-
sively, and somewhat favorably, on Jesus and Christianity during that
period, even serializing his full-length study of Jesus, *Yeshu ha-Notsri*
(*Jesus of Nazareth*) in Shai Hurwitz's journal *He-atid* (*The Future*), beginning in 1908 and continuing through the duration of the Brenner
Affair. So, despite the fact that Klausner contributed to the controversial debate with an article sharply criticizing Brenner, he actually held
some similar views. Moreover, as the editor of the respected Hebrew
Zionist journal *Ha-Shiloach* (*The Fountain*), Klausner also published
articles written in support of Brenner that contained even more favorable appraisals of Jesus and Christianity, and themselves became subjects of heated controversy. Ironically, Klausner himself also became
the subject of intense ridicule in the Jewish press upon the publication
of his book on Jesus in 1922; like Brenner, he was accused of apostasy
and proselytizing for Christianity. Klausner's inconsistent stand during
the Brenner Affair points to the complex and divisive nature of the issues it raised. The wide range of positions taken in the Brenner Affair
reflected the turbulent ideological currents within the world of secular
Zionism and the East European Jewish intelligentsia in general.

In order to understand the larger cultural and ideological context of
the Brenner Affair we must briefly look at the competing ideological
stances of its main protagonists, Brenner and Ahad Ha-Am. As Nurit
Govrin observes, Ahad Ha-Am and Brenner represented two different,
almost polar, perceptions of secular Judaism.[36] Because they were essentially both within the same secular Zionist camp, their conflict must be
viewed as part of an internecine struggle between competing factions
within the movement—one older and more conservative, the other
younger and more radical—in an attempt to control the ideological
direction and definition of secular Zionism. Ahad Ha-Am's vision of
secular Judaism was more positively attached to the Jewish past and
the "spirit of Judaism," the morals and values of Judaism without the

orthodox observance of commandments. His secularism was quite conservative in its conception of the place of tradition and religion for the modern Jew. He advocated a very careful negotiation between the spirit of Judaism as embodied by certain key values, texts, and historical memories, and the spirit of the times: modern thought and culture. Ahad Ha-Am's emphasis on establishing a Jewish "spiritual center" in Palestine reflects his deep concern with recuperating Jewish tradition for the modern Jew. As he put it, the "problem of Judaism" was just as serious as the "problem of the Jews." In other words, ameliorating the existential condition of the Jews must be accompanied by a revitalization of Jewish culture more broadly.[37]

Unlike Ahad Ha-Am, Brenner was primarily concerned with Jews and not with Judaism; he did not limit his view of Jewish life to the question of culture, and sought to solve the "problem of the Jews," not the "problem of Judaism," by seeking a territorial home for Jews as an end itself.[38] Brenner's attitude toward Jewish traditions, values, and history was severely critical, along the lines of Berdichevsky, who, to an extent, served as Brenner's ideological model. Brenner took the notion of the "negation of the Diaspora" to an extreme, calling for the total nullification of all Diaspora (especially rabbinic) culture. His definitions of Jews and Jewishness were much looser than Ahad Ha-Am's, and were based primarily on individual identification with the Jewish struggle; he claimed that "a Jew was anyone who chose to live as a Jew and Judaism was whatever a Jew proclaims it is for him."[39] For Brenner, there was no Judaism outside of the lived existence of Jews, no fixed ideals or absolute rules that defined it; what Jews believed and did in actuality defined Judaism, "if all Jews accepted the teachings of Tolstoy, then this teaching would be Judaism."[40] As Govrin puts it, for Ahad Ha-Am, much like the rabbis, there was a clear fence around Judaism, demarcating the boundaries of what was inside and what was outside, while Brenner sought to smash all such fences in order to create a much more inclusive and fluid definition of Judaism and Jewishness.[41]

Ahad Ha-Am, especially in his more mature writings, saw Judaism, in a modified, modern guise, as a key ingredient of Jewish nationalism, while Brenner saw Jewishness and Judaism as based solely on a national Jewish existence consisting of Jews living on and working their own land, speaking their own language (Hebrew), creating their own (modern) literature, and building a new life for the new Hebrew (not Jewish) man. In fact, Brenner argued for a "total separation of Jewishness from a Judaism that comprises a self-contained structure of teachings, beliefs, ethical ideals and ways of life, positing instead, a Jewishness based on involvement in the present-day existential war of the Jewish people, 'in any manifestation that war exhibits.'" [42] It is from this perspective that Brenner can look toward other religions and their founders for inspiration in a purely objective, posttraditional spirit. Brenner fought against traditional authority, advocating complete freedom of personal expression and ethical ideals, while at the same time striving to create a new Jewish national life that would require revolutionary changes in Jewish ways.

Of course, not all secular Jewish nationalists were as revolutionary as Brenner in his call for total negation of the Diaspora and expunging the role of religion, nor were they as conservative as Ahad Ha-Am in evaluating the role of tradition and its place in the Jewish national future. However, their respective ideological visions constituted two poles of a diverse spectrum of perspectives and philosophies within the realm of secular Zionism and Jewish nationalism more broadly. As we shall now see, during the course of the Brenner Affair this entire cacophonous array of voices informed the countless debates and discussions revolving around Ahad Ha-Am's and Brenner's articles. In this sense, the Brenner Affair, even within its limited scope of topics of debate, served as a window onto the internal dynamics and ideological friction of the secular Zionist intelligentsia.

While living in London in 1910, Ahad Ha-Am published an article, first in Hebrew and then in English,[43] written in response to C. G. Montefiore's book *Some Elements of the Religious Teaching of Jesus: According to the Synoptic Gospels* (1910) from earlier that year, which included an exhaustive and highly sympathetic account of Jesus' life and teachings. In the article, Ahad Ha-Am attacked liberal British Jews like Montefiore and others who had expressed favorable views of Jesus and Christianity in the preceding years, and offered a serious critique of such Jewish reclamations of Jesus and of Christianity. He chastised Montefiore, and Anglo-Reform Judaism in general, for abandoning "the spirit of Judaism," and altering it to be more Christian in his scholarly embrace of Jesus and the New Testament.[44] He ardently rejected the view of English Reformers like Montefiore who had accepted the gospels and Jesus as important parts of Judaism, seeing this as a flimsy pretext for extreme assimilation and a way to curry favor with the Gentiles. Ahad Ha-Am proclaimed that he saw Jesus and the gospels as contrary to the essence of Judaism.

Ultimately, Ahad Ha-Am feared that such positive views of Christianity and Jesus would blur the boundary between the two religions in the minds of assimilated Jews and erode any remnant of Jewish identity among them, eventually leading to mass conversions. Since the turn of the century Ahad Ha-Am had taken a stand against apostasy and rampant assimilation among younger Russian Jews and had long wanted to define an essence of Judaism for modern (non-Orthodox) Jews, partly as a remedy for such thoroughgoing abandonment of all vestiges of Judaism in the name of progressive humanism, freethinking universalism, and assimilation.[45] In the Anglo-Jewish context of the 1910 article, Ahad Ha-Am saw Montefiore's position as a kind of religious syncretism that betrayed the unique spirit of Judaism so important in Ahad Ha-Am's thinking. As a prophet of secular Jewish nationalism, or cultural Zionism more specifically, Ahad Ha-Am had long fought to overthrow the Orthodox version of traditional Judaism without rejecting the "spiritual greatness" of Judaism. He had attempted to adapt this spiritual greatness to conform to a modern sensibility, especially as part of a larger national, Jewish identity. In this respect, he rejected any kind of linking of Judaism to Christianity, and went to great lengths to prove that Jewish ethical ideals were superior to those found in Christianity (a type of "enlightened Jewish triumphalism" similar to that expressed by nineteenth-century Reform thinkers like Samuel Hirsch and Abraham Geiger).

More than just a scholarly discussion of religious ethics, Ahad Ha-Am's article served several important ideological functions: in offering a serious critique of Christian ethics and Christianity more generally in very modern terms, he was able to effectively renounce the fascination with Christianity common among both Liberal Jews in England and progressive secular Jews in Eastern Europe. At the same time, his critique provided him with a forum for articulating his conception of Judaism's moral greatness—again, in modern guise—and its suitability as a religion for the modern Jewish national revival.

Ahad Ha-Am's article "presented a powerful new stimulus to debate the sensitive question: how is a sophisticated liberal-minded Jew
to relate to a modern demythologized Christianity?"[46] The younger,
more radical secular Zionists, led by Brenner (and, to a lesser extent,
Shai Hurwitz), vehemently took Ahad Ha-Am to task for the views he
expressed in his article.

Leading the charge against Ahad Ha-Am, Brenner wrote an article
on the subject of apostasy and Christianity, which appeared in *Ha-poel
ha-tsair* in November 1910 under the pen name Yosef Haver and the
title "Ba-Ittonut u-va-sifrut" ("On the Press and Literature"). There,
Brenner offered biting criticism of the Jewish press's recent obsession
with the issue of apostasy, alleging that this issue had unnecessarily
become one of alarming concern for so many Jewish authors. Brenner
rejected this concern as a nonissue because, like Zhitlovsky, he no longer saw religion as a defining feature of Jewish national identity; instead he advocated a radical secularism which rejected all traditional
religious categories. Freethinking "Hebrews" like himself can seek
spiritual sustenance wherever they find it, from a variety of religions
or from no religion, but in either case, this is not the essence of their
identification as Jews. For Brenner, the uniting factors among Jews are
participation in the national struggle for Jewish existence, working and
settling the land (of Israel), speaking Hebrew, and creating a thriving
(secular) national Hebrew culture. Essentially, Brenner's article conveys
his overall vision of secular Jewish national identity, while the issues of
apostasy, Jesus, and Christianity are really secondary to him.

Brenner lays out his own radical views as a polemical thrust against
Ahad Ha-Am and his sizeable following, mostly the older generation of
Cultural Zionists, who, although primarily secular, were not willing to
completely eliminate religion as a factor in Jewish nationalism. Brenner's
position on the irrelevance of religion for Jewish nationalists as well as
his willingness to see Christianity and Judaism as comparable spiritual
entities must be seen as a provocative rebuttal of Ahad Ha-Am's reigning Cultural Zionist ethos, with its emphasis on the "spirit of Judaism"
as an important part of the Jewish national revival. Brenner articulates
his vision of the place of secular Jews within the Jewish nation in juxtaposition to Ahad Ha-Am, whom he rebukes for retreating from such a
boldly secular Jewish identity, proclaiming: "But for us, his friends and

Jewish freethinkers, we retain no connection to Judaism but we are no less a part of it than those who wear *tefillin* and *tzitzit* [phylacteries and ritual fringes]."[47] Brenner faults Ahad Ha-Am, and especially his recent article, for injecting religion into what should be a purely secular Jewish nationalism, seeing this as a waste of "national energy."[48]

In addressing one of the main concerns of Ahad Ha-Am's article, Brenner wonders if there is indeed any danger posed from Jews accepting Christianity in place of Judaism. He argues that even if one found Christianity to be a "better" religion, with loftier ideals and more spiritual beauty than Judaism, this would not have any bearing on "freethinking Hebrews" such as himself. As a secular Jew, it would make no sense to convert to Christianity, or any other religion for that matter, and adopt the lifestyle of its believers. As atheists, freethinking Jews like Brenner and Zhitlovsky were not interested in converting to Christianity, as they generally viewed religions from a secular, mythopoetic perspective, not from the traditional viewpoint. While Brenner's position shares much in common with Zhitlovsky's secular views of Jewish identity, he seems much less enamored with the particulars of Jesus and Christianity than Zhitlovsky and appears to be more concerned with the cultural stance of dismissing apostasy as a problem and rejecting traditional religious boundaries as part of constructing a new national identity for Jews that is thoroughly secular. For all intents and purposes, Brenner was not all that interested in the problem of Jesus and Christianity, which suggests that his form of radical, secular Zionism represented a true break with the demand of accommodating to Western culture.

In what proved to be the most controversial and inflammatory part of his article, Brenner affirms that, as a freethinking Hebrew, the "Old Testament" has no value for him as a "holy book" or as the "book of books," saying that he finds many contemporary books to be deeper and more meaningful to him than the "Old Testament."[49] He only views the Hebrew Bible as important as a "vestige of ancient memories" and as an "embodiment of the spirit of our people and of the human spirit built over many generations and historical eras."[50] In other words, it is a national text, like many other national texts, just another part of the Jewish patrimony. Brenner adds that he views the New Testament in a similar light, as "our book, bone of our bone and flesh of our flesh . . . part of our spiritual inheritance." He sees no fundamental difference in the asceticism and submission to God of the prophet Jeremiah and that of Jesus—they are of one source—and neither one has any direct relevance for him as a secular nationalist and atheist.

Moreover, Brenner sees no threat "posed to a 'freethinking Jew' by the assertion that Christianity has a higher claim to truth than Judaism."[51] Again echoing Zhitlovsky's thinking on this subject, Brenner claims that it is entirely possible "to be a good Jew and at the same time to be thrilled by the Christian legend of the son of God who was sent to mankind and who atoned with his life for the sins of all the ages."[52] He maintains that how one relates to the "Christian legend of the son of God" is ultimately unimportant and inconsequential and poses no threat to the Jewish nation, even if a Jew is so inspired by this Christian legend that he converts to Christianity. Brenner personally finds the Christian myth strange and detestable, like all religious illusions, which mislead and cause harm. He sees Christianity as representative of religious mysticism more generally, and for an atheist (like Brenner) who does not believe there is a God in heaven, there is no way to believe in His son either. Brenner concedes that as a historical figure, Jesus, like Moses or Buddha or Muhammad, might have had some great qualities—calling him a pure soul and a symbol of perfection—but even this, he posits, is impossible to confirm conclusively. Brenner knew that some would take his words as evidence of apostasy, but alleged that he was not afraid of having his name printed among a list of converts in the Zionist press. As he predicted, his position enraged many in the Zionist intellectual community.

Much of Brenner's article amounts to a radical secularist's critique of religion in general, including both Judaism and Christianity. This makes it even more curious that his detractors would accuse him of inciting conversion to Christianity, a religion whose central story he debunks as "mystical hogwash and dangerous illusion." This stems from the fact that the polemics in the Hebrew press around Brenner's article, and others dealing with Christianity, were often fueled by a variety of motives such as in-fighting within the Zionist intellectual world, preexisting political and ideological battles, personal spats, inflated egos, and competition between Hebrew journals for readers. All of these issues contributed to these ongoing debates and controversies in the Jewish press. In most cases the offending article that elicited the controversy is not that radical or innovative to begin with, but often just seen as a pretext for critiquing an ideological or political opponent. Indeed, Brenner's comments on Jesus and Christianity were hardly original—by 1910, countless Jews had professed such notions—and unlike Zhitlovsky, Asch, or others, Brenner did not depict Jesus in a particularly flattering light. He was unquestionably more interested in the socio-cultural trend of conversion, and its significance for contemporary Jewish life, than in theological or historical musings about the nature or status of Jesus.

Despite his clearly articulated commitment to Jewish nationalism and to the project of Jewish settlement in Palestine, Brenner's article received immediate rebuke by countless critics, both in Palestine and Europe. The most vociferous opposition came from *He-Herut* and focused on Brenner's comments about Christianity and his making light of conversion. In a short front-page article entitled "Heresy or Incitement" (December 2, 1910), the paper bluntly asserted that the author of Brenner's article (he had not yet been identified as such) was attempting to incite conversion to Christianity, and even implied that he was being paid by missionaries to do so. The author selectively quotes some of Brenner's more provocative lines, out of context, to demonstrate that he is rejecting Judaism qua Judaism, and is (seemingly) praising Christianity. He also rejects as an impossible paradox the possibility, raised by Brenner, that one could be a "good, national Jew" and be religiously inspired by the legend of Christianity. This last point proves that notwithstanding its hyperbolic bluster, *He-Herut* both perceived and rejected Brenner's central ideological premise about expanding the definition of Jewish national identity. Brenner followed up his original article with a short clarification in the December 9 issue of *Ha-poel ha-tsair* called simply "A Question," in which he rejected the charges leveled against him in *He-Herut* as ridiculous sensationalism, a hysterical response by narrow-minded people who, upon seeing the words "New Testament" and "Christianity" in an article, level trumped-up charges like incitement and missionizing to stir up interested readers. He laments the state of the Jewish press for this kind of libelous sensationalism, and makes it clear that he is the author of the first article (clearing up the confusion based on the pseudonym he had used).

Despite Brenner's clarification, many other papers and individual

authors remained fixated on his position on conversion, often accusing him of aiding Christian missionaries. The editor of the London
paper *Ha-Yehudi (The Jew)* offered a bitingly satirical condemnation of
Brenner's views (December 15, 1910), citing Brenner's article as proof
that during the period of revival in Israel, Jews were actually being
led to the Vatican to be converted.[53] Another article, appearing in S.
M. Lazar's Cracow paper *Ha-Mitzpeh (The Vista)* (December 30, 1910),
linked Brenner's article to missionary activity in Palestine, especially
to the British Jewish convert and missionary S. Feingold. The author
accused Brenner of, at least tacitly, supporting missionary efforts by
equating the New Testament with the Torah, and seemingly giving
assimilated Jews the nationalist camp's stamp of approval to convert to
Christianity.[54] Some articles opposing Brenner also alluded to other
Jewish writers who expressed a favorable attitude toward the "prophet
from Nazareth." Most notably, Shmuel Tschernowitz, writing in *Ha-
Tsefira (The Siren)* (March 9, 1911), grouped Brenner with Zhitlovsky
and Asch, condemning Brenner's embrace of Jesus in a rather sarcas-
tic tone and accusing all three writers of "worshiping false gods."[55] It
should be pointed out that these were essentially secularist, not Orthodox, papers leveling such charges against Brenner. They were so
concerned with the possibility that his provocative stance could be exploited for missionary purposes that they largely ignored the serious
critique he offered of the place of religion in defining Jewish national
identity, only seeing his radical secularism as opening the door to widespread conversions.

However, Brenner's article, and his stance in general on the separation between religion and nationalism, did cause many secular Zionists to reconsider the question of the relationship between the two. For
Ben Zion Katz, editor of *Ha-Z'man (The Times)* in Vilna, as well as
for many others, Brenner's radical articulation of a complete separation
between secular nationalism and Judaism (saying "we secular Jews have
no part in Judaism") was troubling.[56] In an article of March 3, 1911, Katz
wonders if young nationalist Jews like Brenner, who look favorably on
Christianity in some kind of enlightened way (like Tolstoy), yet write in
Hebrew, live in Palestine, and work for the cause of the Jewish nation,
should have their nationalism called into question. (Katz later wrote in
his memoirs that he opposed both Ahad Ha-Am's harsh stance against

Christianity, and Brenner's claim that the New Testament should be seen as a Jewish book; Katz rejected Brenner's notion, arguing that he had forgotten how much Jewish blood had been spilled in the name of the gospels. Katz felt that one could express certain ideas in a scholarly work about Christianity, but should refrain from doing so in more popular, publicistic articles.)[57] Others, such as Shimon Bernfeld, writing in *Ha-Tsefira* (March 16, 1911), whose article coined the term "The Brenner Affair," saw Brenner's stance as part of the generational conflict between the "young ones" and their elders, and, unlike Brenner, did not think that one could separate Jewish nationalism from Judaism.[58]

Joseph Klausner provided one of the more sophisticated and nuanced responses to Brenner's views on religion and nationalism. Writing in his own journal, *Ha-Shiloach*, in an article entitled "Freedom and Heresy" ("Herut ve-epikorsut," February 1911), Klausner argues that enlightened, freethinking Jewish nationalists must recognize the important place of the past and of religion for sustaining the Jewish nation. Even if they do not believe in the religious doctrines themselves, they must see them as important national treasures. Thus, Klausner criticizes those, like Brenner, who simply negate the Jewish past and its traditions, and sees them as arrogant in their disregard, and even disdain, for the Jewish past.[59] He keenly observes that the main idea of Brenner's article is that one can be a "national Jew" while rejecting all of the religious claims of Judaism. Klausner notes that this idea itself is not new, crediting Ahad Ha-Am with propagating this notion before Brenner; but, for him, it is how Brenner promotes this idea that is problematic. By invalidating the past in toto, and by maintaining that Judaism has no role whatsoever to play in Jewish national life, Klausner contends, Brenner has gone too far. He has crossed the line from legitimate freedom of opinion (*herut*) to outright heresy (*epikorsut*).

Furthermore, Klausner, like other detractors of Brenner (most notably Ahad Ha-Am, as we shall see), suggests that Brenner's argument for the relative equality of Judaism and Christianity amounts to an insult to all of the generations of Jews who suffered or gave their lives to maintain their commitment to Judaism and not convert to Christianity. Klausner maintains that by claiming there is no fundamental difference between Jeremiah and Jesus, Brenner effectively nullifies the entire history of Jewish martyrdom. Klausner himself saw Jesus as an intrinsically Jewish figure, but went to great lengths to show how his teachings diverged from the Jewish mainstream, ultimately becoming "non-Judaism" (we will explore Klausner's writings on Jesus below). For Klausner, Brenner's radical atheism and religious relativism is an affront to the historical legacy of Jewish identity, which was maintained at a very high price. Like Ahad Ha-Am, Klausner is offended by Brenner's disdain for religious sentiment altogether, especially concerning his remarks about "some father in Heaven," which he sees as disparaging to all monotheistic people. Moreover, Klausner's basic argument is that Jewish national life depends on such beliefs and is undermined by their utter rejection, as Brenner espouses. In the final analysis, Klausner affirms that religion and nationality are inseparable for Jewish identity, viewing attempts by Brenner, as well as Zhitlovsky and other radical secularists, to discard religion altogether as harmful to the Jewish national cause.

Many of Klausner's central points echo those of Ahad Ha-Am, his mentor in many ways, who functioned as one of Brenner's principal detractors throughout the course of the affair. After all, Brenner's article had been a thinly veiled attack on Ahad Ha-Am himself, who did not let it go unopposed. Ahad Ha-Am first responded to Brenner's article with a number of personal letters to friends and colleagues (including Klausner). In the earliest letter he wrote after Brenner's article appeared, he refers to the author (he did not yet know it was Brenner) as one of the "impudent youth" of his day [60] and calls his belittlement of the Jewish belief in a Heavenly Father a "national insult" and an act of *chutzpah*, especially considering the extent to which Jews have sacrificed and suffered over the years for their belief in God. [61] In a letter to his friend who sat on the board of the organization Hovvevei Zion (Lovers of Zion) in Odessa, which subsidized the publication of *Ha-poel ha-tsair*, Ahad Ha-Am raises the subject of stopping the subsidy because of Brenner's article. In addition to his correspondence and articles, it was this campaign by Ahad Ha-Am to stop the subsidy for the paper that placed him at the center of the Brenner Affair.

Ahad Ha-Am's first public rebuttal of Brenner came in an article in the May 1911 issue of *Ha-Shiloach*, entitled "Torah from Zion" ("Torah mi-tzion"), in which he criticized the Palestinian Jewish youth—Brenner chief among them—for being attracted to foreign influences such as

Christianity, and converting to Christianity in significant numbers. Ahad Ha-Am vehemently rejected Brenner's call for a total separation of religion and nationalism, arguing that religion remained a central factor for Jewish national identity even if not in its traditional sense; the mythic significance of God for Jews and Jewish history could not be ignored. In explicit juxtaposition to Brenner, Ahad Ha-Am forcefully argued that "someone who says that he has no portion in the God of Israel, in that historical force which has given our people life and influenced that life, its spirit and its progress for thousands of years . . . can be a decent human being, but he is not a national Jew even if he lives in Eretz Israel and speaks Hebrew."[62] This proclamation unequivocally refutes the major premise of Brenner's position and, as some would argue, actually represented a departure from Ahad Ha-Am's own earlier stance that one could reject the Jewish religion and still remain a "national Jew." Fundamentally, Ahad Ha-Am opposed Brenner because of his positive treatment of Christianity—a national insult in Ahad Ha-Am's eyes—and on account of what he "saw as Brenner's attempt to blur the differences between Judaism and Christianity, and his tendency to cut the connection with the national past."[63] Brenner's extreme negation of Jewish tradition ran counter to Ahad Ha-Am's "enlightened Jewish triumphalsim."

To a considerable degree, Ahad Ha-Am's harsh reaction to Brenner, and his previous attacks on Shai Hurwitz for his views on Christianity, must be seen as part of an ongoing intergenerational conflict within the Zionist intelligentsia, dating back to the turn of the century, in which Ahad Ha-Am and his generation opposed the "young ones" (tse'irim) led by M. Y. Berdichevsky and Brenner. Ahad Ha-Am and his circle consistently viewed the "young ones" as going beyond the pale in their ideological vision and attempted reformulation of Jewish identity and culture, which was more closely in tune with external ideals and philosophies, namely European (Christian) ones. Some of the more conservative elements within the secular Zionist world saw the "young ones" as rebels who were out to destroy Judaism, and promote assimilation and conversion to Christianity or apostasy more generally. The intergenerational nature of the conflict appears clearly when we look at the bulk of those who supported Brenner in his battle with Ahad Ha-Am and his other numerous opponents. Even if they did not conform ideologically to the more extreme wing of the "young ones" camp, almost all were important younger figures in the Zionist world who challenged Ahad Ha-Am and his generation in some way.

In addition to his numerous critics, several prominent, (mostly) young Zionists rallied behind Brenner in support of his stance on the separation of religion and nationalism. For one, David Ben-Gurion wrote an article supporting Brenner in the Labor paper in Jerusalem, *Ha-Achdut* (*Unity*) (February 17, 1911), entitled "On the Slope" ("Ba-midron").[64] Ben-Gurion claimed that until recently it was widely accepted that the question of religion and the question of nationalism were separate; one could be a nationalist Jew, working for his people, while completely rejecting the Jewish religion. As far as Ben-Gurion was concerned, this should not even be a matter of controversy among secular Zionists.

The prominent Labor Zionist ideologue A. D. Gordon (himself slightly older, but very influential within young Zionist circles in Palestine) also entered the fray shortly after hearing Ahad Ha-Am speak publicly in Palestine against Brenner and the threat of apostasy among the Jewish youth. Gordon wrote Ahad Ha-Am a letter explaining Brenner's original article and criticizing Ahad Ha-Am's views on the young Palestinian Jewish intelligentsia's stand on Christianity and apostasy.[65] Gordon suggested that for Brenner and other Jews living in Palestine, apostasy was not as central an issue as it was for Jews in the Diaspora, since Jewishness was more easily and naturally expressed in Palestine without the fear or threat of Christianity looming. This implied that Jews in Palestine had a national, extrareligious way to express their Jewishness, unlike in the Diaspora, which thereby removed the threat that Christianity had posed to Diaspora Jewry. Like Brenner, Gordon suggests that conversion is a "Diaspora problem" that can be resolved once and for all by Jews settling in Palestine. In this sense, the Brenner Affair and the debate over Jesus and Christianity was one of the key issues involved in the parting of the ways of European and Palestinian Zionism over the roles of tradition, religion, and the proper relationship to Western/Christian culture.

Other writers supported Brenner more explicitly for his position on Jesus and Christianity. An article by the essayist Ben Israel (the penname of Y. L. Pupes), entitled "Concerning the Question: Whither?" ("Le-she'elat Le-an?"), appearing in *Ha-Shiloach* (February 1911), was one of the first to staunchly endorse Brenner's views on Christianity. Like Brenner (and other Jewish scholars), Ben Israel saw the gospels as "part of the literature of Israel and a fruit of the Hebrew spirit of the previous hundreds of years."[66] While this appears similar to Brenner's claim that the New Testament is "bone of our bone, flesh of our flesh," Ben Israel went even further than Brenner in his positive evaluation of Christianity as against Judaism. He understood the New Testament as springing from the soil of the Hebrew Scriptures, and posited that it was only on account of later historical developments that the New Testament became "distant" from the Jewish Scriptures. Ben Israel concerned himself primarily with the relationship between early Christianity and Judaism, seeing in Christianity some "improvements" over the legalism of Pharisaic Judaism; he contrasts Judaism, centered on law, with early Christianity, centered on moral ideals, which can serve more universally as "guideposts or lighthouses for mankind." In this respect, for Ben Israel, Christianity surpasses Judaism.

Ben Israel's article elicited a new round of harsh responses similar to those that first followed Brenner's article; some viewed his ideas as even more dangerous than Brenner's. Ahad Ha-Am wrote a very sharp response to Ben Israel's article in a letter to Klausner (March 1, 1911), who had opened himself up to criticism by agreeing to publish Ben Israel's article in *Ha-Shiloach* in the first place. In another letter, Ahad Ha-Am writes that "Ben Israel's article is actually less insulting and painful than Brenner's because in many instances where it appears he is favoring Christianity it is just a result of the flowery language he uses."[67] Ben Israel committed suicide in April of that year, and some wondered whether the harsh responses to his article might have had any effect on his decision to end his life.[68] Ben Israel's idealization of Christianity as part of a critique of Judaism had became somewhat common among radical critics within the East European Jewish intelligentsia; Zhitlovsky, Brenner, and Hurwitz had all incorporated positive assessments of Christianity, to some extent as part of larger critiques of the limitations of Judaism.

Although only five years Ahad Ha-Am's junior, Shai Hurwitz acted as one of his most stinging critics, and served as a voice of the "young ones" generation in many respects. He himself was no stranger to controversy, and had tangled with Ahad Ha-Am several years earlier over

his own article "Le-she'elat qiyyum ha-yahadut" ("On the Continu-
ance of Judaism," *Ha-Shiloach*, April 1904), rejecting Ahad Ha-Am's
notion of a sustaining "essence of Judaism" that would help preserve
modern Jewish culture and identity without a traditional religious
commitment. It was therefore no surprise that along with Brenner,
Hurwitz led the charge of those attacking Ahad Ha-Am's views in his
1910 article, along with sharply criticizing his opposition to Brenner's
article. In an article in his own journal, *He-atid* (April 1911), entitled
"Le-harhavat ha-gevulim" ("Toward an Extension of the Boundaries"),
Hurwitz called for a radical secularization and expansion of the definition and scope of Jewish national identity. He criticized Ahad Ha-Am's
views on Christianity on a number of different counts. It is interesting to note that in the same issue of *He-atid* that his article appeared,
Hurwitz also published other articles dealing positively with Jesus and
Christianity, such as S. A. Horodetsky's assessment of Jesus' Jewishness, entitled "Judaism and Christianity" ("Yahadut v'notsrut"), and
an installment of Klausner's *Yeshu Ha-Notsri*.[69] Horodetsky, a Zionist
historian of Hasidism and Jewish mysticism, was one of the first Hebrew writers from this period to actually assign a positive appraisal to
the teachings of Jesus, seeing them primarily as an "embodiment of
Judaism."[70] Horodetsky claimed in his *He-atid* article that "Jesus was
a Jew in all of his heart, who lived as a Jew and whose thoughts were
Jewish." In fact, in the context of an article on Hasidism in *He-atid* in
1908, Horodetsky viewed Jesus as a "Jewish expression of emotional-
ism and myth, which later had its parallels in Hasidism."[71] He makes
several observations regarding the similarity, both in form and content,
between the teachings attributed to Jesus and those of the Baal Shem
Tov, nearly seventeen hundred years later.

Perhaps self-consciously commenting on the contents of his own
journal, Hurwitz acknowledged in his April 1911 article that "certain
young Jewish intellectuals quite naturally feel an intellectual affinity for
aspects of Christianity. This affinity confirms for many of them their
innermost link to universalism, their birthright to that extension of
their Jewishness which is Christian European culture."[72] Hurwitz recognized, like Zhitlovsky, that for progressive secular Jews, approaching
Jesus and Christianity from a sympathetic, enlightened perspective is
inextricably linked to participating in "Christian European culture."

Hurwitz therefore chided both Ahad Ha-Am and Klausner for greeting this "academic radicalism" with such horror, and for proclaiming these intellectuals advocates of "non-Judaism," which would only result in alienating them even further.[73] Hurwitz suggested that Ahad Ha-Am and Klausner were tightening the boundaries of Jewishness at the precise time when they should be loosened and expanded.

In his own book on Hurwitz, Stanley Nash comments on the preoccupation with Jesus among some of the secular Zionist intellectuals from the early part of the century, claiming that this phenomenon "reflect[s] the search for the new man and the new Hebrew (man) during this period."[74] In other words, interest in Jesus was part of a wider ideological quest for new ideas, ideals, and expressions of Jewish identity and culture. In this light, for Hurwitz, publishing Horodetsky's views on Judaism and Christianity or Joseph Klausner's study of Jesus in his journal was part of "redeeming 'not yet sanctified' subcurrents of Judaism and hence, 'extending the boundaries' of Judaism," and furthermore, the "reclaiming of Jesus was . . . an affirmation of Hebraism's breadth . . . because for writers like Hurwitz . . . pure 'Hebraism' was equivalent to the most 'human' and 'natural' of ideals, the identification with Jesus represented a commitment to humanize—to rejuvenate and to restore—to 'Hebraize' Judaism."[75] Thus, embracing Jesus and Christianity was a byproduct, a symptom, of the attempt to universalize Jewish culture, to "extend the boundaries" of Jewishness.

Hurwitz had already offered his views on Christianity in a controversial 1909 *He-atid* article on Hasidism, "Hasidism and Haskalah" ("Ha-Hasidut ve-ha-Haskalah"), in which he proclaimed that Christianity is "more creative, more ethical, even more Jewish than Hasidism," seeing Christianity as "the first religious manifestation within Judaism of the emancipation of the spirit from Scripture, emotion from the Law, the individual from the collectivity."[76] Hurwitz's article met with fierce opposition, with many authors harshly polemicizing against Hurwitz in the Hebrew press. In a fascinating example of how far these polemical debates could go, there was a "trial" in 1908 between Hurwitz and one of his attackers, Shimon Menachem Lazar, before a secular Zionist "court of honor" in Lvov, that was well attended and covered by the Jewish press throughout Eastern Europe. Hurwitz charged Lazar with libel for accusing him in *Ha-Mitzpeh* of missionizing. During the trial, one of the witnesses against Hurwitz, Shimon Bernfeld, was questioned by a judge: "Hurwitz says that there is poetry in Christianity, but have not other well-known Jews—Hess for example—said such things? Are they also missionaries?" Bernfeld responds: "I think that this is a lie. I do not know if Hess said such things. Jews who say such things have no portion in Judaism."[77]

This exchange shows how ideological opponents could latch on to rather benign sayings about Christianity and use them to anchor serious personal attacks. Also, the fact that in 1908 a secular Zionist such as Bernfeld could maintain that one has no "portion in Judaism" for saying there is "poetry in Christianity" indicates that many East European Jewish intellectuals still harbored deep-rooted animosity toward that religion. (Zhitlovsky made this point explicit in his rebuttal to Ansky.) Especially against the background of assimilation and conversion, many Jewish intellectuals feared that any positive position on Jesus or any aspect of Christianity, even when made in an academic context, or referring to a demythologized, contemporary view of Christianity, could be taken out of context as an endorsement of outright conversion and total assimilation. The subtlety often involved in Jewish reclamations of Jesus or reinterpretations of Christianity, as well as in the reevaluations of all religious issues in a "poetic" or secularized form, was often lost.

Not only do the Brenner Affair and other such controversies enlighten us as to why positive Jewish appraisals of Jesus or Christianity typically met with so much fierce opposition, they also reveal the wider ideological currents that led to such positive appraisals in the first place. Jews such as Brenner, Hurwitz, and Ben Israel, or even less radical writers like Horodetsky and Klausner, looked upon Jesus and Christianity more sympathetically than traditionally minded Jews largely because of their own expanded notions of Jewishness, or their changing views on the nature of the relationship between Judaism, Jewish history, and Western history and culture—including Christianity. For these writers, reclaiming Jesus as a Jewish figure with laudable merits of some kind showed their willingness to challenge and reject traditional Jewish attitudes and taboos concerning Jesus as part of their attempt to overthrow Jewish tradition more generally; it also helped to serve the goal of presenting Judaism and Jewish ideals as more universal and in line with "Christian European culture." Finally, as radical secularists and Jewish nationalists, these writers, especially Brenner and Hurwitz, expressed their views on Jesus and Christianity as part of defining a new Jewish national identity not based in any way on traditional religious categories or old boundaries between Jews and Christians.

As an important postscript to the Brenner Affair and an example of how Jewish writing on Jesus continued to elicit antagonism in the Hebrew press well into the twentieth century, we must briefly consider the controversy surrounding the publication of Joseph Klausner's *Yeshu Ha-Notsri* in 1922. Klausner had been a leading figure of the Zionist intelligentsia and Hebrew literary scene since the beginning of the twentieth century as editor of *Ha-Shiloach*, and as a scholar of Jewish history and literature. Unlike Brenner, Klausner was only a moderate secularist and belonged more to the mainstream than to the radical margins of secular Zionist thought in the early decades of the century. Along with his scholarly interests in Hebrew literature, Jewish messianism, and Second Temple–era history, Klausner had maintained an ongoing interest in the connection between Jewish culture and world culture, or "Judaism and Humanity,"[78] and bridging the two was part of his life's work. In this context, Stanley Nash claims that Klausner's interest in Jesus and early Christianity was part of his lifelong pursuit of reconciling "Jewishness" and "humanness"[79] and of his attempt to demonstrate that Judaism gave birth to a religion that conquered half of humanity; in other words, Christianity's real strength and greatness was its innate Jewishness.[80] In his book, the first modern full-length history of Jesus in Hebrew, Klausner stresses the Jewish character of Jesus and his teachings, while also showing where Jesus' teachings depart from Judaism; he addresses the question, "how can Jesus be both Jewish and the source of something not-Jewish: Christianity?"[81]

Klausner stresses that Jesus was a "product of Palestine alone," not subject to Gentile influences, arguing that all of Jesus' teachings can be traced to Jewish sources (384–85, 386–87). Indeed, Jesus was, according to Klausner, a "chauvinistic" Jew, contrary to Christian perceptions. Moreover, essentially following Geiger and Graetz, Klausner posits that Jesus was observant of Jewish law—only his disciples were not—standing apart from later Christian dogma about him. Klausner emphasizes Jesus' positive attitude toward Judaism, qualifying his critique of the

Pharisees, and seeing him as a good "messianic Jew," although Jesus' practice did conflict with "normative Judaism" in some ways (365–68). Klausner maintains that the ceremonial laws had a national function, which Jesus neglected or seriously diminished, and, most importantly, that Jesus' ethical teaching contradicted "national Judaism" (371–74). Like Ahad Ha-Am, Klausner faults Jesus' ethical teaching for its excessive emphasis on mercy and love and its disregard for the ideal of justice. In general, Klausner contends that Jesus' overemphasis on ethics to the exclusion of *halakha* undermined "national Judaism," causing Jesus to be rejected by Israel (390).

Klausner argues that Jesus' disproportionate emphasis on individual morality, what he terms "exaggerated Judaism," was a danger to statecraft and a threat to Jewish national life (374). Judaism for Klausner is an "all-embracing, all inclusive, political, national, social culture" combining ethics and laws, mercy and judgment. Ultimately Jesus' teachings did not embrace the whole of life, and therefore were not Judaism (396–97). Klausner claims that Christianity is flawed because it separates ethics from political reality, and Christians have never lived up to Jesus' high ethical standards. Despite this criticism, Klausner praises the ethics of Jesus, especially the Sermon on the Mount, and even maintains in conclusion that Jesus was "the most Jewish of all Jews," asserting that "if ever the day should come and this ethical code be stripped of its wrappings of miracles and mysticism, the Book of the Ethics of Jesus will be one of the choicest treasures in the literature of Israel for all time" (414).

Klausner's evaluation of Jesus thus contains striking ambivalence. On the one hand he decisively praises Jesus as the "most Jewish of all Jews," declaring his ethics to be a great achievement, and claiming that his teachings were firmly rooted in Jewish sources. Klausner even labels Jesus a Jewish "chauvinist" (a favorable category in Klausner's view), who ministered to the Jews and not the Gentiles. On the other hand, he repudiates Jesus' moral code as a misguided form of "exaggerated Judaism" that emphasized the individual at the expense of society, ultimately undermining Jewish national life and becoming "non-Judaism." David Berger has offered a persuasive explanation for this ambivalent analysis of Jesus, claiming that "Klausner the nationalist wanted to reclaim Jesus for the Jewish people without exempting him from the critical scrutiny that every Jewish instinct required."[82] In other words, just like Geiger and his contemporaries of the previous century, Klausner attempted to identify the positive aspects of Jesus' teachings—and by extension, Christianity—as essentially Jewish, while also accounting for why Jesus' teachings in their entirety no longer constitute Judaism. His scholarship was every bit as motivated by apologetic and polemical concerns as that of his predecessors. One of the elements that made Klausner's book distinctive, however, was the secular, nationalistic prism through which he evaluated Jesus and his teachings.

Despite both the nationalistic and the apologetic quality of Klausner's work, shortly after the book's publication many writers accused Klausner of apostasy and proselytizing, condemning the book robustly in the Jewish press and polemicizing bitterly against Klausner himself. Much of the harsh reaction came, as might be expected, from the traditional Jewish press and Orthodox writers, such as the Orthodox scholar Aaron Kaminka, who dismissed Klausner's book as a "truckling and kow-towing to the Christian religion and an assertion of great affection for the foggy figure of its founder, a denial of the healthy sense of our saintly forefathers . . . who rejected with loathing those fables and inventions, knowing the hero of those stories to have been no more than a 'mocker of the words of the wise.'"[83] Among the mostly secular supporters of the Hebrew renaissance, Klausner's book was received quite positively "as a great and important addition to Hebrew literature and to Jewish history."[84] Yet, even among those who admired the book and Klausner's scholarship, there often existed a sense of anxiety that Klausner had taken on such a controversial topic, which had the potential to offend Jewish and Christian readers alike. Indeed, the book "evoked so much controversy that even Ahad Ha-Am called the Hebrew work 'a public scandal.'"[85]

After the translation of the book into English by the Christian scholar Herbert Danby in 1925, numerous responses to it appeared in the English press. Danby himself claimed about Klausner's book that "the nationalist motif has assumed such enormous proportions as to dominate the writer's outlook."[86] Danby astutely identified Klausner's book as "a most unexpected by-product of the rise of Jewish nationalist instinct and the revival of Jewish culture," even calling it an attempt to reclaim Jesus "as a figure in the gallery of Jewish worthies . . . an attempt to rescue him from the hands of Christendom."[87] Some liberal Jews, most notably C. G. Montefiore, criticized Klausner's book for precisely this nationalist conception of Judaism; most Reform Jews at that time still strongly rejected such a conception and therefore objected to Klausner's vision of Judaism, which was founded primarily on secular nationalist rather than religious principles. For Jews like Montefiore, who had rejected the national component of Judaism and no longer saw it as an all-encompassing national culture, Klausner's critique of Jesus for his emphasis on individual morality was misguided. Montefiore takes issue with Klausner's "nationalist and secular attitude towards both Judaism and Jesus."[88]

It seems appropriate to conclude this chapter with Montefiore's critique of Klausner for being exceedingly secular and nationalist in his conception of both Jesus and Judaism. Throughout this chapter we have examined the deep-seated connection between such secular and nationalistic conceptions of Judaism and views of Jesus, seeing how the two have been interlinked as part of attempts by numerous East European Jewish intellectuals to forge new definitions of Jews and Jewishness. After all, Montefiore and his brand of liberal Jewish universalism, in which Jesus figured significantly as a symbol of such Jewish universalism of the past and future, had raised the ire of Ahad Ha-Am, spurring his nationalistic critique of Christianity and liberal Jewish reclamations of Jesus, and thus instigating Brenner's article and the entire Brenner Affair. These opposing critiques highlight the stark contrast between the universalistic, religious conception of Judaism typical of Reform Judaism, and the secular nationalist conception of Judaism articulated by Zionist thinkers. Within the Zionist camp, however, looking at the Brenner Affair exposes the sharp fault lines that divided the older, more conservative wing of Zionists (mostly) in the Diaspora led by Ahad Ha-Am, and the younger, radical wing (mostly) in Palestine led by Brenner, over the question of defining Jewish identity vis-à-vis attitudes toward Jesus and Christianity. Representing an interesting mix of such muscular, secular nationalism and liberal universalism is Zhitlovsky's brand of secular humanism combined with a Yiddish-based cultural nationalism, in which Jesus is revered for both nationalistic and universalistic reasons. Indeed, the *tseylem frage* debate between Zhitlovsky and Ansky reveals the tensions between universalism and particularism that plagued secular Yiddishists in general. In the following chapter we will trace some of these tensions between secular universalism and cultural nationalism as we examine the place of Jesus and Christianity in the emergence of Yiddish literary modernism.

Three Yiddish Modernism and the Landscape of the Cross

> The word hangs naked on the cross.
>
> —Melekh Ravitsh, 1922

Yiddish Literature Crossing Boundaries

The changing cultural climate revealed by the Crucifix Question and Brenner Affair controversies became increasingly manifest in Yiddish and Hebrew literature in the first half of the twentieth century as more and more writers made use of the figure of Jesus as well as other Christian symbols and motifs. While David Roskies claims that "for all their radicalism, Yiddish writers could not have broken the Jesus taboo had it not been for prior developments in Christian Europe (such as the quest for the historical Jesus),"[1] I propose that this extraordinary trend in Yiddish literature must also be viewed as emerging from concurrent developments in Jewish Europe.[2] As we saw earlier, the Jewish recovery of Jesus had begun with Moses Mendelssohn and the Berlin Haskalah over a century before, and since the latter half of the nineteenth century had slowly seeped into enlightened Jewish circles in Eastern Europe as well. This phenomenon of modern Jews reclaiming Jesus as a fellow Jew was firmly rooted in Jewish intellectual and literary circles by the beginning of the twentieth century, thereby rendering the figure of Jesus a powerfully alluring symbol for many Jewish writers, especially those of an avant-garde bent. As with much of the Jewish scholarship on Jesus from the nineteenth century, the separation of Jesus from Christianity allowed Jewish authors to conceive of and portray him in exclusively Jewish terms, sometimes in ways that were sharply critical of Christianity and contemporary Christians. Herein lies the central tension that permeates the entire process of modern Jews recovering Jesus: in addition to Jews and Jewish culture becoming more "Westernized" through incorporating Jesus and other Christian motifs, these motifs typically became Judaized.

The prominent Yiddish literary critic Shmuel Niger addressed this phenomenon in some of his studies of Yiddish literature, observing that "for a long time Yiddish writers have been writing about Jesus and Christianity."[3] He asserts that Zhitlovsky was not the only one to do so, as many "other Yiddish writers, historians, publicists, and poets have also written about this subject." Yet the Jesus that these Yiddish writers created differed sharply from the one found in the works of their secular European contemporaries, as Niger maintains that "one could enumerate a considerable list of Yiddish stories, poems, and *poemas* where the Jesus-figure is often depicted as a Jewish figure, and where the legends surrounding him are depicted as Jewish legends."[4] Niger again addresses this phenomenon in a treatment of Sholem Asch's novel *The Nazarene* (1939). In discussing Asch's attempt to "bring home" the legends of Jesus and Mary, Niger lays out the challenges facing the Jewish artist—like Asch—who wants to render these mythic figures Jewish, and lists the steps needed to realize such a transformation. He writes that "he [the artist] must bring the material that, so to say, has become apostasized back into the bosom of our father Abraham; he must Judaize it. He must purify it, he must free it of all those things that attached to it while in foreign and, at times, hostile circles. He must return Rabbi Yeshu, son of Joseph, the rabbi from Galilee who was dragged away to the pagans in Rome, to the Galilee, to Judea, to the Land of Israel, to the Jews of his time."[5] What Niger describes here amounts to a programmatic act of literary reclamation, an adjunct to the Jewish scholarly project of reclaiming Jesus as a Jew with all of its polemical subtexts.

Especially in the tumultuous and bloody years of World War I, the Bolshevik Revolution, and the Russian Civil War and accompanying Ukrainian pogroms (1914–21), Jesus-figures and Christian motifs pervaded the writings of avant-garde, modernist Yiddish authors in both Europe and America. Some, as Niger suggests, attempted to portray Jesus as thoroughly Jewish, representative of the suffering that Jews experienced at the time, while others saw him in more universal terms as an emblem of human suffering and tragedy so appropriate for literary responses to the unfolding terrors of the surrounding world. Many writers also depicted Jesus in a redemptive context as a failed prophet or Messiah, who, like the poets themselves, was unable to save the world from violence and bloodshed as it lurched forward toward total apocalypse and chaos. At times, many of these various themes and uses of Jesus even appear in the same work. Thus, the figure of Jesus and Christian images such as the cross served these Yiddish modernists as malleable literary symbols in myriad ways: aesthetically, ideologically, culturally, and politically. They played a crucial part in the process of creating a modernist style, persona, and vision that was at once Jewish and universalist. By employing Jesus and numerous Christian motifs in their treatment of themes such as suffering, tragedy, war, and redemption, these Yiddish writers touched on many of the complex issues raised in the fierce debates raging in the Jewish press during the preceding years. Did establishing Jesus as a figure within the modernist Yiddish literary canon serve as a way for modern Jewish writers to subvert Christian cultural claims on the figure of Jesus? Or was it merely a way to share in these claims as part of a broader cosmopolitan culture? Were these writers trying to flex their muscles as avant-garde mavericks by brazenly incorporating images that had been (and to a large degree still were) taboo in Jewish culture? Or were they asserting the same basic premise as Zhitlovsky and Asch, who argued for the essential Jewishness of Jesus and early Christianity in the first place?

In this chapter, I attempt to provide some answers to these questions by examining works by several modernist Yiddish writers containing overt Christ or crucifixion symbolism. These writings form part of what I call the "landscape of the cross," a virtual subgenre in modernist Yiddish literature that steadily emerged in the years during and following World War I and the Bolshevik Revolution. We will see both the ubiquity and the centrality of this subgenre in the Yiddish literary world as we observe how the Jesus imagery in these works is profoundly connected to their authors' modernist ethos and self-understanding. I contend that these works, with their combination of cosmopolitan universalism, Jewish martyrology, symbolic syncretism, and occasional anti-Christian polemical stridency, reflect the paradoxical currents that informed Jewish modernism in general: a tension between old and new, Jewish and Christian, particular and universal, secular and religious, personal and national, resounds in these works.

Thus, the appropriation of these Christian cultural and literary symbols with all of the historical-cultural connotations inherent in this process provided these Yiddish writers with a stage for acting out the central problems of Jewish modernity. By portraying the previously taboo Jesus as a Jewish redemptive figure and as a symbol of universal tragedy these modernists allowed themselves to adopt the new, the foreign, and the other (Jesus), while simultaneously embracing the old, the traditional, and the native (Jewish messianism). The radical and the revolutionary became framed within the historical and the classical, resulting in a distinctive and innovative form of Jewish culture.

Within the realm of Yiddish literature the period immediately following the 1905 Revolution in Russia witnessed a widespread acceptance of new, non-Jewish paradigms by Yiddish writers of this generation. This included the adoption of Western European literary styles, aesthetics, themes, and motifs, as well as mythical and folkloric archetypes, as appropriate sources of inspiration. The effects of turn-of-the-century European literary trends, most notably the diverse set of movements collectively known as modernism, on Yiddish writers from this period played an especially significant role in opening the door to Christian images and themes in Yiddish literature. Sholem Asch and Lamed Shapiro, as well as the rest of the writers to be discussed in this chapter, belong to this generation of Yiddish writers, which can be defined as modernist rather than simply modern.[6] They constitute a second generation of Yiddish writers in Eastern Europe, emerging on the heels of the pioneering classic trio of modern Yiddish fiction, *di klassiker*—Mendele Moykher Sforim (S. Y. Abramovitsh), Sholem Aleichem (Sholem Rabinovitsh), and Y. L. Peretz—who began writing in the 1860s, 1870s, and 1880s. While *di klassiker* were by no means immune to the influences of their European literary contemporaries, the second wave of Yiddish authors came of age in the first three decades of the twentieth century and more explicitly embraced the various styles and trends associated with European modernism. This experimentation with modernism was part of a growing cultural cosmopolitanism that, to a large extent, defined this generation. Not content with the folksy parodies of shtetl life, or Haskalah-inspired bildungsromans often associated with nineteenth-century Yiddish and Hebrew literature, writers like Lamed Shapiro, Sholem Asch, Zalman Shneour, and many others began to "examin[e] the darker side of man's psyche, his drives and his sexuality."[7] Their stories touched on aspects of Jewish life and realms of the human psyche that had been earlier ignored, such as the Jewish underworld; bitter class struggle in the shtetl; lust, violence, and suicide; and the problems of abnormal psychology. Peretz had earlier begun to experiment with some of these themes, especially abnormal psychology. His incorporation of certain aspects of modernist style in his writing can be seen as a harbinger of the flood of modernism that enveloped this next generation of Yiddish writers. This new openness and penchant for experimentation was part of a process of rebelling against Jewish traditions, religious and literary, in the search to transform both Jewish literature and Jewish life.

As these Yiddish modernists embraced secular artistic and literary traditions that had been considered taboo in the premodern Jewish world, the figure of Jesus held a particular attraction as the most taboo graven image of them all. Firmly established at the core of Western-Christian traditions of art and literature, both religious and secular, the symbols of Christ and crucifix invoked within the Jewish artist age-old feelings of revulsion, as well as a powerful attraction and desire to embrace the previously forbidden, both in form and content. Ruth Wisse asserts that "the cross haunted the Jewish imagination as a symbol of a theory of love perverted into the practice of hate which the Jew was somehow challenged to redeem."[8] Seeing themselves as part of a broader European, if not wholly universal, literary movement, modernist Yiddish writers expressly rejected any kind of parochial limitations placed on the styles and subject matter that they could incorporate in their work. As Seth Wolitz observes, many of these authors saw themselves as "pioneers who were creating [a] Jewish secular culture in the context of Western civilization."[9] They often freely blended Jewish themes and motifs with non-Jewish ones, and at times favored Christian over Jewish motifs. Wolitz claims that for the group of modernist Yiddish poets in interwar Poland known as Yung-Yiddish (Yiddish Youth), "the Dybbuk or a Golem and other Jewish motifs did not appeal to them as much as the motif of Christ on the cross," whom they viewed "as a fellow brother in misery."[10] However, I suggest that in utilizing these Christian images and symbols, they invested them with new Jewish meanings and used them to address issues such as Jewish suffering and loss with some of the most potent symbols of the Western canon. The very process of Jews more freely employing the central symbols of Western-Christian civilization resulted in the creation of a new, distinctively modern, Jewish culture, which was both universal and particular at once.

Furthermore, the proliferation of Christ-figures and Christian motifs in modern Jewish literature must be seen as part of a larger undercurrent in the overall process of modernization: the secularization of religious concepts and texts. As freethinking Jewish intellectuals and artists struggled to modernize Jewish culture and society they frequently adapted such traditional Jewish concepts as messianic redemption, exile, prophecy, martyrdom, and apocalypticism, as well as various biblical motifs, in an attempt to anchor their revised visions of Jewish culture in classical Jewish ideals and sources. This tactic of reinterpreting and transforming traditional religious concepts and themes instead of completely eradicating them can also be seen in the universal move toward modernity in the West. Seth Wolitz captures the essence of this phenomenon in modern Jewish literature when he characterizes it as part of a broader trend of "cultural nationalism," which involves "effort(s) to save a people's authenticity, modernize it, and create the ambience for its greater participation in the world with all its political implications."[11] This process frequently manifested itself in the work of modern Jewish thinkers and artists, in the form of a constant struggle with the past in order to wrest from it all that was redeemable and bury all that was not.

One part of this process involved the attempt by modern Jewish writers to reclaim the heretics and false messiahs of the Jewish past and thereby turn them into heroes for the present. This phenomenon was widespread in modern Jewish literature (Yiddish and Hebrew) and thought, and unquestionably contributed to the fascination with Jesus witnessed during this period.[12] Modern Jewish writers saw in figures such as Shlomo Molcho and Shabbetai Tzvi (infamous false messiahs from the medieval and early modern periods), the Marranos (forced Jewish converts during the era of the Spanish Inquisition), and the excommunicated Jewish philosopher Benedict (Baruch) Spinoza, as well as Jesus, tragic heroes who had been vilified by the dominant rabbinic culture. They now needed to be rehabilitated as part of an endeavor to subvert traditional Jewish norms and construct a new, revitalized, secular Jewish culture.

The figure of Shabbetai Tzvi is most closely related to that of Jesus, in that after his failed messianic campaign ended in apostasy he too was unanimously renounced and vilified by the traditional Jewish establishment. Likewise, in the modern period enlightened Jews (from Theodor Herzl to Gershom Scholem) have frequently vindicated him and attempted to resuscitate his image.[13] In fact, authors such as Asch and Uri Tsvi Grinberg wrote empathetically about both Shabbetai Tzvi and Jesus in their fiction and poetry, while the Hebrew writer A. A. Kabak became famous for his epic novels about Shlomo Molcho and Jesus.[14] Asch published his play *Shabbetai Tzvi* in 1908, only a year before "In a Carnival Night" appeared, while Grinberg's poem "King Shabbetai Tzvi" was published in 1933 in the Polish Yiddish newspaper *Di velt* (*World*) under the pseudonym Yoysef Molcho (itself an allusion to the other false messiah, Molcho). As a preface to the translation of this poem in the *Penguin Book of Modern Yiddish Verse*, the editors explain that "in the 1920s Greenberg [*sic*] became interested in the whole gallery of Jewish messianic figures and rehabilitated them from a modern national perspective as great, misunderstood visionaries."[15] It is therefore by no means surprising that during the same period (1934) Grinberg also wrote a sympathetic Yiddish poem about Shlomo Molcho (a Marrano) entitled "Me and My Brother from Portugal."[16] Whether they were writing in Yiddish or Hebrew, or had socialist or Zionist leanings, modern Jewish writers mined the Jewish past to find literary heroes for the present.

Opening Doors: Asch and Shapiro Inscribe the Cross

The writing and thought of Sholem Asch, whose groundbreaking story "In a Carnival Night" was at the heart of the Crucifix Question in the East European literary and intellectual world, can be firmly situated within many of these prevailing trends. His fascination with the figure of Jesus and his bold use of Christian imagery and motifs throughout his literary career are explicitly connected to his understanding of Jewish history and his attempt to create a modern Jewish culture that synthesizes traditional and secular elements in a unique and often sensational way. It is only through examining some of Asch's central concerns that we can begin to understand "In a Carnival Night." Like other modern Jewish intellectuals who attempted to lend revised secular meanings to traditional concepts, Asch constantly grappled with age-old religious themes in an effort to make sense of modern Jewish life. His writing was permeated with questions of a spiritual-religious nature, issues of finding "self and soul" in the modern world once tradition has been abandoned.[17] Asch's entire body of work is permeated with the related motifs of martyrdom (*kiddush ha-shem*) and messianism, with a particular focus on the tension between the two. In the introduction to his 1921 novella "The Sorceress of Castille" (itself a tale about martyrdom with Christological overtones in which the female Jewish protagonist is depicted as a Madonna-like martyr), Asch states that "two elements of Jewish history have always interested me: martyrdom and the messianic strivings which always followed acts of martyrdom. These two elements of Jewish history have long captured my imagination and my creative desire. Recently, I have begun to attempt to realize my literary dream."[18] Asch's best-known work on the subject of martyrdom is *Kiddush Ha-Shem* (1919), his fictional account of the Chmielnitski massacres in 1648–49 in Ukraine (published as a companion piece with "The Sorceress of Castille" in 1921), in which he builds fantastic tales of Jewish martyrdom out of Nathan Hanover's historical chronicle of the events. However, from his earliest writings, including "In a Carnival Night," the themes of martyrdom and courageous suffering in Jewish history frequently reappear. Asch was not alone among modern Jewish writers in focusing on the martyrological aspect of Jewish history, yet in Asch's writing it occupies a very central place.[19]

It is worth noting here that since the death of Rabbi Akiba at the hands of Roman soldiers in the second century of the common era, there has been an extensive history of martyrology in Jewish tradition, in which suffering and death in the name of God were accorded a positive religious connotation. Especially in the medieval context of conflict with Christianity, martyrdom offered a means to justify Judaism by proving its righteousness and virtue among the nations and before God, because, "through Jewish martyrdom all the nations [would] recognize the one true God."[20] This tradition of "martyrdom religion" became particularly strong in Ashkenazic lands after the Crusader massacres in the eleventh and twelfth centuries. For these Jews, the notion of "catastrophe as punishment, the central component of the biblical-rabbinic view, was no longer experienced as applicable to explaining what took place . . ."[21] The Jews of the Rhineland (Mainz, Speyer, Worms, etc.) could not reconcile the self-perceived piety of their own communities with the enormous destruction visited upon them without abandoning the classical paradigm for explaining catastrophe. They sought an alternative means of explanation, namely the concept of *yissurin shel ahavah* ("afflictions of love"). This conception held that "suffering is an opportunity awarded by God to the most worthy for the display of righteousness and for the garnering of otherworldly rewards. Destruction was thus divorced from sin."[22] This notion also generated similar concepts, such as the idea that Jews suffer for the sake of God, alleviating God's pain, in a sense, and that as the "suffering servant" of God, Israel vicariously atones for the iniquities of the world through its pain and sacrifice.[23] This strand of Jewish thought, so present in much of Asch's writing, is very strongly intertwined with Christian concepts of vicarious suffering, and therefore it is not altogether surprising when Asch incorporates Jesus into this Jewish tradition of martyrdom. In fact, for almost all modern Jewish writers Jesus' death is understood more within the Jewish tradition of martyrdom than the Christian tradition of vicarious atonement and sacrifice. Part of the appropriation of Jesus from Christianity involves Jews reinterpreting the very meaning of his death.

The synthesis of Christian and Jewish traditions was part of Asch's overall belief in the essential Jewishness of Christianity and its founding figures. In fact, Asch's "interest in Jesus, Paul, and Mary . . . stemmed from their being Jews and essential figures in Jewish history, and he wanted to help bridge the two-millennia gap between Judaism and Christianity."[24] Regarding Jesus specifically, Asch stated that "I have never separated Christ from the Jewish people."[25] In 1908 Asch set out to write a novel about Jesus and embarked on a trip to Palestine to gather local material for the novel. At this point, especially during his visit to Jerusalem, Asch's ideas about the interconnectedness between Judaism and Christianity began to take root. He recalled years later that "since that time I have never thought of Judaism or Christianity separately. For me it is one culture and one civilization . . ."[26] Asch repeatedly articulated this belief in the common core of the two religions and expressed his profound empathy for the central figures of Christianity throughout his literary career. When Asch suspended work on his Christ novel after finishing part of the first chapter, "In a Carnival Night" became his vehicle for publicly expressing his emerging ideas about the place of Jesus in the world of Judaism. The story also sharply highlighted the connection for Asch between the themes of messianism and martyrdom, which continually pervaded his writing.

In "In a Carnival Night" Asch explicitly invoked the figure of Jesus in his exploration of the interconnected themes of messianism and martyrdom.[27] This story—lauded by Zhitlovsky and condemned by Ansky—was Asch's first fictional attempt at inscribing Jesus (and Mary) into the Jewish tradition of messianism and martyrdom that occupied so much of his attention. He boldly incorporated the *Jesus redivivus* motif into what would have otherwise been an unremarkable tale of Jewish martyrdom in the Middle Ages. As in so many of his later stories of Jewish martyrdom, Asch presents a Jewish community—this time in sixteenth-century Rome—undergoing trials and tribulations at the hands of its Christian oppressors. The leading families of the Jewish community are forced to embroider tapestries that will adorn the Christian Carnival procession that is at the heart of the story, and the elders of the community are made to march naked through the streets in a humiliating act that signifies utter Jewish servility and submission to the Church. As in many of Asch's later stories, the Jews are depicted as bearing their suffering in silent dignity, as passive victims whose only real strength is their piety and willingness to become martyrs in the name of God. Wealthy Jewish daughters quietly offer up their bridal trousseaus in an ultimate act of self-sacrifice in order to provide their Christian overseers with adequate adornments for their Carnival and save the Jewish community from the Church's wrath. The Jewish elders bear their indignity with stoic silence, only concerned with trying to cover up their nakedness as they run through the Roman streets among jeering crowds.

In this story, and throughout his larger body of work, Asch tends to cast the Jews with all of their sufferings in the Diaspora as the "true Christians." *They* are the ones who constantly suffer and die for their God, giving their lives as the ultimate sacrifice. Their path is consistently a *via dolorosa*, as seen in this story when the Jewish elders are forced metaphorically to bear their cross as the Christian revelers heckle them during the Carnival procession. Asch takes the age-old tradition of Jewish martyrology into new territory by rendering the Jews as a "people of Christs" with Jesus as the quintessential emblem of their suffering. Like the Reform thinkers I surveyed above, especially Kohler and Emil Hirsch, Asch also attempts to illustrate that the Jews are indeed better disciples of Jesus' moral doctrines than those who call themselves Christians, and, moreover, they act as living exemplars of central "Christian" ideals such as love, forgiveness, and self-sacrifice. In turn, Asch depicts the Christians as barbaric pagans who have completely abandoned the teachings of Jesus in propagating a religion *about* Jesus instead of the religion *of* Jesus. This Christological understanding of Jewish history accompanied by a scathing condemnation of historical Christianity was only possible if Jesus and his life and teachings were rendered in a completely Jewish light. For a Jewish writer of fiction like Asch, this had different ramifications than for his Reform predecessors who wrote works of history and theology.

In "In a Carnival Night," as throughout his later writings, Asch depicts Jesus in a distinctly Jewish manner. He refers to him as "the Jew from the town of Nazareth," and it is implied that from the moment he descends from the cross and sets foot on the streets of Rome his fate is the same as that of his fellow Jews. Asch depicts Jesus as thoroughly identifying with contemporary Jews, and, typically, as being identified as one, too. The Romans on the street with Jesus are busy preparing for the Carnival and therefore do not notice the "man-god" as he passes by. The very act of Jesus' descent from the cross represents his willingness to forsake the divine status that the Christians have bestowed upon him, in favor of his identification as a human and as a Jew. Besides the miraculous act of descending from the cross, a mythical/fictional device that is never actually explained, Asch's Jesus distances himself from the Christ of Christian legend. He covers up his stigmata so as not to be recognized as the crucified Christ returned (although this eventually happens at the story's climax). Furthermore, Jesus is repulsed by the "praise and song" Christians offer him as they bow to his wooden image on the cross. Jesus' thorough identification with the historical plight of his fellow Jews and his repudiation of those who call themselves Christians is fully articulated in a fantastic scene in which he addresses the Jewish Messiah.

Asch facilitates Jesus' monologue to the Messiah by employing the rabbinic legend about the Messiah being chained to the gates of Rome awaiting God's call: "The man-god went through the Augustus Gate, which is located at the outskirts of Rome. There, enveloped by night, he encountered the Messiah sitting on a stone, bound to the wall with black chains on his legs. He held the shofar in his hand, with a pitcher of anointing oil by his side, waiting for God's word to free him and usher in redemption" (222). In the presence of the true (but shackled) redeemer of the Jewish people, Jesus approaches the Messiah and asks his forgiveness for all that "they" (the Christians) do in his (Jesus') name. This critical scene is almost assuredly the first example in Yiddish fiction of Jesus himself begging forgiveness for all of the atrocities committed in his name. This theme was certainly touched upon in the nonfiction writings of Reform rabbis and other nineteenth- and twentieth-century authors, but Asch's bold fictional portrayal of Jesus himself coming off his cross and asking the Jewish Messiah to forgive him is a truly powerful and unprecedented tactic. Not only does it serve as a biting condemnation of the historical legacy of Christian anti-Semitism, but it also is part of Asch's attempt to separate Jesus from historical Christianity and reclaim him for the Jews. Like the historians Geiger and Graetz, Asch presents Christianity—through the mouth of Jesus himself—as an inauthentic religion based on the corruption of Jesus' teachings and the exploitation of his martyrdom. Asch's Jesus accuses the Christians, whom he refers to as *fremde* (foreigners or strangers), of "ripping the shroud off my body and turning it into banners which they dipped in my blood and then used to bring tears and sorrow to my brothers with my name on their lips" (222). He further states that the Christians distorted his teachings, changing his message of peace into one of war, and his message of forgiveness into one of vengeance.

The Jews of Jesus' own time are not completely blameless in this process, as Jesus relates that he had brought his teachings to them originally, to their study houses and synagogues, and was rejected by them as if he were a leper. If anything, this assertion reinforces the general vision that Asch consistently embraces: Jesus was a Jew bringing Jewish teachings to his fellow Jews. He was rejected and cut off by them and subsequently appropriated by the "strangers" who raised their banner in his name only to pervert his message and persecute his people. In this sense, Asch's vision as embodied in this story and elsewhere in his work is truly a Jewish *reclaiming* of Jesus. The transfer of ownership over Jesus had already occurred once at the time of his death when the strangers/Christians began to formulate a religion in his name, and now, Asch was reasserting the intrinsic Jewishness of Jesus and his teachings.

David Roskies has claimed that "In a Carnival Night" set the mold for the school of "ecumenical idealists," those Jewish writers who saw the possibility for Jews and Christians to reconcile, and that Asch believed "that Jewish-Gentile antagonism was a thing of the past and that enlightened Jews now recognized the essential humanity of the dominant Christian culture."[28] However, it is crucial to note that Asch's embrace of Jesus, as we see explicitly in this story, coincides with a harsh denunciation of Christianity and Christian anti-Semitism. In juxtaposition to the cruelty exhibited by the local Christian community, Jesus himself is seen as identifying with the Jewish plight, and throwing in his lot with his fellow Jewish martyrs. Asch's Jesus is disassociated from Christianity, allowing Asch to portray him as a positive Jewish figure without accepting the essential humanity of the dominant Christian culture. Roskies' assertion that Asch thought Jewish-Gentile antagonism was "a thing of the past" is not borne out in Asch's writings. His message to the Christians is more along the lines of that emphasized by the Reform writers like Hirsch, Kohler, and I. M. Wise: Christians must eschew their corrupt Christian doctrines and adhere to the authentic teachings of Jesus, which were essentially Jewish to begin with and would therefore dictate a profound improvement in their treatment of and attitude toward contemporary Jews.

The climactic episode of Asch's tale depicts Jesus proclaiming his solidarity with his fellow Jewish martyrs in word and deed. In concluding his monologue to the Messiah Jesus exclaims that "together with my brothers and sisters, I will bear shame and humiliation as their [Christians'] song and praise offend me" (222). In the next scene, as the Carnival procession unfolds with the humiliation of the Jewish elders, the reader discovers that Jesus has joined the "runners" in their painful procession before the unrelenting Christian mobs. The narrative reveals that, to the shock and bewilderment of the spectators, "he, the man-god, was among the runners. They had whipped and chased their god. . . . Covering his naked body with the shroud of Joseph of Arimathea, Jesus raised the cross high over the bowed heads of the spectators and passed though their midst . . . " (225). In this scene traditional typologies become totally inverted: it is the barbaric Christians who are cast as would-be deicides as they unwittingly beat and taunt their own "man-god," while Jesus with his cross raised high becomes emblematic of the Jewish people and their suffering at the hands of the Christians.

This depiction of Jesus as the paradigmatic Jewish martyr was central to Asch's work, and also figures significantly in other works by modern Jewish writers and visual artists. Asch revisited this theme in a later, far more powerful story, "Christ in the Ghetto" ("Kristos in geto," 1943, to be discussed in the following chapter), which portrayed Jesus in the Warsaw Ghetto coming down from the cross and assuming the figure of a dead Hasidic rabbi who had been gunned down by a Gestapo officer. In his guise as rabbi, Jesus prevents a Polish mob from rioting against the Jews by instilling compassion and love in their hearts. For Asch, then, Jesus' essential teaching was of brotherly love, an ideal not often achieved by historical Christians but that could be recovered by upholding a mythic vision and projecting it as the light for the future. The dominant feature of both of these stories, however, is Asch's depiction of Jesus as a loyal, martyred Jew, an emphatic act of Jewish reclamation.

This act of reclamation is expanded upon by Asch in the enigmatic final scene of "In a Carnival Night" (which oddly is not included in the

English translation) to include the figure of Mary (Miriam), the mother of Jesus. In this strangely esoteric scene, which reads like an apocalyptic parable, the biblical matriarch Rachel is portrayed as a majestic vision in white who brings light to a world of darkness. She carries ripped Torah scrolls and prayer shawls in her apron and knits shrouds with which to cover all her martyred children.[29] A young girl follows after Rachel with outstretched arms, pleading with her, "Let me, mother, let me help you sew the shrouds" (228). The "daughter" is Miriam (Mary) joining her "mother Rachel" in claiming matriarchal responsibility for the suffering of all their children. Asch effectively places Mary squarely in the Jewish matriarchal pantheon through her identification with Rachel, allowing him to fully recover Christian symbols and archetypes as part of a Jewish mythic past. Mother and daughter—synagogue and Church—are joined together. But for Asch, Mary is not the emblem of the daughter religion, the Church. In his revised legend of the past, Miriam, like her son, is part and parcel of Jewish myth and collective memory. She relives the pain of her son's crucifixion and laments the fact that now "they slaughter all my children in my son's name" (228). Like Jesus addressing the Messiah in the previous scene, Asch's Mary attempts to gain acceptance among the Jewish people, as represented here by the matriarch, Rachel, by pledging allegiance to her and condemning the actions of those (Christians) who exploit her son's sacrifice by committing atrocities in his name.[30]

As Zhitlovsky implied, Asch's story attempts to abolish Jesus, and Mary's "outsider" status among Jews, returning them to the fold, as it were, by depicting them as devoted Jews who are not responsible for the sins of Christians, even when these violent deeds were committed in their name. Furthermore, it must be seen as part of Asch's larger undertaking, also shared by Zhitlovsky, of merging Jewish and Christian-European civilization into one unified "European-Jewish world." Ansky's observation that the "whole idea of the story hinges on the discovery that Mary and Jesus were Jews" is true, to a point. But Ansky fails to recognize that Asch, through his story, and Zhitlovsky, through his essay, were doing more than merely currying favor with the Gentiles by embracing the central figures of Christianity in such a positive way. In fact, they were subverting the dominant Christian-European culture

by investing the core Christian myths with an essentially Jewish meaning, and subsequently incorporating these myths into works of Jewish
literature that contributed to the development of a modern Jewish cultural canon.

One of the key Yiddish writers in this new cultural canon was
Lamed Shapiro (1878–1948). Although he was one of the least prolific
prose writers of the second generation of Yiddish authors, Shapiro
made his mark in the Yiddish literary world with a number of stylisti-
cally complex and thematically daring short stories dealing with the
effects of pogroms on Jewish society and the individual psyche. Every
aspect of his writing is infused with various modernist styles, which
effectively allow him to treat this grave subject in a chillingly graphic
and boldly innovative way. Traces of expressionism, naturalism, deca-
dence, and psychological realism are all evident in many of Shapiro's
works. His graphic portrayals of violence and in-depth psychological
character studies bring a modernist tone and sensibility to his writings that starkly set them apart from those of *di klassiker*. These factors are especially salient in Shapiro's trademark pogrom stories—"The
Cross," "The Kiss," "In the Dead Town," and "Pour out Thy Wrath"
(written in 1909) and "The Jewish Government" and "White Chal-
lah" (written in 1918)—in which the pogrom is not treated solely as a
social-historical factor in Jewish life, but rather as a window through
which to explore the complexities of the human psyche in relation to
such brutal and traumatic experiences. Among these stories, "The
Cross" ("Der tseylem") stood out, not only for its shockingly vivid
depiction of violence and gore, but especially for Shapiro's bold use
of the primary Christian symbol as the indispensable axis of his story.
After being at the heart of the Crucifix Question debate and gaining
him much renown, "The Cross" remained Shapiro's signature story
and major claim to fame for years, a fact that he came to bemoan later
in his career.[31]

Avraham Nowersztern observes in an article on Shapiro's pogrom stories that "the content of 'The Cross' itself had very little to
do with the controversial discussion that took place in the pages of
Dos naye lebn, which was primarily concerned with what attitude the
Jewish intelligentsia should adopt toward Jesus and Christianity."[32]

Zhitlovsky understood the story to be a rejection of a more "universalist humanistic" approach toward Christianity and European civilization motivated by the sense of betrayal young Jewish revolutionaries like Shapiro felt in the wake of the pogroms. Zhitlovsky's highly politicized reading of "The Cross" does appear to have some merit, but he fails to recognize that Shapiro's story is not as ideologically programmatic as Asch's. While Shapiro's utilization of the cross does partly serve as an indictment of a brutal Christian world that practices murder while preaching love, there is also another level on which it operates. Nowersztern argues persuasively that for Shapiro the cross functioned primarily as an aesthetic tool, a literary device, used to deal with the problems and tensions at the center of his story. Shapiro employed the cross not only as a religious-historical icon, but as a rich literary symbol that allowed him to explore such critical and timely issues as the construction of identity in the modern world, and the tensions between memory and forgetfulness. "The Cross," then, is more than just a story about a pogrom, and Shapiro's use of the image of the cross does more than merely condemn the horrors of Christian anti-Semitism; it confronts the quintessentially modern crisis of identity formation and the subsequent breaking of traditional boundaries that this condition typically entailed. The story addresses the most primitive, animalistic human drives that are triggered through primal eruptions of violence, such as a pogrom. Above all, it conveys the power of nature to liberate humans from the shackles of morality, ideology, and community that bind them. Shapiro boldly utilizes the cross as the cohesive device that drives his narrative along and brings these various themes to the surface.[33]

The story begins in the wilderness of the American prairie, three years after the pogrom that forms the center of the story. This frame story introduces us to the central protagonist, a man with a cross carved into his forehead, through the eyes of a second narrator who has been the man's traveling companion in their wanderings across America. The protagonist and his companion roam freely across the rugged contours of the prairie living a barebones existence; their lives are simple and unshackled. They are both nameless, traveling without passports, cut off from civilization, not recognizing any borders or boundaries. The central protagonist with his "child's smile" has been transformed into a child in the bosom of nature, creating the feeling of both unfettered freedom and forgetfulness.[34] It is as if he had been born anew into an American Garden of Eden, liberated from memory and civilization. The only thing that links him to his gruesome past is the cross etched into his forehead. The cross keeps the past alive on his very flesh. It is a core physical identity marker, not something superfluous like a name or a passport that can be easily left behind.[35] In this first scene Shapiro introduces two of the major tensions of the story, between nature and civilization, and between remembering and forgetting, with the cross serving as the nexus of these juxtapositions.

In "The Cross" nature is depicted as a realm of liberation where the protagonist can escape his past and build a new life based on a new identity. Ironically, access to this realm of nature is only made possible through violence and mayhem in the form of a pogrom that awakens his most primitive impulses. In this sense nature and violence are intimately connected for Shapiro as "both through nature and through physical violence, people could purge that weaker part of themselves, break those civilizing shackles called humanism, politics, and culture to become 'iron men.'"[36] Nature is the refuge from human morality and civilization, the only place to exist once the moral order of civilization has completely broken down. In the midst of the long and grisly pogrom scene that the protagonist relates to his curious companion, he muses: "What does nature, the *universe*, know of dirt and shame? In the universe there are no such things as dirt and shame."[37] This allusion to the fundamental amorality of nature—of the universe itself—comes at a time when the protagonist is having a struggle with his own morality. The savage brutality and sheer frenzy of the pogrom awakened within him immoral urges and a lust for violence that he had never experienced before: "until that night I had not known of true rage, which intoxicates like strong wine; of rage that suddenly boils in the blood, streams through the whole body, smashes into the head, and floods all thoughts" (147). After wildly lashing out at the pogromists in self-defense, he is viciously beaten, bound with rope, and thrown at the foot of his mother's bed, where the pogromists then beat and rape her. Already changed by the chaos around him and fueled by the hatred and resentment he feels for his mother, the protagonist takes guilty pleasure in watching his mother tortured. As he struggles to free himself from the cords that restrain him, both literally and metaphorically, he loses consciousness, only to awaken moments later and undergo the ultimate act of transformation: the sign of the cross is carved into his forehead by the short peasant who has just raped his mother.

Once marked by the cross, an emblem of Christian salvation, martyrdom, and forgiveness, the protagonist plunges into the depths of utter chaos. His narration of the story becomes fragmented and his grasp on reality becomes tenuous. He struggles to find one "point" of reality—from without or from within—that can help him make sense of things. Yet the cross has caused him to forget himself. As he lies in the dark, still bound by his mother's bed, he notices the wound on his forehead: "on my forehead I feel a burning wound, it burns sharply and makes me forget my other wounds" (152). The process of forgetting his wounds, both physical and psychological, is an integral part of the transformation that he undergoes. In order to break free from the world of chaos and destruction that surrounds him he must liberate himself from the bonds of civilization and self. The first step in accomplishing this comes when he frees himself from the ropes around his hands: "After still more effort—and at my feet lie the torn, frayed ropes, at my feet lie the broken shards of gods" (154). This physical unshackling is accompanied by a metaphorical liberation from God, from Law, and from Man. The protagonist, empowered by the cross on his forehead, experiences a "transvaluation of values," as he is transformed into an *Ubermensch* or "iron man" who is not subject to the normal confines of humanity, reality, or even time.[38]

The first act that embodies the protagonist's new value system is the "mercy killing" of his tortured mother. Barely able to recognize his mother as more than a "bloodied something," he grabs a table leg and smashes it on her head while emitting a "suppressed roar" that sounds so strange he can hardly recognize it as his own voice. From that point on, all boundaries are blurred. The protagonist emerges from his house into a savage world of violence in which he cannot find his place. Drifting between Jewish self-defense forces and bands of pogromists, he does not know where he belongs: "I found myself in the ranks of the self-defense unit and—among the mobs of pogromists. I felt like a storm-driven leaf. The cross burned on my forehead" (156). He crosses freely over the boundaries separating these two opposing communities as if he were above the fray. Even when he passes by the short peasant who had branded him with the cross, he pats him on the shoulder and winks at him, obviously not concerned with petty acts of revenge. The man with the cross is a victim no longer. The cross on his head has redeemed him not from sin, but from the possibility of sinning. Emancipated from civilization and its values, he is free to act out his most primitive urges and impulses. The ability to act on one's impulses and exert physical strength are the cardinal tenets for his new "transvalued" code of behavior. The distinction between victim and victimizer has become unclear and inverted.

The ultimate inversion occurs when the man with the cross himself becomes a savage pogromist, effectively erasing his own victimhood. Before this process culminates he witnesses an act of murder and madness that highlights the identity confusion that prevails. He sees a sixteen-year-old pogromist brutally murder an old Jewish man with an axe. Afterward, the boy is chased down an alley by a young Jew from the self-defense unit with a gun in his hand. With the pogromist backed against a fence the Jew raises his gun, only to turn it on himself and fire. The young peasant loses his mind and runs off screaming. The protagonist, having followed the two down the alley, breaks out in a hideous laughter and kicks the young Jew's corpse, which lies on the street convulsing like a worm (157). (The last part of this episode is mysteriously left out of the English translation.) For the "*tseylem* man" the Jew is the guilty one on account of his inability to kill the young pogromist. He could not successfully accomplish the transformation from victim to murderer that the protagonist himself is about to consummate.

This transformation is completed when he goes to the house of a young Russian woman, Mina. His partner and would-be lover from the revolutionary cell to which they both belong, Mina becomes the sacrifice in his sadistic ritual of redemption. Finding himself banging at her door, he is at first puzzled as to why he is there. Then, he sees Mina and it becomes clear to him: "A flash blazed in my mind, and for a moment fear overtook me. I understood where I was and what I would do. Immediately, I became calm" (158). Mina barely recognizes him and is silent when she first sees the cross "glowing" on his forehead. He relates to her the entire lurid experience he has just endured with intermittent smiles and laughs that frighten her. Then, "slowly and calmly" he rises to attack her. He notes that she tried to defend herself and he muses: "how could her strength suffice against the man with the cross on his forehead?" (159). He then rapes her, but does not divulge to us the "despicable details" of the act. When he is finished, he strangles her, then collapses on a chair and falls asleep instantly. The utter fury unleashed by the protagonist functions as a cathartic sexual act. Afterwards he feels "fresh, animated, and calm." The wound on his forehead no longer hurts, "it only itched a little," and he claims that his "mother's soul had found its peace" (160). Through rape and murder his inner conflicts are resolved and his liberation from the shackles of morality and civilization is completed.

The role that the cross plays in this process is crucial. After the protagonist briefly contemplates taking a knife and slicing away the cross on his forehead, he "thought to let it remain—*As a frontlet between thine eyes*. Ha! Was it these frontlets that our old, dear God meant?" (160). The cross replaces the *tefillin* as a reminder of the law, and the "law" it represents is that of pure animal instinct and uninhibited inclinations. A multilayered subversion occurs. Not only does the pogrom victim become a murderer, but the Jewish ritual object, the *tefillin*, is transformed into a cross, and the original meaning of the cross itself— love, salvation, and martyrdom—has been replaced by a new doctrine of murder, lust, and physical power. As Roskies observes, "Nothing captured the paradox of freedom-through-coercion and liberation- through-violence as well as the symbol of the cross. Was the hero a victim, a suffering Christ, or Cain, the murderer marked for life?"[39] He appears to be both at once, a suffering victim who is transformed into a murderer, not through the mark of Cain, but through the cross, the symbol of Christ himself. If, as Ruth Wisse claims, the cross "haunted the Jewish imagination" as a symbol of love "perverted into the practice of hate which the Jew was somehow challenged to redeem," then Lamed Shapiro was cynically taking up this challenge. However, unlike in Asch's works, the cross is not restored as a true symbol of love in Shapiro's fiction. Instead, Shapiro reconciles the seeming contradiction of salvation and brutal violence represented by the cross. The cross redeems the protagonist from the chaos and violence that has engulfed his world by allowing him to commit an act of violence, which frees him from that world.

What, then, can Shapiro's shocking tale tell us about his stance regarding the Crucifix Question, which the story itself had elicited? Should we concur with Zhitlovsky, who saw Shapiro's position as "purely nationalistic, dictated by a boundless hatred of the cross?" Or does Nowersztern's claim that the content of "The Cross" had very little to do with the issues that were raised in the Crucifix Question debates hold more merit? I suggest that both critics are partly right in assessing Shapiro's pioneering story, as I believe that Shapiro's use of the cross functioned on many levels. As Zhitlovsky asserts, Shapiro does utilize the "boundless hatred for the cross" that existed within the popular Jewish imagination in order to effectively render it as a locus of violence in the modern world. However, this neither confirms his own position regarding how enlightened Jews should relate to Jesus and Christianity, nor is it the only consideration in employing the cross as the central symbol of his story. For Shapiro, the cross was also part of a universal canon of literary symbols that Jewish writers such as himself could freely use. While for Asch, employing Jesus and other Christian symbols in his writing was part of an ideological program that aimed to redraw the boundaries between Christian and Jewish culture, civilization, and history, for Shapiro it was primarily an aesthetic choice in creating fiction that helped to construct a modernist literary universe in which these boundaries could be breached. Both Asch and Shapiro were opening the door for other Jewish writers and artists to follow in their footsteps, freely incorporating assorted Christian images and symbols—with the figure of Jesus being most common—in their artistic works. Often combining religious, political, and stylistic concerns—like Shapiro—these writers inscribed Jesus the Jew into the emerging secular canon of modern Jewish culture. We can now examine the various trajectories this process traversed in the decades that followed the emergence of the Crucifix Question.

Modern Myths of the Apocalypse:
Poets, Prophets, Christs, and Messiahs

In 1922, Shmuel Niger wrote a salient essay entitled "Modern Myth" in which he attempted to explicate the prevalence of apocalyptic themes in Yiddish literature during the preceding several years. The essay asserted that "in apocalyptic times one can only create apocalypses" and that "a fantastic world can only be captured [artistically] by fantastic means."[40] In other words, Niger was suggesting that in the revolutionary times in which he was living, a radically new mode of art and literature was required to adequately render and express the turbulent experiences of life. The realism that had served an earlier generation of Yiddish writers no longer sufficed. Niger also addressed the need of the current generation of writers and artists to create a new mythology of heroes and demigods, prophets and Messiahs, in order to fulfill the creative aspirations of mankind. He specifically alludes to the prophetic vision of the poet himself who builds "towers to the heavens" and from there thunders down God's vision for the future in his own voice.[41] Niger believed that chaotic, cataclysmic times call for the creation of founding myths that can provide new and stable foundations to allay the chaos and regenerate mankind. He viewed the primitivism of modernist styles like Cubism and Dadaism, the *nakete dikhtung* ("naked poetry") of the Yiddish poet Melekh Ravitsh, and the outcry of the Yiddish expressionists like Uri Tsvi Grinberg as reflecting this need to return to a primordial time and create new myths in order to recenter the world and start anew.[42] Niger's essay implies that the central task of the modernist artist is to construct the culture of the future on the ruins of the past. In order to better understand this phenomenon we must situate the mytho-apocalyptic literature Niger explored in his essay within the larger cultural-historical context of modernism as a pivotal force in European (non-Jewish) and Jewish cultures.

The entire phenomenon or movement known as modernism was part of a vast cultural upheaval that shattered the foundations of Western art and literature at the end of the nineteenth and beginning of the twentieth centuries. Traditional forms collapsed, resulting in crisis—a condition that is part and parcel of modernism. Alienation, discontinuity, and shock were defining features of this trend, as authors and artists attempted to forge new cultural forms and styles distinct from past traditions, to create modern myths for a posttraditional generation.[43] In many ways these essential features of modernism are fundamentally characteristic of the modern Jewish revolution in general. Benjamin Harshav's concept of the modern Jewish revolution is helpful in delineating the cultural process in which twentieth-century Jewish modernists were intricately involved. Harshav defines this revolution as "a veritable explosion of modernity within one or two generations," and emphasizes that "Jews eagerly joined the 'general' modern culture in manners both extrinsic and intrinsic; while many took up the languages and entered the cultural institutions of the extant European nations, others created a European-type secular culture of their own in Hebrew and Yiddish, accepting European genres and modes of discourse and infusing them with elements transformed from the Jewish tradition."[44]

This intermingling of Jewish and non-Jewish cultures exposed the modern Jewish artist, writer, and thinker to both complementary and competing models for cultural creativity. The inclusion of crucifixion motifs in Jewish art and writing constitutes one example of the synthesis of these competing models in which traditional Jewish culture serves as the thesis, Christian-Western culture the antithesis, and these modernist works constitute the synthesis, something wholly new that draws on both conflicting sources. (Other binary opposites such as particular and universal, self and nation, old and new, also became reconciled.) In this manner, the figure of Jesus could become "part of the modern gallery of Jewish literature."[45]

To be sure, hybridity and intermingling of disparate sources and styles was an essential feature of European modernism in general. However, for the East European Jewish artist, arriving fresh, as it were, into the cultural discourse of the West, a certain amount of catching up had to be done. Harshav has suggested that "when the East European Jewish intelligentsia, in one grand leap, landed in the general twentieth century, Yiddish poetry undertook not only to catch up with Europe's appreciation of the classics and the modernistic trends, but also to take an active part in the discussion of the most timely cultural problems and in the artistic movements of the environment."[46] Thus, different trends, movements, and even "periods" coexisted in Yiddish literature, especially in the early interwar years.

Modernist movements, consisting of circles of poets and writers and a variety of literary journals, rapidly surfaced in the various centers of Jewish cultural life—Warsaw, Kiev, New York, Moscow, Berlin—in the first few decades of the twentieth century. These movements or groups, such as Di Yunge ("The Young Ones") in New York (1909–19); Yung-Yiddish and Di Khalyastre ("The Gang") in Poland (1918–24); the Eygens ("Our Own") group in Kiev (1918–1920), which later became associated with the journal *Milgroym* (*Pomegranate*) in Berlin (1922–24); the Moscow group Shtrom ("Current") (1922–24); and the Inzikhistn ("Introspectivists") in New York (1920–39), typically conceived of themselves as the avant-garde of a new Jewish culture.[47] As such, they attempted to create a secular Yiddish culture that reflected both Jewish and universal concerns. Combining European modernist forms, themes, and images with Jewish ones, they always sought to "pass the new into Yiddish as easily as possible."[48] Furthermore, as modernists and as Jews these writers and artists often underwent a "modernist crisis" in amplified terms, since the modernist motifs of exile, alienation, uprootedness, destruction, and the like had always been integral aspects of the Jewish Diaspora experience, even though the mechanisms for expressing this experience had previously been different. In this sense, the defining ethos of modernism reflected intrinsic Jewish sensibilities. While the revolutions, wars, and general turmoil of the early twentieth century deeply influenced many modernist movements and trends, the particular plight of European Jews (especially in Eastern Europe) with their own devastating losses during this period profoundly affected the nature and content of modernist Jewish literature and art in a unique way. The numerous pogroms in Eastern Europe from 1903 until 1921, in addition to the widespread general violence and mayhem of the time, invested much of Yiddish modernism with a dark, mournful, apocalyptic mood, and a grotesque, bloody appearance, perhaps matched only by German expressionist poetry following World War I.

In fact, German expressionism profoundly influenced the works of the Khalyastre group of Uri Tsvi Grinberg, Melekh Ravitsh, and Peretz

Markish, as well as M. L. Halpern, and their poetry was often referred to as Yiddish expressionism. For both the German and the Yiddish expressionists the poetic "I" was at the center of the universe and everything was refracted through it. The creative power of the artist, not the subject matter, was the focus of expressionism. Unlike the impressionists, who relied on "seeing" and observing the world, the expressionists emphasized "envisioning" in an "attempt to create a visionary world."[49] The need to turn inward propelled the creative impulses of the expressionist writer, who related to world events through a highly personalized language of the soul and the psyche. The German expressionist manifesto by Kazimir Edschmidt (1917) asserts that for expressionists, "reality needs to be created anew within the soulscape of the artist . . ."[50] This type of internal, psychic, visceral emotional response to external, physical, historical conditions was essential to Yiddish expressionism as well. The historical condition of East European Jewry was reflected and refracted through the psychic landscape of the expressionist poet. In an article appearing in the second issue of Uri Tsvi Grinberg's avant-garde journal *Albatros* in 1922, the Yiddish literary critic Max Erik declared that Yiddish expressionism was for all intents and purposes a "new language," reiterating the central ideal of "the new" to which the Yiddish avant-garde was constantly aspiring. He included the poets Grinberg, Markish, and Ravitsh, as well as the poet-novelist Moyshe Kulbak, in his analysis of the "new language" that these poets had created.[51]

In the very same year Peretz Markish declared in an essay in another modernist Yiddish journal that the role of the poet as a subversive revolutionary figure was to "destroy the old and bring on the new."[52] This new language was dominated by a sense of crisis, rupture, chaos, and gloom. A palpable tension existed between past and present, as the expressionists saw the world, and indeed the entire cosmos, as standing on the abyss of total destruction. They transformed Yiddish into a vehicle to deal with universal if not cosmic concerns: death, disenfranchisement, loneliness, and the decline of civilization. They often linked together violence and regeneration in an apocalyptic vision of complete annihilation followed by rebirth and a new order. As Niger had suggested in his essay, also written in 1922, these modernists were creating mythic literature of fantastic proportions in order to allay the chaos of their day; thematically and linguistically, the ordinary would no longer suffice.

Uri Tsvi Grinberg's short-lived journal *Albatros* (1922–23), with its combination of avant-garde art and Yiddish expressionist poetry, constitutes a quintessential example of this new type of Yiddish modernism. Among its most distinguishing features is its overt preoccupation with the figure of Jesus and crucifixion motifs. This preoccupation reflects many attributes of the expressionist poetics of its editor (Grinberg) and main contributors. The journal identifies itself as the vanguard of the new—its subtitle is "Journal for the New Poetic and Artistic Expression"—and the motto of its nucleus of poets—Di Khalyastre—proclaims:

> We young ones, a joyous, frolicking gang,
> We're walking down an unknown path,
> In deep melancholy days,
> In nights of terror
> *Per aspera ad astra*! [to the stars through difficulties][53]

This conveys the sense that these poets were fearless young rebels, blazing new paths in Jewish culture during an era of profound turbulence. Among the first articles in the inaugural issue are three expressionist manifestoes written by Grinberg ("Proclamation" and "Manifesto to the Opponents of the New Poetry") and Melekh Ravitsh ("The New, the Naked Poetry"). Also included in this first issue are excerpts from Grinberg's *poema* (long narrative poem) "Velt barg arop" ("World in Decline") and Peretz Markish's "Veyland" ("Woeland"), both of which employ numerous apocalyptic motifs—especially Christ and cross symbolism—that potently express the central concerns and prevailing style of this circle of poets and artists. As Grinberg edited the journal and wrote much, if not most, of it, he set the tone and mood for all of the works appearing in its pages, and his explicit poetics need to be addressed in some detail.

In the manifesto of his poetic vision that initiates the first issue of *Albatros*, Grinberg graphically articulates his tortured self-understanding as a poet and his role in the world disintegrating around him. He proclaims that his manifesto is a bridge to a new world for the "convulsing generation" in which he lives. The poet is the "heroic wounded man" with a million heads; he is an individual and the world all at once, a concept that clearly reflects the blurring of boundaries between self and world that reigned in Grinberg's poetic universe, and in expressionism more generally. For Grinberg, poets are themselves the "clearest expression of the convulsion" of the world and "their bodies convulse from carrying on their naked shoulders dark globe-pain [*globusvey*]."[54] The poet (like Jesus and Atlas) vicariously bears the pain of the world, acting as the suffering servant of the modern age. He excruciatingly purges his innermost feelings and experiences in the form of poetry: a bone-crunching service to mankind, as the voice of the "convulsing generation." In a torrent of Christological images Grinberg delineates the plight of the poet: "Albatrosses of the young Yiddish poetry. Spiritual food: [their] own flesh; veins; nerves. To drink: their own bone-goblets of pulsating blood. And black *shabbos* bread—our showbread—[is] suffering. What is yet missing in the kingdom of holy poverty? We, the frolicking caravan of God's poor ones. Albatrosses. Poets."[55] Like the Christian concept of Jesus redeeming mankind with his body and blood, Grinberg's poet also nourishes the world with his flesh and blood, providing it as a type of holy communion, and his sacrificial offering—like Jesus—is his suffering.

Grinberg laments the state of the world and of his generation, which exists in the "open-mouthed endlessness, whose tongue glows on the Saharan crossroad [*tseylem-veg*]: Eldorado–Nirvana."[56] The world is in a kind of limbo between spiritual enlightenment, represented by Nirvana, and carnal materialism, represented by the lost city of gold, Eldorado. Grinberg sees the present as a time of renewal, crisis, and revolution of the spirit. The world is abandoning religion and all that is holy: "the world and the red century stand in decline."[57] The apocalyptic vision of a world in decline, in its twilight, that pervades much of Grinberg's poetry from this period is articulated in his proclamation. He exclaims that black crosses lurk behind the backs of his generation, adding that poetry must reflect this abysmal state of the world: "Such songs must be sung. Savage. Chaotic. Bloody."[58] He claims that maybe other kinds of poems can be composed after the rebirth of the world, but in the meantime, "We are naked. Disheveled. Unfurled. A horror-and-shame gospel of veins and bones from the chaotic, turbulent generation which stands at the crossroads [*tseylem-veg*] Eldorado–Nirvana."[59] In Grinberg's bleak vision of the state of the world, "apocalyptic imagery fuses with the cross motif that had become established as a modern expression of the traditional Jewish apocalyptic symbolism of destruction and exile."[60] In other words, for Grinberg the cross and the entire matrix of images associated with it function as symbols with a wide range of meanings; this image matrix forms a central part of Grinberg's modern myth, and allows him to convey the misery of the human condition, the particularly dire plight of the Jews, the self-sacrifice demanded of poets, as well as the decline of civilization at large at the time of the apocalypse.

Grinberg's contemporary and fellow member of Di Khalyastre, Melekh Ravitsh, shared his poetics and apocalyptic symbolism to a large degree. He articulated the seven essential features of his newly conceptualized "naked poetry" in the first issue of *Albatros*.[61] In his manifesto Ravitsh accords the most value to poetry (and art in general) that is primal in nature. He begins by musing: "what does it mean to be a poet, to be an artist?" He suggests that it must be something instinctive and natural, part of one's nature. He claims that "talent and craft have nothing to do with the new, the naked poetry."[62] Basic human instincts are key for Ravitsh in creating "naked poetry"; guts are valued over brains. "Naked poetry" grabs the human spirit and the heart. Ravitsh talks of new worlds being born, seeing the era in which he lives as a time of regeneration and rebirth in which new forms are taking shape: of people and of poetry (a much more optimistic assessment of the times than Grinberg's). Like many of his expressionist peers, Ravitsh demonstratively favors an anti-aesthetic approach to poetry and art, exclaiming "*pfui* to aestheticism!"[63] The naked poet, he asserts, depicts real things, not just aesthetic ornament. In his most striking move, Ravitsh concludes his formulation of the meaning of "naked poetry" by employing the symbolism of the crucifixion:

Thesis vii, "And they hung him on a tree"

The word hangs naked on the cross. The proud INRI laughs at it. It [the word] wanted to be the king and redeemer of pain. Blood drips from its hands and feet. But it takes the secret of pain that lives in it and the secret of joy into the grave. It didn't exclaim: "my God, my

God why have you forsaken me!" "After you served beauty, after you served lies, I forsook you."[64]

Here Ravitsh demonstrates how central a symbol the crucifixion had become for the Yiddish avant-garde; not only did it serve as an emblem of human suffering—personal, Jewish, and universal—it also was used to represent the tragic impotence of the word as the would-be savior of the world. Ravitsh conveys the failure of the word, of poetry and literature, to save the world from its suffering. By extension, the master of the word—the writer—is implicated as a failed redeemer who cannot manage to unlock the potential sealed inside the words he uses. The word then dies a martyr's death like Jesus on the cross, taking this secret wisdom to the grave. By serving beauty—lies—and not pursuing the truth of the world's pain, Ravitsh implies that the word, and those who wield it, are abandoned by God.

Moreover, Ravitsh playfully reinterprets the Christian metaphysical concept of the Logos ("the word") as Jesus himself, by reading it hyper-literally; he suggests a reverse transformation of sorts in which the crucified Jesus physically becomes *dos vort* (instead of "the word" becoming flesh), hanging on the cross, naked with bloody, dripping wounds. In Ravitsh's formulation then, the crucified Jesus, with his nakedness and tortured suffering, embodies the "naked poetry" Ravitsh is attempting to create. The figure of Jesus becomes a metaphor for modernist Yiddish poetry itself! Not all were happy with these Christian images playing such a central role in Yiddish modernism. In a letter to the editor in the third issue of *Albatros*, Max Erik deplores such Jewish mimicry of Christian modes and motifs. He proclaims that "we haven't even noticed how we have taken everything from them, everything. Their hours and their longings, and their Mephisto and even their man with the cross."[65] Erik looks back to a time when Jews possessed their own language and culture, rather than adopting those of the non-Jewish milieu. His remarks articulate similar misgivings to those that Ansky expressed concerning Jews adopting Christian mythology rather than relying primarily on their own cultural treasures. Nonetheless, despite these objections, Jesus and the cross became an integral part of the cultural repertoire available to Yiddish modernists as they composed their modern myths.

As Grinberg's and Ravitsh's manifestoes attest, the apocalyptic vista created by avant-garde Yiddish poets in forming their modernist mythologies often partook of classical religious imagery and messianic motifs, including especially the symbols of Jesus' passion. Wolitz observes that "the cross, the bloodied Christ . . . the tolling bells, the steeples, form a continuum upon which the Khalyastre poet and artist express their exaltations, *umet* (sorrow), and ultimate isolation all in a heavy grotesque mode against the backdrop of night."[66] In Grinberg's poetry this nightmarish landscape dominates; he frequently refers to it as a *Golgota velt* ("Golgotha world"), intimating that the entire world is suffering the agony of the crucifixion: "Dark glowing red. Anguished twilight. Golgotha world."[67] These poets regularly adapted traditional images from classical religious texts, such as the Hebrew and Christian Bibles, in order to convey the epic scope of their vision, and in many cases the poets saw themselves as prophetic visionaries bringing God's message of impending doom to the nation.[68]

Grinberg and his expressionist peers cultivated this mode of prophetic apocalypticism, with Grinberg himself forcefully claiming the mantle of prophetic seer. Melekh Ravitsh, in the section of his memoirs in which he recounts his years in Warsaw in the 1920s, conveys the prophetic and even messianic mood that animated the Yiddish literary scene at that time. He mentions that the literary critic Zalman Reisen deemed Peretz Markish to be a "young prophet," a fact he repeats in another essay on Markish. In further elaborating on the literary scene in Warsaw, Ravitsh speaks of young people coming to literary gatherings and waiting to hear the "new redemptive word. The messianic word, the word from [the] prophet, the young prophet. Intelligent Jewish masses—waiting for a prophet."[69] With this anecdote Ravitsh imparts just how much modernist Yiddish literature—especially poetry—functioned as a type of secular scripture. It was eagerly awaited by a young Jewish population starving for redemption in modern terms from a world that was chaotic, bloody, and tumultuous, and empty of the old religious comforts and sureties. Ravitsh claims that young Jewish intellectuals, especially assimilated ones, now craved Jewish heroes and prophets, turning to Yiddish literature in addition to or even instead of Polish literature to provide salvation.[70]

The role and function of the prophet in these works often became confused or even conflated with the figure of the Messiah, who was traditionally linked to the End of Days in classic apocalyptic narratives, such as the books of Daniel and Revelation.[71] The Messiahs and Christ-figures that appear in the apocalyptic works of these Yiddish expressionists are frequently identified with the speakers of the poems if not the poets themselves, and are typically depicted as tragically failed redeemers. Using messianic symbolism was a way to couch contemporary ideological concerns in terms of traditional Jewish cultural referents. Eli Lederhendler sees this phenomenon as a "post-traditional celebration of tradition" meant to cement the Jewish national bond for modern Jews who have largely abandoned the traditionalist way of life.[72]

Contemporary ideas were often expressed in terms full of the rhetorical symbols of messianism. This signified an ideological messianism over against a theological messianism. Modern Jewish thinkers, writers, and ideologues tapped into what Lederhendler calls a "subterranean source of messianic inspiration in the popular Jewish imagination."[73] He further claims that "references to the constancy of the age-old messianic faith or to the national destiny of the Jews lent depth to a nationalist conceptualization of Judaism."[74] Although Lederhendler asserts this in regard to Russian *maskilim* and proto-Zionists of the 1870s and 1880s, it is also applicable, with some qualification, to the case of Yiddish writers in the first third of the twentieth century; they also frequently employed messianic symbolism as a means to lend coherence and authority to various secularized notions of Jewish national identity and destiny. Except for Grinberg, who harbored strong Zionist sentiments even in much of his Yiddish writing let alone in his later Hebrew works, the majority of Yiddish writers who incorporated the rhetorical symbols of Jewish messianism in their writings had no overtly Zionist or nationalistic motivations; their approach might more aptly be seen as cultural nationalism. They saw in traditional messianic symbolism a rich storehouse of legends and heroes from which to create modern, secular Jewish literary works that would have broad popular appeal, a strong dramatic flair, and an epic sweep. Yiddish modernists also often used these messianic motifs with bitter irony.

In his book on messianic themes in American Yiddish poetry, Yisrael

Pomerantz argues that Yiddish poets were drawn to the Christian mythology of Jesus because of their attraction to the idea of a martyred/suffering Messiah. Thus, they often incorporated the Jewish legends of the Messiah chained to the gates of Rome, or presented Jewish messianic figures like Shlomo Molcho or Shabbetai Tzvi in a way that resembled the figure of Jesus. He contends that, for the most part, the American Yiddish poets flirted temporarily with both the secular universal (read socialist) model and with the Christian model of the Messiah (Jesus) before arriving at a more Jewish image of the Messiah, based on both rabbinic and popular sources.[75] However, his theory neglects the fact that many of these writers saw Jesus as a purely Jewish Messiah. The problem must be addressed as to whether the writers viewed Jesus as a Christian messianic figure to whom they were attracted for various reasons, or whether they approached him as an intrinsically Jewish figure, or—a third possibility—whether they conceived of Jesus as a universal symbol of redemption, neither Christian or Jewish. These distinctions are fuzzy, and it is therefore difficult to ascertain which approach is predominant with a given author—whether he sees himself adopting Christian messianic legends about Jesus because of the strong dramatic content they contain, or whether he construes these legends as Jewish ones to begin with, as Niger suggested.

In Ansky's *tseylem frage* essay he also addresses the issue of Jewish authors and artists adopting Christian legends and reworking them as Jewish ones. He posits that it is acceptable to reconcile with the "Christian legend" (the story of Jesus) in two particular ways: by incorporating aspects of the legend in such a way that they inspire Jewish artistic creations, or by assimilating European artistic works and cultural manifestations, which are permeated by Christian themes. When considering the use of Jesus as a messianic figure by Yiddish writers in light of this sort of re-Judaization of Jesus we uncover the creation of Jewish narratives that compete with the established Christian narratives and legends about Jesus. In other words, establishing Jesus as a figure within the Jewish legendary pantheon of Messiah figures served as a way for modern Jewish writers to subvert Christian cultural claims on the figure of Jesus and firmly anchor him within the realm of Jewish cultural discourse.

Grinberg, like many of his expressionist-oriented contemporaries, was preoccupied with the figure of the Messiah in general and Jesus in particular. As part of the apocalyptic thematic that pervaded the poetry of Yiddish expressionists like Grinberg, Moyshe Leyb Halpern, Moyshe Kulbak, and Peretz Markish, the figure of the Messiah is often central. Sometimes Jesus is alluded to in this redemptive framework, although typically not as *the* Messiah, but rather as *a* messianic figure, and a failed one at that. The theme of a tragic, lonely redeemer waiting to be accepted by his people recurs frequently in Grinberg's poetry and that of his contemporaries, especially Hey Leyvik (who will be discussed below).[76] In many of these instances the suffering and torment associated with Jesus' failed attempt to redeem the world inform these depictions; it is Jesus as a cosmic failure that so often captivated these writers.

Moyshe Leyb Halpern's expressionist epic poem "A nakht" ("A Night") is one of the first modernist works to contain extensive messianic-apocalyptic motifs and Jesus/crucifixion imagery. Written in response to World War I, "A nakht" first appeared as a twenty-one-part *poema* in the 1916 anthology *East Broadway*,[77] and Halpern later included his revised, twenty-five-part version of the *poema* in his first book of poetry, *In Nu York* (1919). Even before the war, though, Halpern had demonstrated a strong interest in the figure of Jesus and the crucifixion theme. In a poem written in 1913, "In der fremd" ("In a Foreign Land"), which addresses Halpern's experience of immigrating to America, he includes allusions to the figure of Jesus as his brother, as well as a scene in which the poem's narrator is metaphorically crucified like Jesus:

> It seems that I myself—I now hang on a cross . . .
> A wreath lies on my head . . . a wreath of thorns . . .
> Blood drips from my hands and feet. . . . and all around the cross,
> My tormentors strike up a grim dance.[78]

Through the use of such "self-crucifixion" imagery, the poetic speaker expresses his personal sense of torment and alienation, a theme that recurred in the work of Halpern, Grinberg, and several other Yiddish poets.

In "A nakht" Halpern weaves together the personal, the historical, and the apocalyptic into one nightmarish vision. The horrors of Jewish history and visions of the End of Days are refracted in the dreams of the poetic "I" where they merge with personal conceptions of death and destruction. The poetic speaker presents a surrealistic panorama of events—real and imagined—that graphically convey images of pogroms and persecutions alongside personal feelings of torment and tragedy, conflating collective memories with personal ones. Chana Kronfeld asserts that Halpern's work disrupts "the very distinctiveness of the personal and the collective."[79] The unfolding of history—Jewish and cosmic—transpires solely within the psyche of the poem's narrator. As Avraham Nowersztern observes, the poem moves fluidly from "apocalyptic vision" to "personal nightmare" as cosmic apocalypse and individual death are interwoven.[80]

In depicting this personal nightmare of cosmic proportions Halpern draws on many classical images of messianic figures—including Jesus—and the End of Days, often subverting them both with true modernist zeal. As the poetic speaker entertains the various possibilities for salving the wounds of the world, all forms of redemption, traditional and modern, are rejected. Halpern's narrator renounces the prayer shawl (*tallis*), the crucifix, and the flag—the latter representing such modern ideologies as Zionism and Communism—as useless, empty symbols, which should be spit upon (202). Elsewhere, messianic figures are portrayed as hapless and ineffective, themselves victims of the world's violence and suffering. This sort of blunt antipathy toward messianism and religion in general reverberates throughout much of Halpern's work, especially permeating "A nakht."

Halpern's poetic voice in "A nakht" depicts Jesus as a failed redeemer whose messianic status must be dismissed as well; as a Messiah, or a god, Jesus is of no use to those who suffer:

And here—while he hangs on a burning cross
With a wounded heart and wounded hands,
What good for you will be the glow you see around his head,
He still hangs there on the cross?

Dream yourself to be as blind as the night.
It's no use. The blood that runs from the cross,
Will run and run and cry in you,
As it did a thousand years ago.

Dream yourself to be, as quick as the wind.
It's no use. You won't be able to flee from yourself.
The earth and sky will pass away
And you will remain alone. (188)

Halpern stresses the inefficacy of an inanimate Jesus hanging on the cross. However, unlike the other messianic figures he debunks in earlier passages, the poet appears to be drawn toward Jesus, who for him embodies suffering and death—the reigning realities in Halpern's apocalyptic vision. Jesus symbolizes the continual mood of inner crisis and torment felt by the poetic speaker and therefore a certain solidarity exists between the two.[81] Halpern thereby implies that Jesus is valuable to the modern poet not as a redeemer, but as the archetypal victim of the world's cruelty.

Halpern links the affliction of Jesus' crucifixion to the individual and to the Jewish people as a whole: "The blood that runs from the cross, / Will run and run and cry in you, / As it did a thousand years ago." Halpern joins the crucifixion and Wandering Jew motifs in creating a synthetic typology of Jewish historical suffering that becomes embodied in the consciousness of his poetic self. As Halpern's poetic speaker imagines himself reliving the trials and tribulations of Jewish history, from slavery in Egypt through exile and hardship in Christian Europe, his suffering and persecution become emblematized by the crucifixion:

And they stretch me out
On a large black cross.
They strike me with nails
And they call this my throne.
The wounds in my feet and hands burn
As hellfire burns;
I cry in my pain and distress
And I pray for death.
The cross begins to roam
Over forest, field, and stone.
The cross moves and I hang
Stretched out lengthwise. (212)

The passage continues with the poetic voice describing his journey on the big black cross, racing across the countryside of a "foreign land"—

Europe—leaving destruction in his wake. He proceeds to describe the endless wandering and running that becomes his fate—only now, the black cross runs behind him as he traverses "mountain, steppe, and valley" (212). The suffering described by the speaker reflects the historical plight of Europe's Jews in the Middle Ages, as he has become the Wandering Jew, embodying the collective fate of the nation. In this context, the cross comes to represent both the persecutors and the persecuted; it is the people worshiping the cross who persecute the Jew(s), and the Jew(s) whose fate it is to be crucified on the cross:

> They drive me out like a demon
> With biblical verses and prayer.
> I run over trail and path,
> I hear chasing behind me.
> I see more and more crosses
> Running toward me.
> I see myself as if through smoke,
> On the crosses up high.
> I close my eyes and run,
> Church walls rise.
> I see myself hanging alone,
> Bleeding on every stone. (213)[82]

Again, Halpern clouds the distinction between individual and national memory, making it difficult to determine whether the torments and crucifixions experienced by the poetic speaker reflect his own internal experiences and feelings, or are representative of the collective historical experiences of the Jewish people. Nowersztern proposes that "in Halpern's poetic vision Jesus is not crucified in one particular time and place. He wanders further with the cross in a continuous apocalyptic drama, and thus merges with the poetic-I in the *poema*."[83]

In the year following the publication of Halpern's revised version of "A nakht," Uri Tsvi Grinberg published his own nightmarish, apocalyptic poem, "Golgota" ("Golgotha," 1920), in which he combines a strong prophetic spirit and autobiographical sensibility with powerfully graphic, phantasmagoric images of death, destruction, and personal torment in the form of crucifixion. This poem predated Grinberg's *Albatros* by two years and proved to be a precursor of many such apocalyptic,

crucifixion-infused epics from those years. In "Golgota" Grinberg blurs
the boundaries between past and present, nation and individual, and
the poet and Jesus. He inserts his poetic self into the historical frame
of Jesus' last days rather than applying Christological imagery to contemporary scenes. The poem opens with the narrator asserting that he
is illuminated in prophecy, quickly establishing its prophetic mood. His
body and soul are mystically and tenderly "enveloped in the mild night
glow and holy dreaminess."[84] The dream topos is accentuated, as the
poetic speaker "dreams of the kingdom of Heaven with glassy eyes," an
allusion to Jesus, who also had such dreamy visions. Indeed, the narrator approximates Jesus himself, as he talks of the Bethlehem road, the
seaside city of temples, and how he will "make childlike" (*farkindn*) the
kingdom of Heaven for millions. He is clearly a prophetic-messianic
figure, showing the way to the "holy east." He beckons his listeners to
bow their heads and be anointed with the purest olive oil. Here, Grinberg conflates image fragments from the gospels' narrative of Jesus' life,
classical Jewish messianic tropes—anointing with oil, ingathering of
exiles—and his own idyllic vision of the Land of Israel.

The ultimate conflation of the poetic "I" and the historical Jesus occurs in the second section of the poem, in which the two figures meet
on the road to Golgotha. The speaker encounters a worn and emaciated
man, bearing his likeness, who carries a black cross on his shoulder.
He addresses the woeful figure: "where are you going!?—I asked /—To
Golgotha to Pilate."[85] A mysterious transformation then takes place in
which the poetic "I" assumes the identity of the man with the cross on
his shoulder:

> The man in my likeness disappeared in an instant.
> I stand all alone with the black cross.
> I don't know where Bethlehem is. All around, to the four ends of the
> world is red flame.
> A violent sunset burns all around.
> There is no other city on the earth, everything is Golgotha . . .
> I stand in Golgotha with a black cross and wait for Pilate.—[86]

The poetic speaker suddenly finds himself alone on the way to his own
crucifixion at Golgotha. By locating his poetic persona on the fate-
ful path of the historical Jesus, Grinberg effectively appropriates the

power of Jesus' passion. He employs these symbols to situate his poetic speaker on the edge of the apocalyptic abyss; the world is burning with the red flames of Golgotha, which for Grinberg signify the utter chaos and destruction of the modern world. The narrator's fate is shared by the entire world: all will meet their end at Golgotha, hanging on the cross. In this fashion, Jesus and his crucifixion become transformed into the ultimate universal symbol for the modern apocalypse. Grinberg, like many of his modernist contemporaries, utilizes the symbolism of the crucifixion (Jesus, the cross, Golgotha, Pilate) as the most potent means of expressing the dire plight of his entire generation.

Yet, Grinberg refracts this plight through the consciousness of the self by placing his poetic speaker on the cross; once universalized, the crucifixion becomes an ahistorical condition, perpetually experienced by all those who truly suffer. The concrete manifestations of the crucifixion now convey the innermost anguish and torment of the poetic "I":

Nineteen hundred and twenty years . . .
Every morning I am broken open on a burning red cross.
My body is thin.
My bones can be counted through my emaciated skin.
Yet blood drips from my wounds.
I don't know where all this blood came from.
Under my feet an abyss opens.
The blood falls into it.[87]

Not only does the poetic "I" suffer these daily crucifixions, perched over the deep abyss, but millions of mourners sit at his feet every night. Like Jesus, the poetic voice calls out to God: "Why hast thou forsaken me?" Yet he inserts a very poignant addendum to this scriptural phrase, observing that his plea to God "reverberates in the void from a dead world. / Neither God nor people hear it."[88] This reinforces the pervasive sense of abandonment that dominates the poetry of Grinberg and his fellow Yiddish modernists; in the modern world the poet is abandoned by God as well as by his own people.

This passage also suggests that the poet endures his own personal martyrdom as an individual artist and a national redeemer of sorts who is worshiped, mourned, and crucified by his nation. Grinberg conceived of himself as a poet in prophetic-redemptive terms: a prophet-Messiah, like Jesus, who is rejected by his people and ultimately crucified. Moreover, he felt that poets in general experience this kind of rejection from their nation; indeed, Grinberg asserted that "the modern poet must suffer at the hands of the people."[89] While for Melekh Ravitsh the crucified Jesus could embody the "naked poetry" of Yiddish modernism, in Grinberg's work he came to represent the poet himself.

Grinberg also portrayed the reigning antimessianic or demonic forces that emerged at the dawning of the apocalypse. He published his first major expressionist epic poem, "Mephisto," in 1921. It was hailed by the Yiddish literary historian Zalman Reisen as "one of the most significant Yiddish documents of today's zeitgeist, a book of sorrow and self-torment."[90] Much of the poem paints an interior psychic landscape of the poetic voice, sketching assorted surreal, often somber images: an expressionist "soulscape" or *neshome landshaft*. The mood is always dark and heavy as the speaker renders a nightmarish vision of a demonic, tumultuous world in decline. Grinberg's poetic voice opens the poem declaring that "gods die, nations expire" but Mephistopheles (the devil) lives on. In fact, the speaker always has Mephisto right at his side. Like the majority of traditional apocalyptic narratives, Grinberg's *Mephisto* includes a cosmic battle between good and evil forces at its very center. God and Mephisto battle for control of the world, and the ramifications are momentous as the world's fate hangs in the balance. The poet continually opposes the sacred and the profane realms, often drawing on religious symbols to represent the former and carnal desires to represent the latter. In one scene the Torah and the cross are connected as symbols of holiness in a world overrun by desecration that:

blasphemes . . . the image of God!
and the ark curtain [*paroches*] waits,
the cross waits!
and the Torah scroll waits . . .[91]

After a section in which the action takes place in a synagogue, with someone reading the "tochacha"[92] and invoking the horrors of life and the pains of the flesh, the next section laments the tragic plight of Jesus:

And woe to Jesus son of Joseph who hangs on the cross
In dark churches or on roadside posts in the village,

When he opens his eyes in darkness in the middle of the night—
He suddenly sees Pilate, the Lord of Golgotha—
"So you're the king of the Jews? Then you deserve a crown of thorns!"
And he lays a new wreath of thorns on his head
And he snickers and snickers . . .[93]

Jesus is portrayed sympathetically as a holy figure of suffering; in a world that is ruled by the powers of Mephisto, all that is holy must suffer and be humiliated as Jesus is by Pilate. The depiction of Jesus in this passage emphasizes his Jewishness as well; he is identified as Yeshu ben Yosef, using the standard Hebrew version of his first name and his Jewish patronymic ("son of Joseph"). Also, Pilate's reference to him as the king of the Jews reiterates his Jewish origin and national allegiance even though he now resides in churches and Christian villages. The figure of Jesus thus serves Grinberg in myriad ways. It allows him to evoke the traditional Christian typology of Jesus as the personification of holiness, suffering, and sacrifice while simultaneously establishing him as a Jewish historical figure of great national significance: a king of the Jews. Grinberg's utilization of Christian tropes and typologies is transformed into an act of Jewish cultural appropriation, which served Grinberg's nascent, militant nationalism.

Grinberg published another apocalyptic *poema*, "Velt barg arop" ("World in Decline"), in 1922 in fragments, both in Markish's journal *Khalyastre* and in his own *Albatros*. It has never been published in full, and possibly was never completed. Again, Grinberg paints a prophetic, apocalyptic vision of human decline and the abandonment of morality, religion, and civilization as a whole. The *poema* opens with a carnivalesque scene, a chaotic nightmare of sorts. Jesus-figures hang on trees everywhere, and the world is depicted as "sinful and whoring" (405). The poetic voice declares "we are deep wounds in the wounded body-world" and people are living "without souls! only by the power of blood" (405–6). He invokes the primordial sin of Eve, proclaiming that today "we eat apples from a thousand apple trees" (406). A whirling naked circle of dancers consumes all in its path with flames, including the Jesus-figures hanging from the burning trees, symbolizing total desecration and the destruction of the possibility of redemption. Grinberg's poetic voice proclaims that there is no love and no God in this world; a great deluge and sunset (*shkiya*) have replaced them. The earth is dark and blind, and the world is dying.

As in "Mephisto" the figure of Jesus plays a dual role in this poem as well. The difference between the historical-Jewish Jesus (Yeshu) and the theological-Christian Jesus (Yezus) was crucial for Grinberg; this distinction makes it possible for him to portray the depravity of the Christian world as it mocks its own god, while simultaneously presenting Jesus as a symbol of Jewish suffering at the hands of the Christians. Grinberg depicts (quite unsympathetically) the nihilist revolt against religion and moral authority that was occurring in European civilization, and he shows the rejection of Jesus to be central to this revolt. Blasphemous gangs run wild (*hefker*) without *tallis* and *tefillin* or crucifixes on their breasts (implying that Jews and Christians both participated in these gangs). The blasphemous gangs go from cross to cross beckoning Jesus to come down and join them, as there are no believers left to worship him save dogs and outcasts (410–11).

The Madonna travels with a group of whores looking for Jesus. A naked Mary Magdalene dances along, a Jewish god is crucified, and the wild crowd wants him to come down and join them in their dance. The scene has the feel of a pogrom as the wild gang desecrates Torah scrolls, scattering them in the muddy streets.[94] It is the eve of a "black Sabbath" and as the world sits *shiva* (the traditional Jewish custom of mourning), a void opens up below. Nakedness is a recurring motif; people have become stripped of all externals, including clothes. Only raw, primal emotions and feelings remain (an example of Ravitsh's "naked poetry"). Grinberg deftly combines a plethora of conflicting images—the most sacred juxtaposed with the most profane—in creating a nightmarish vision of civilization run amok.[95]

The poem's final scene is one of Golgotha, which, as we have seen above, for Grinberg became the central symbol of the modern apocalypse; Jews are now hanging on trees while "brother Jesus" is lamented for his wounds. The general apocalyptic mood of destruction and desecration has taken on a distinctly Jewish feel. The poetic voice calls out "it's not your lament! it's our pain, the Judah-Christ pain!" and "our Madonnas go about wantonly [*hefker*] in the cities" (418). This suggests a deep bond between the Jews and Jesus, who share the "Judah-Christ pain." While Jesus—the Jew on the cross—is metaphorically spurned by Europe's Christians, contemporary Jews actually suffer the wrath of Christian Europe's rebellion. The very last image portrayed is of rotting bodies hanging on every cross. (Grinberg employs this image again, in a slightly modified form, in his "Royte epel fun vey-beymer" ("Red Apples from Pain Trees") in the following issue of *Albatros*, with the poetic voice proclaiming "Jesus' bodies rot on the poles everywhere."[96] With these gruesome images Grinberg implies that the decay of European civilization brings with it the maltreatment of Europe's most ubiquitous Jew: Jesus. Grinberg transforms the symbols of Jesus' suffering into both universal—even cosmic—and Jewish emblems of contemporary catastrophe.

Another apocalyptic fantasy with overt Christ symbolism and messianic motifs, Ber Horovitz's *poema* "Yeshu ha-Notsri" ("Jesus of Nazareth")[97] appears in excerpted form in the second issue of *Albatros* immediately following Grinberg's controversial *poema* "Uri Tsvi farn tseylem" ("Uri Tsvi in Front of the Cross").[98] It shares many of the same apocalyptic themes found in Markish's "Veyland" and Grinberg's "Mephisto" and "Velt barg arop," including visions of the conflagration of European civilization. The excerpt opens with the phrase "And it shall come to pass at the End of Days" (in both the original Hebrew and a Yiddish translation), an apocalyptic signature phrase that Halpern also uses in "A nakht."[99] The prophetic speaker in Horovitz's *poema* declares that at the End of Days, Messiahs everywhere will be liberated from their crosses, and with their nail-pierced bloody hands will take up their crosses and go together en masse through cities and villages, gardens and deserts, to converge on Rome. In Rome the legendary Jewish Messiah in chains will be unshackled to await their arrival; he is the last Messiah, the Son of David. This implies that the Messiahs on crosses—representing the images of the crucified Jesus throughout Christian Europe—are pseudo-Messiahs or preliminary Messiahs, who must be freed in order to liberate the true, final Messiah. Yet after he is freed, the poem foresees the Christ-Messiahs erecting their crosses and creating an "unending forest" that will be set ablaze by heavenly flashes of lightning and cause an apocalyptic conflagration that engulfs the entire earth. This vision concludes with the vanquishing of the cursed and bloodthirsty Edom (Rome, Christianity)—representing the forces of darkness—leading the way to a rebirth of the now-purified world with a luminous sun rising in the east that is white as snow—possibly an allusion to a rebuilt Jerusalem.[100]

The poem's vision of the End of Days is an inventive conflation of traditional apocalyptic narratives—Jewish and Christian—with a distinctly contemporary twist. Horovitz draws freely from the imagery of the Book of Revelation, conjuring images of Armageddon and the destruction of Babylon, yet his flaming forest of crosses unequivocally alludes to modern-day Europe: the kingdom of the cross. Indeed, Horovitz subverts the original meaning of the Book of Revelation, as the Babylon destroyed here is not pagan Rome, but Christian Rome, which is a metonymy for all of Christian Europe. In a move that must be read as a symbolic appropriation of the figure of Jesus, the crucified Messiahs serve as agents of Christian Europe's final destruction. These Messiah figures reject their role as crucified saviors, liberating themselves from their crosses in order to join the true Jewish Messiah in Rome and then assemble these crosses into an "unending forest" that is consumed by a heavenly blaze. Thus, they help the true Messiah vanquish Edom—an empire they involuntarily helped to establish— and restore Jerusalem as the rising sun of the east.

The sort of denunciation of contemporary Christian civilization witnessed here typically accompanied the appropriation of Jesus-figures and Christ symbolism by these modernist Yiddish writers. As was the case with their maskilic predecessors in the previous century, their adoption of a positive stance toward the figure of Jesus often involved an underlying polemical tendency, and corresponded to a critique of some aspect of Christian culture. Approaching these subjects under the guise of literary modernism did not erase these tendencies, and in some cases, the cultural clash with Christianity intensified. Like much of the Yiddish expressionist poetry from this period, Horovitz's and Grinberg's poetry represents the conjunction of modernist apocalypticism, social critique, and a revised anti-Christian polemic. Moreover, these Yiddish modernists, who had by and large rejected traditional Jewish beliefs about the Messiah, were exploring the relevance of these traditional categories in purely secular terms. The redeemer was now the poet, or the political revolutionary (a Herzl or a Lenin) who brought a new message of redemption to the people. Yet often these radical visionaries were rejected or their message was not easily realized. The neoclassical myths these modernists created, based on legendary messianic figures, allegorically addressed the major social, political, cultural, and religious crises of their times.[101]

The Night Crucified:
Jesus as a Universal Emblem of Tragedy

The Yiddish modernist portrayal of Jesus was not entirely confined to the genres of apocalyptic *poemas* and messianic dramas. While many of the works examined above present Jesus as a tragic figure in the context of his failed messianism and suffering on the cross, a more romantic, personalized, even humanized vision of Jesus as the very ideal of human suffering also emerged in this period. Not isolated from general trends in European literature, Yiddish authors had long been able to witness modern literary renderings of Jesus as a symbol of suffering humanity; as Ursula Brumm, speaking of modern literature in general, has observed, "in a secular age Christ becomes a literary symbol for the man who suffers innocently for his brethren."[102] Yiddish poets began to depict the palpable and visceral human pain manifest in the image of Jesus on the cross in ways that liberated such images from the confines of Christian theology, and saw Jesus in universal—and sometimes Jewish—terms. One of the common features of many of these poems is the way in which the narrator addresses Jesus directly as he fixes his gaze on the crucifix, a bold reversal from the age-old Jewish tradition of averting one's eyes from all images of the "hanged one."

One of the first to take up this theme was Hey Leyvik, a leading Yiddish poet in New York, who first depicted Jesus as a tragic hero in 1915 in his poem "Yezus" ("Jesus"). Leyvik, who belonged to a generation of Yiddish poets in America, Di Yunge, that was consciously modernist in form and content, focuses on the universal aspects of Jesus' suffering without directly alluding to the Jewish experience. In a way that Itzik Manger and others later emulated, Leyvik envisions Jesus as a thoroughly universalized tragic figure who has been abandoned by the world:

> Covered in gray up to their necks they lie sleeping,
> Head to head and hands to hands, their feet facing the window;
> Over them in some corner entangled in cobwebs
> Jesus hangs on a cross, his mouth contorted and his eyes closed,
>
> Both his hands and feet are pierced with nails,
> His entire body is meager and bare naked, his shame not concealed.
> Below a dried-out lamp sways on a chain—
> There is nobody to tend to it with wick and oil.
>
> Covered in gray up to their necks they lie sleeping,
> Occasionally someone rises—he crosses himself and lies back down,
> Jesus hangs alone and naked, lonesome in a dusty corner,
> His feet twisted, his head bent and his eyes closed.[103]

The setting of the poem appears to be a hospital or possibly a prison, both places where men in institutional gray would be crammed together in a room, and a crucifix would hang on the wall. In either case, the sleeping masses—whether inmates or people in general—are depicted in stark opposition to Jesus on the cross: they lie covered from head to toe surrounded by others while he hangs naked and alone in a dusty corner. Jesus is abandoned by the world, tragically neglected among the cobwebs just like the dried-out lamp located beneath him; the image of the lamp ironically suggests Jesus' proclamation in the Gospels that he is the "light of this world" (John 8:12). However, like the lamp of the poem, Jesus is not tended to, his flame left to flicker and die out. Leyvik underscores the chasm that exists between the idealism of redemptive dreamers like Jesus and the realities that the world presents to them; his martyrdom seems to be in vain, as attested to by his state of neglect on the cross.

The poem also potently emphasizes Jesus' vulnerability and humiliation as he hangs naked, exposed for all to see. In accentuating the grotesque quality of Jesus' physical appearance—contorted mouth, bent head, bloody hands, and twisted feet—Leyvik reveals his fascination with the torment and anguish implicit in the very graphic image of Jesus that hangs on the cross (especially in Eastern Europe, where the realism and detail of crucifixes can be extraordinary). This fascination was shared by other Jewish writers and artists of East European origin and suggests that the ubiquity of the image of the crucified Jesus in the Slavic landscape captivated their imagination, if not always their sympathy. Leyvik later declared concerning his attraction to Jesus that "I saw him simply as a prisoner."[104] This sense that Jesus was a man trapped on his cross, forced to become a god by a Christian world, which now barely had time for him, haunted Leyvik as well as many other Yiddish poets of that period.

In a poem entitled "Jesus to the Children" ("Yezus tsu di kinder"), Leyvik's contemporary on the American Yiddish scene, Moyshe Leyb Halpern, depicts Jesus as a tragic, lonely figure who, despite "possessing the earth and the sky," longs to have his own children like an ordinary person. His divinity has robbed him of the simple human joys that he now craves.[105] For Halpern, as with Leyvik, Jesus became the embodiment of the suffering, alienated individual, as well as a romantically tragic figure in his own right. Indeed, Ruth Wisse observes that for Halpern, "Jesus thus bec[a]me . . . the ironic symbol of his own lonely torment."[106]

Leyvik also explored the tension between the human and the divine nature of Jesus in a long poem entitled "Er" ("He," 1918)[107] in which Jesus is fully humanized and his innermost feelings are expressed in Freudian terms. The narrative structure of the poem is a dialogue between Jesus and the poetic "I" that seems to be modeled on a psychoanalytic session in which the poetic voice functions as the therapist to whom Jesus—the patient—comes to confide his problems. Jesus articulates the anguish he suffers on account of being deified and losing his simple humanity; he laments being made a god and held aloft, when in reality he feels forlorn and lonely. Toward the poem's end Jesus accuses his listener of not being able to understand his plight: "You've never been a god to people, / You've never been a Jesus, / You've never hung on a cross."[108]

His most painful emotions stem from his relationship with his mother, Mary. He despises her for treating him as a god rather than as her mortal son, and describes her acts of adulation toward him in terms laden with sexual tension and violence: her "warm and passionate kisses" nauseate him, he wants to crush her "Madonna head" when she bows to kiss his feet, and he's dreamed for years of committing matricide.[109] Leyvik presents Jesus as a deeply tormented figure subject to both emotional and physical affliction—he suffers from epileptic seizures—who cannot reconcile his human needs and longings with his divine status. Leyvik's Jesus experiences a conflict between his inner feelings and desires and the expectations placed on him by the people he is intended to redeem. Many other Yiddish authors depict a similarly conflicted Jesus, yet in Leyvik's poem, he has been driven to murderous deeds because of his existential despair. He carries a bloodied knife and a hammer (possibly an allusion to the symbols of the 1917 Revolution) and recounts taking part in a pogrom, asking rhetorically why he alone should ignore the new commandment to kill that now fills the world. Thus, Jesus is both tormented victim and brutal victimizer at once. With such powerfully jarring images, Leyvik composed a complicated and darkly rich portrait of Jesus that stresses his human frailties and ultimately renders him a tragic figure of immense proportions.

By the end of the 1920s the creation of a "landscape of the cross" in modernist Yiddish writing had spread beyond expressionist circles. The neo-Romantic poet and balladeer Itzik Manger, for example, utilized the symbolism of the crucifixion in fresh and innovative ways in his earliest collection of poetry, *Shtern afn dakh* (*Stars on the Roof*, 1929). Manger moved beyond the typical expressionist trend of employing crucifixion and cross motifs as part of an apocalyptic vista of destruction and decay, instead using these symbols to evoke more ordinary feelings such as sadness and tragedy on a mundane level. In his poem "Ecce!" the poetic voice addresses a beggar who comes to him and offers to sing to him about sadness and death. He exclaims

> Hey beggar! Let's crucify
> The hour of midnight.
> And at the foot of the cross
> Only sing and laugh!
> All paths that stray
> Gravitate toward the cross.
> Whether Jesus is crucified,
> Or the night, whether I, or you![110]

This demonstrates what a multivalent symbol the crucifixion had become, universalized and abstracted—the night crucified—in order to create a sorrowful mood in the poem. Crucifixion for Manger symbolizes the common fate shared by all people—not just Jesus—as well as by nature. In his poem "Ich bin der ovent" ("I Am the Evening"), the evening proclaims that it is crucified on the cross, but tells a sojourner not to bow down before it (as if it were Jesus). Here, Manger creates a plaintive landscape in which the sunset, the evening, and the trees are all described in terms of the crucifixion, "the blood from the sunset plays on the crucified hands" of the evening, and "a cross sleeps in every tree."[111] This fanciful image of a crucified landscape reflects a broader trend present in much of Manger's poetry, the personification of nature, but it also reveals the extent to which the crucifixion motif had been expanded and absorbed within Yiddish poetry.

These examples also point to Manger's tendency to accord a central place in his poems to Christian characters and landmarks, as priests, churches, monks, saints, and the figures of Jesus and Mary inhabit many of his early works. As Janet Hadda remarks, "from the outset, Manger also employed the landscape of Christianity . . . in poems where it functioned as a cultural backdrop."[112] For Manger, depicting this Christian cultural backdrop to Jewish daily life in Eastern Europe and readily incorporating Christian images and motifs were part of his larger project of creating a universally valid poetic form that would help to reinvigorate and inscribe Jewish culture in the East European Diaspora. It also reflected his attempt at creating a nonethnocentric realism in his poetry. In an essay appearing in his own literary journal, *Getseylte verter* (*Measured Words*), Manger praises his generation of writers and poets for honestly rendering this Christian landscape, while he castigates the founders of Yiddish literature for blatantly ignoring it.[113] He marvels at how Abramovitsh's literary persona, Mendele Moykher Sforim, lovingly surveys and details the rural landscape all around him while "not even once did he observe the cross, which stands in the very middle of the path, or the figure which hangs on that cross."[114] Manger also indicts Sholem Aleichem and Peretz for patently neglecting the cross and the figure of Jesus, which so thoroughly populated the Christian countryside that their many characters inhabit.

Manger and other Yiddish poets and writers of his generation clearly made up for this "blindness" on the part of the *klassiker* by foregrounding the markedly Christian features of their East European environment. For example, crosses often appear as part of the native Slavic landscape in Uri Tsvi Grinberg's early poetry (1915–18), especially in his idyllic descriptions of Serbian villages.[115] The crosses are typically depicted as golden or red, gleaming in the sunlit sky atop churches and rooftops. Unlike the Yiddish masters, these modernists explicitly portray the Christian landscape—especially the cross—in sometimes romantic ways, revealing a growing consciousness of (and sometimes an attraction to) the Christian rhythms of European life. In fact, in one of the first poems he published, "Pascha-Nakht" ("Easter Night," 1921), Manger depicts thousands of Christian worshipers "pouring out their souls" in longing for redemption. The poem ends with their hopes being dashed as the poetic voice declares, "And the man on the cross hangs there frozen / Cold and mute!"[116] Manger's ending implies that despite the belief of the faithful Christians, the man on the cross does not have the power to redeem. Rather than a mockery of Christian belief—which was quite common in traditional Jewish texts, ancient and modern— Manger's poem appears to be a lament for the tragic condition of living in an unredeemable world, a tragedy equally felt by devout Christians longing for redemption and by Jesus, the would-be redeemer "frozen" on the cross.

Manger's contemporary, Rikudah Potash, produced an interesting twist on Manger's call for Yiddish poets to be conscious of their Christian surroundings. In her poem "Poylisher harbst" ("Polish Autumn"), in which she intimately depicts Polish rural life, not only does her speaker observe the Christian landscape, but is also observed by it: "In the middle of the road Christ hangs nailed on a cross / He also saw how I wandered about."[117] Unlike Manger's "frozen" Jesus on the cross, Potash's Christ plays an active role by calling attention to the poetic speaker's status as a foreign element to this village scene.

As was the case for Grinberg and the *Khalyastre* poets, Manger's interest in the cross constitutes more than just a realistic fascination with the Christian dimensions of his environment—it also involves his ongoing quest for powerful poetic images of mythic proportions. Whether symbols of the cross and the crucifixion were used to express the tragic suffering of a generation, the pain and mortality of individuals, or the bittersweet beauty of a somber sunset, Manger saw in them universal emblems of tragedy and sadness that were unparalleled in their ability to instantly elicit such moods. It is therefore in this spirit that Manger typically employs the symbol of the cross. In the opening article of the first issue of his *Getseylte verter*, in which he challenges a new generation of poets to lead the way in a poetic revival of sorts, Manger proclaims that "the suffering of our generation has inscribed blood and scattered crosses over all the paths of the world. Christ's head sobs symbolically in our dream. Our wounds need consolation."[118]

In the following issue of the journal Manger laments the fate of the individual in similar terms in an essay dedicated *in memoriam* to Hugo von Hofmannsthal: "I believe: every twilight is fatal, and through every twilight steps a man, who carries his sadness like a cross on his shoulder. Only in the deep hours of dusk does the Golgotha path organically expose itself with all of its sorrows, with all of its heroics, with all of its deaths."[119] Manger's conception of a "Golgotha path" (*Golgota-veg*) is more quotidian than Grinberg's nightmarish, apocalyptic "Golgotha world" (*Golgota velt*), as it represents for him the ordinary trials and tribulations of life, which inevitably end in death.

In his poem "Aleyn" ("Alone") the poetic voice sings a lament of his utter loneliness and is accompanied by a chorus of evening shadows, wind, and snakes, who join in pronouncing his loneliness. At one point the speaker declares in a variation on the poem's central refrain, "Now I am alone, and the night is with me, / And a red cross burns on my door."[120] Hadda speculates that this image may refer "to the practice, used in times of plague, of marking the doors of the infected with a red cross."[121] (This image also ironically evokes the lambs' blood marking Israelite doorposts in the Exodus story.) Yet, it seems to me more likely that Manger chose to emblematize the loneliness of his protagonist with the symbol of the burning red cross because for him the cross embodied loneliness; it had become a metaphorical repository for an entire spectrum of human feelings and experiences. It was precisely the range and fluidity that the cross possessed as a literary symbol that made it so compelling for Manger and other modernists who similarly utilized it. Manger displays the metaphorical versatility of the cross/ crucifixion symbol in a line from the poem "In tsug" ("In a Train"), essentially a romantic lyric: "And every moment you become nearer to me, / My longing also hangs crucified in the wind."[122]

As the cross came to symbolize human suffering and tragedy writ large in Manger's work, the historical Jesus' particular plight no longer seemed unique. Manger conveys this sense most pointedly in his poem "Di balade fun dem layzikn mit dem gekreytsikn" ("The Ballad of the Lice-Ridden and the Crucified"), in which a lice-infested traveler confronts a roadside Jesus on his cross. The man "awakens the crucified from his sleep" to demand acknowledgment that his own pain equals that of Jesus. He makes the point that while his own suffering passes unconsoled, Jesus' suffering is constantly rewarded by his followers who adore and worship him: "Two women rock you on the wind" (the Virgin Mary and Mary Magdalene), and

> For your every wound there is a mouth,
> Which consecrates your body, crucified man.
> For your every thorn there is a [bent] knee,
> Which consecrates your cross, crucified man.[123]

The lice-ridden man thereby expresses his resentment for Jesus attracting so much loving attention for his misfortune, while he is shunned and ignored.

Manger was not alone in making this point, as many Jewish writers chose to foreground this apparent inequity, especially in works that deal with collective Jewish suffering in a historical context (to be further explored in the following chapter), in which Jesus' suffering is no longer seen as unique or even monumental. In an ironic way then, Jesus becomes paradigmatic of human suffering when, in fact, modern man suffers to an even greater degree than Jesus did/does. Manger's poem concludes with Jesus acknowledging the holiness of the lice-ridden man's suffering:

> Jesus stammers:—lousy one, I believe,
> That three times holy is your tear and dust!
> And from the cross trickles a silver cry,
> The lice-ridden man smiles and happily departs . . . [124]

In the end, Jesus provides the traveler with the consolation he was sorely lacking; Jesus' tears bring a smile to the face of the lice-ridden man and in so doing confuses the issue once more as to which of them is truly the more tragic figure.

The works examined in this chapter testify to both the prevalence and the diversity of Jesus and crucifixion motifs in modernist Yiddish literature in the early decades of the twentieth century. Following on the heels of the reclamation of Jesus, which had begun over a century earlier in Western Europe, these writers continued to blaze the path that the bold stories of Asch and Shapiro had initiated in 1909. Each author casts Jesus according to his particular ideological or poetic vision, depicting his own version of Jesus in order to pursue a decidedly modernist and secular agenda. The case of the Jewish authors who utilize this literary device presents us with a significant example of how modern European literary trends and genres could be absorbed by Jewish writers and adapted to address particular Jewish concerns. The act of reclaiming the figure of Jesus and all of the symbolism associated with his life and death allowed these writers to create a new literary home for him in the emerging canon of secular Jewish culture, wresting him from the Christian cultural context in which he previously resided. In the next chapter, we will see how this process helped to transform Jesus and the crucifixion into emblems of Jewish suffering and persecution, in Yiddish literature and beyond.

Four The Passion of Jewish History

> Like Jesus, the Jews have not ceased to mount Golgotha;
> like him, they are always nailed to the cross.
>
> —Joseph Bonsirven, 1937

Whose Crucifixion Is It Anyway?

In 1937 the French Jesuit scholar Joseph Bonsirven published a book entitled *Les juifs et Jésus* (*The Jews and Jesus*), in which he surveyed modern attitudes toward the figure of Jesus.[1] Bonsirven's book reflects trends in certain circles of both Jewish and Christian scholarship by asserting the Jewishness of the historical Jesus and acknowledging the scourge of Christian anti-Semitism. He observes that in light of this history, for the Jews, the cross cannot be "the symbol of a self-sacrificing love, nor the sign of a redeeming hope, nor an emblem of peace, but the symbol of persecution, oppression, discrimination, the stake, and the gibbet."[2] Besides identifying the inimical position of the cross in the Jewish cultural consciousness, Bonsirven understands the plight of Jews throughout history in terms of the crucifixion; this Jesuit theologian saw the Jewish experience as a perpetual ascension of Golgotha. He expresses Jewish suffering in explicitly Christological terms. He sharpens this notion by citing the British Jewish writer Israel Zangwill's claim that the Jews are not only "the People of Christ, but the Christ of the peoples."[3] Bonsirven was not alone among Christian thinkers in the twentieth century who, especially in the wake of the Holocaust, began to interpret Jewish victimization by drawing from a rich storehouse of Christological symbols, in particular the application of the symbolism of Jesus' passion to the interpretation and depiction of catastrophic events in Jewish history.

170   Another French Catholic writer, Francois Mauriac, furthered this trend in his foreword to Elie Wiesel's *Night*, where he makes sense of Wiesel's experience in the Nazi death camps, and the Holocaust in general, by drawing on a Christian interpretive framework. For Mauriac,

Wiesel the survivor is like "Lazarus risen from the dead" and, moreover, he may resemble his brother, "the Crucified, whose cross has conquered the world."[4] As a Christian writer, it is not surprising that Mauriac imposes an understanding on Jewish suffering that draws on his own tradition, seeing the Holocaust survivor as a kind of Christ-figure resurrected from the ashes of the death camps. Subsequent Christian theologians, even progressive ones, have continued to offer such readings of the Holocaust and Jewish history in general. Franklin Littell, in his 1975 book *The Crucifixion of the Jews*, presents a view of the Holocaust that conceives of Jewish suffering in boldly Christological ways. Even though he painstakingly berates Christians for their complicity in the persecution of the Jews, and chronicles the evils of Christian anti-Semitism and the need for new Christian theological self-definitions that consider Jews in a new light, Littell consistently describes the Jewish experience of persecution and oppression by means of the vocabulary of Jesus' passion. He speaks of the Holocaust and its aftermath as the "crucifixion and resurrection of the Jewish people."[5] He also sees in the "crucifixion" of European Jewry "the shocking possibility that this event may be the confirmation of the calling of the Jewish people to be the Suffering Servant . . ."[6] In the last paragraph of the book, Littell ponders that "when the Body of Christ is discovered at Auschwitz, it will be raised from among the victims, not hidden among Catholic and Protestant and Orthodox guards and administrators."[7] Littell's postulations assume a fundamental link not only between Jesus and the Jews, but also between the *fate* of Jesus—to be martyred in the name of God at Golgotha—and the *fate* of Jews throughout history. The views of these Christian thinkers raise many questions as to how one depicts events of Jewish catastrophe, and on whose terms Jewish suffering is to be expressed. As the above examples attest, certain Christian writers, especially religious ones of various stripes, readily employed the passion of Jesus in confronting the horrors of Jewish history.

As exceptional as it may be for these Christian writers to adopt such a reading of the Jewish historical experience, it is not all that surprising that they would draw from their own tradition in order to make sense of Jewish history. Especially in the aftermath of the various quests for the historical Jesus in which the Christian separation of Jesus from

Judaism had been largely reversed, it became more common for some Christian writers to view Jewish suffering sympathetically, in Christ-like terms. However, it is far more remarkable to examine how, since the nineteenth century, modern Jewish historians, theologians, writers, and artists have also turned to the symbols of Jesus' passion in reckoning with the tragedies of Jewish history. As part of the wider trend of reclaiming Jesus as a Jew, which began at the end of the eighteenth century, numerous Jews have used the crucifixion as the ideal paradigm for explicating and depicting the Jewish historical experience of persecution and suffering, both in general, and in particular historical contexts. In Joseph Salvador's study of Jesus from 1838, he argued that the "Hebrew people played an important role as a symbol of suffering humanity, as a Christ people" and that "the evangelists themselves wanted to realize on a new level in the passion of Jesus the long and terrible passion of the Hebrew people."[8] In Salvador's lachrymose conception of Jewish history, then, the ongoing suffering of the Jews can be understood as part of their spiritual/historical mission as a "Christ people," whose suffering served as a model for Jesus and for all of humanity. In this sense, Salvador was not appropriating the passion motif from Christianity, but demonstrating that it was an intrinsically Jewish experience to begin with.

Salvador's views of Jewish history as defined by suffering—*Leidensgeschichte*—were in line with those of other Jewish historians of his time such as Leopold Zunz and Heinrich Graetz, but he was the first to express this view in terms of the conceptual framework of Christ's passion. In the late nineteenth century, Reform Jewish thinkers such as Kaufman Kohler, Emil Hirsch, and Joseph Krauskopf developed Salvador's notion of the passion of Jewish history as they began to formulate Christological understandings of the Jewish historical experience, seeing the Jewish nation as the embodiment of "the man of sorrows from whose wounds flow the balm of healing for the nations."[9] For them, the Jewish experience of victimization and martyrdom surpassed that of Jesus himself; by appropriating the heretofore exclusively Christian symbolism of Jesus' passion and applying it to their understanding of Jewish history, these thinkers were helping to radically transform the crucifixion into the paradigmatic archetype of Jewish suffering.

This chapter explores the ways in which modern Jewish writers and artists have expanded this historiographic and theological trend by boldly adopting the crucifixion as an appropriate archetype—literary and visual—for representing Jewish suffering. The power such symbolism has in conveying the injustices and persecutions that the Jews endured in the European Diaspora profoundly captivated the East European writers and artists of the twentieth century with whom the greater part of this book is concerned. The works I will consider in this chapter typically combine a palpable anti-Christian polemic, if not rage, with a desire to recognize Jesus as a paradigmatic Jewish martyr, and thereby frame Jewish suffering in traditionally Christian terms. A love-hate syndrome existed in which the Jewish artist/writer was simultaneously repulsed by Christian violence and anti-Semitism, and attracted to Jesus as an emblem of Jewish martyrdom. At times this ambivalence resulted in a tension between claiming or adopting Jesus as a paradigm of Jewish suffering, and the more polemical and aggressive move of appropriating Christological symbolism as intrinsically Jewish while implicating Jesus as being in some way complicit in Jewish persecution. Like their Reform predecessors, these Jewish modernists often saw the Jews as a "people of Christs," with the crucifixion as the quintessential symbol of the passion of Jewish history. This appropriation of the passion is structured around a central irony: the martyrdom of the Jew, Jesus, had become (indirectly) the primary cause of the martyrdom of countless Jews through the centuries, and now, Jesus' crucifixion was seen as the paradigm for all subsequent Jewish martyrs.

By identifying the entire nation as a people of Christs, all of the profound meaning and significance traditionally associated by Christians with Christ and his passion became transposed to a distinctly Jewish, collective context. But unlike such Christian authors as Bonsirven, Mauriac, and Littell, or the Reform writers of the nineteenth century, the Jewish modernists with whom I am concerned here were operating in a largely secular context as the avant-garde of a new Jewish culture. In fact, a large part of the modernist syncretistic approach to Jewish culture involved creating new literary and visual archetypes capable of expressing the travails of the Jewish nation. Indeed, most of the works we have examined that formed the "landscape of the cross" were created in the aftermath of intense Jewish suffering, such as the pogroms in Ukraine in 1919–21. World War II and the Holocaust also presented these Jewish modernists with another historical trauma that called for a response. In the following pages, I will explore how writers such as Grinberg, Markish, Asch, and others incorporated Christian images and archetypes in response to such Jewish tragedies. We will see that at times, especially during and after the Holocaust, these images were rejected by many in Jewish literary and intellectual circles as unsuitable for Jewish cultural discourse.

"While You Were on the Cross": Jesus Confronted by the Passion of Jewish History

The association of the crucifixion with Jewish suffering was not limited to the writings of Reform rabbis or expressed solely by Jewish historians; there are many examples in modern Jewish literature in various languages of writers employing the symbolism of Christ's passion in order to express the pain of Jewish history, ancient and contemporary. Claiming the crucifixion as an appropriate if not inherently Jewish symbol provided these writers with new ways to treat the theme of Jewish suffering. It allowed them to move beyond more common traditional motifs such as the binding of Isaac, the expression of suffering in the books of Lamentations and Job, and Rabbi Akiba and other mythologized Jewish martyrs, which had been previously employed by Jewish authors, both traditional and modern, in dealing with the themes of Jewish martyrdom and persecution. In some cases, older motifs became combined with the symbols of the passion in depicting Jewish suffering in a modern context.

The motif of the binding of Isaac (commonly referred to in Jewish sources as the Akedah—Hebrew for binding) is one of the oldest Jewish archetypes of collective martyrdom. Based on the story in Genesis 22 of God's command to Abraham to sacrifice his son Isaac, the Akedah became a myth central to traditional Jewish thought about martyrdom, and a recurrent motif and image etched in the Jewish cultural consciousness. While early Christian exegetes saw in Isaac and his near sacrifice a prefiguration of the fulfilled sacrifice of Jesus, for Jews, especially beginning in the Middle Ages, "Isaac represented the Jewish people, constantly being called upon to make the supreme sacrifice as martyrs. History recounts many instances of parents killing their children in the face of persecution and calling upon the story of the Akedah as justification."[10] Especially in its medieval midrashic versions, in which Isaac is said to have actually been sacrificed and later resurrected, the Akedah became a prevalent symbol of Jewish martyrdom. Shalom Spiegel chronicles how this strain of legends helped locate Isaac as the paradigmatic sacrifice in Jewish consciousness and inscribed the Akedah as the model for understanding various forms of Jewish martyrdom, especially in cases such as the Crusader massacres in the eleventh and twelfth centuries, where fathers sacrificed their children and then themselves.[11] This model was frequently used by premodern and modern authors (and artists) alike in responding to various types of Jewish historical catastrophes. In the twentieth century (if not earlier), Jewish artists and writers began experimenting with conflating the Akedah and crucifixion motifs. Itzik Manger and Marc Chagall especially linked these two symbols together in their work, ironically following the Christian theological move of linking the Akedah and the crucifixion together as an example of Old Testament prefigurations of the life and death of Jesus. These modern conflations of the Isaac and Jesus models of sacrifice and martyrdom are indicative of the modernist penchant for symbolic syncretism. They both became widely used literary and visual archetypes of national, as well as personal, suffering. Indeed, in her discussion of modern Hebrew poetic applications of the Akedah, Glenda Abramson claims that "in Israeli art, far more than in the literature, the symbolism of the Akedah is transmuted to Christian symbolism and demonstrates the conflation of the two images of innocent sacrifice, more easily rendered visually than verbally. . . . In a few paintings, the cross appears in conjunction with the symbolism of the Akedah."[12] Ziva Amishai-Maisels also confirms that modern Jewish artists, especially in response to the Holocaust, often employed the Akedah motif—sometimes together with the crucifixion motif—as a visual symbol of the most recent Jewish national calamity.[13]

Despite the persistence of older motifs such as the Akedah, its frequent use in conjunction with crucifixion imagery points to the emergence of Christological symbolism as a new and competing paradigm of Jewish suffering. Toward the end of the nineteenth century, under the influence of the Jewish reclamation of Jesus in historical and theological circles, Jewish writers in both America and Europe began to recognize the power inherent in applying the symbols of Jesus' passion to the historical plight of the Jews. Most often the adoption of the passion motif included a trenchant polemical thrust against Christians, who were depicted as the persecutors of the "people of Christs" rather than the true worshipers of Christ. One of the first authors to seriously employ this motif was the American Jewish poet Emma Lazarus (1849–87), who was influenced by the historical writings about the Jewish Jesus emanating from American Reform circles in the 1870s and 1880s, and frequently used Christological imagery in her many poems dealing with Jewish historical themes, especially in the early 1880s in the aftermath of the Russian pogroms of 1881 and 1882.

Lazarus, who is best known for her poem "The New Colossus," which sits at the base of the Statue of Liberty, incorporated in her poetry countless allusions to the long exile of the Jews with its many persecutions and expulsions, and frequently conveyed this suffering, which she saw as majestic and noble, through her use of Christological imagery. In a prose poem entitled "The Exodus (August 3, 1492)" Lazarus portrays the suffering of Jewish exiles from Spain, including one "youth with Christ-like countenance."[14] In her poem "The Valley of Baca" (based on Psalm 84), which presents a grand history of Jewish suffering, the narrator recounts a similar vision:

> I saw a youth pass down that vale of tears;
> His head was circled with a crown of thorn,
> His form was bowed as by the weight of years,
> His wayworn feet by stones were cut and torn.[15]

Typically, Lazarus's so-called "Jewish poems" depict historically rooted episodes of medieval Jewish persecution at the hands of their Christian neighbors, in which she accentuates Jewish martyrdom and underscores the irony of the Jews being Christ-like victims who are punished for their rejection of Christ. Possibly the most profound example of this

Christological rendering of Jewish history is found in Lazarus's poem "the Crowing of the Red Cock," in which the poet declares,

> Where is the Hebrew fatherland?
> The folk of Christ is sore bestead;
> The Son of Man is bruised and banned,
> Nor finds whereon to lay his head.
> His cup is gall, his meat is tears,
> His Passion lasts a thousand years.[16]

Like the historian Joseph Salvador, or the rabbis Kaufman Kohler and Emil Hirsch, the poet Lazarus depicts the history of the Jews as a continuous ascent up Golgotha, a passion that "lasts a thousand years." She symbolically conflates the passion of Jesus as portrayed in the gospels with the historical experience of the Jewish people. As Shira Wolosky argues, Lazarus "goes beyond reclaiming Jesus as a Jew and actor in Jewish history. She makes Christ her defining figure of Jewish identity, with the Jews, as a historical people, themselves the body of Christ."[17] Wolosky further claims that Lazarus subverted Christian typological thinking by rejoining the Jew and the figure of Christ as the "Suffering Remnant" or "remnant lost," as she calls it in her poem "The World's Justice."[18] I suggest that this subversion or inversion continues even further as Lazarus turns the "crucifiers" (the Jews) into the crucified, and the worshipers of the crucified (the Christians) into the "crucifiers." This inversion, which many later Yiddish authors such as Sholem Asch, Zalman Shneour, and Uri Tsvi Grinberg also utilized, highlights both the innovative and the polemical nature of this type of writing.

While Lazarus may have been one of the first to present this Christological conception of Jewish history in poetry, it soon became more and more common for Jewish writers of all stripes (and artists as well, as we shall see below) to understand contemporary episodes of Jewish suffering and victimization in such terms. This was especially the case in the aftermath of the various pogroms that recurred throughout the first decades of the twentieth century in tsarist Russia, Poland, and Ukraine, starting with those in Kishinev. In the period immediately following the initial pogroms in Kishinev in the spring of 1903, the American Jewish press frequently compared the Jewish pogrom victims to Jesus and discussed their suffering in Christ-like terms.[19] Both

Jewish and Christian authors compared the Jewish victims to Jesus in terms of suffering, martyrdom, etc., as well as pointing out the irony of the Christian Gentiles killing Jesus' own people in his name.[20] In one striking example of this trend, the American scholar of Jewish literature Israel Davidson (1870–1939) wrote a poem that appeared in the *Jewish Exponent* (September 4, 1903), entitled "Eli, Eli, Lama Sabachtani." The poem explicitly identified Jews with the crucified Christ by applying the symbols of the crucifixion to the Jews, or, more specifically, to the figure of the Wandering Jew:

> The Tartar savage drank the blood of his kin,
> And ate the heart of his fellow, and then,
> With hands uplifted heavenward called on Christ.
> And down from the cross the meek-hearted Jew,
> Who offered his life on the altar of love,
> Looked with infinite agony upon the crowd,
> That worshipped his name but defied his word . . .
> And from his heart the blood, so long congealed,
> Began to ooze once more, and drop by drop . . .
> It fell in the sea of Israel's blood . . .
> But out of the depth, behold,
> The bleeding ever-wandering Jew,
> Christ-like on the flaming cross appeared.
> O'er his head a halo of suffering,
> On his brow a crown of torture hung,
> And deep from his heart the cry
> That once the death of Heathendom sounded,
> Now in deep sonorous, solemn foreboding,
> Through the world of Christ resounded,
> "Eli, Eli, Lama Sabachtani."[21]

Davidson's poem, more so than the poems of Lazarus, graphically captures the perverse irony of Jesus' followers—the Russian Christians in this case—savagely attacking his own people—the Jewish pogrom victims—ostensibly in the name of Jesus himself. The poem also depicts a remarkable episode of symbolic transformation in which Jesus' crown of suffering and martyrdom is passed to the people of Israel, as represented by the Wandering Jew, through the blood that flows from each of them; out of this ritual-like commingling of blood, which stands for the historical persecution of the Jews, the Wandering Jew emerges as the new Christ, crucified on his cross with halo and crown, exposed before the world of Christendom. Davidson depicts Jesus himself as stirred by the suffering of his fellow Jews and disgusted by the acts of his supposed followers, a theme that, as we have seen, was fully developed in subsequent years by writers such as Asch and many others. Moreover, the way Davidson meticulously applied the central symbols of Jesus' passion—cross, halo, crown of thorns, calling out to God—to the suffering Jew also became part of the stock repertoire of images used by later Jewish writers and artists in various combinations; it represented a radical transformation of the passion motif into an accepted Jewish literary and visual archetype.

The poem's ironic act of transformation and subversion of traditional types is amplified by Davidson's use of the Wandering Jew to epitomize the Christ-like suffering of Jews throughout history. The myth of the Wandering Jew originated in medieval Christian legends about a Jew who meets and rebuffs (or strikes) Jesus on the way to his crucifixion, and is condemned to wander the earth until Jesus' return. By the seventeenth century the figure of the Wandering Jew (or the Eternal Jew, also known in German as Ahasver) had taken on deeply anti-Jewish connotations, and came to represent the Jewish people as a whole. The motif of the Wandering Jew became widespread in European folklore, often reflecting a variety of localized beliefs and superstitions concerning the Jews, and also became common in modern European literature and art.[22] In many of the later treatments of the Wandering Jew figure, he became depicted more positively as a historical narrator of sorts—predicated on the notion that he is the eternal wanderer—and was used as a historiographic device.[23]

By the beginning of the twentieth century, the topos of the Wandering Jew made its way into modern Jewish literature and visual arts as a sympathetic figure embodying the Jewish historical experience of suffering and exile, as is the case in Davidson's poem. Jewish writers and artists cast off the theological and popular enmity connected to the character in Christian legends, transforming the Wandering Jew into a positive archetype, and a means for expressing Jewish historical consciousness as well. Many of the Yiddish writers discussed in this book, such as Moyshe Leyb Halpern, Uri Tsvi Grinberg, Peretz Markish, Zalman Shneour, and Itzik Manger, employ the Wandering Jew figure (implicitly or explicitly) as a witness, chronicler, and survivor of Jewish history, often narrating or recounting acts of persecution and violence committed by Christians.[24] Jewish visual artists such as Samuel Hirszenberg, Marc Chagall, Ben Shahn, and many others also adopted the Wandering Jew motif as a visual symbol in depicting the plight of Jewish victims and refugees.[25] In this way, these authors and artists reclaimed this figure from Christian legend, where he is a negative marker of everything Jewish, and presented him as an emblem of Jewish suffering and perseverance, a martyr and hero—on par with Jesus—who symbolizes all of Jewish history. In many modern works of Jewish writers and artists, such as Davidson's poem, the Wandering Jew and Jesus compete for the crown of Jewish martyrdom, sometimes merging into one conflated figure. At other times the Wandering Jew serves as a witness to Jesus about the passion of Jewish history.

As we have witnessed in the previous chapter, in the realm of Yiddish modernism in the interwar period Jesus and the crucifixion became common symbols as well. Poets like Grinberg, Markish, and Halpern incorporated an array of Christian motifs and images in creating a darkly apocalyptic poetic landscape. Indeed, these and other Yiddish poets and writers from this period also began to associate Jesus and the crucifixion with the historical plight of the Jewish people, figuring Jesus as a paradigmatic Jewish martyr and depicting Jewish suffering and martyrdom in terms of the crucifixion. As Moyshe Leyb Halpern's central protagonist in a 1920 play proclaimed about Jesus, " . . . he who hangs on the cross belongs to us. He is ours, our martyr . . ."[26] However, there exists a noticeable ambivalence about the reclaiming of Jesus and the crucifixion as literary symbols of Jewish suffering in these works. Despite the power these images can bring to a text as rich metaphors and multivalent motifs, they are weighed down by a historical burden that must be removed. Yiddish poets wrestled with the dichotomy of the figure of Jesus as a Christian god/Messiah—more associated with the Christian persecutors of the Jews—and as a quintessential Jewish martyr—representing the Jewish victims of Christian violence—often attempting to embrace the latter while rejecting the former. We will now examine three poems from this period that in applying a Christological understanding to Jewish history also confront Jesus with a historical chronicle of Jewish suffering, playing up the dichotomy between Jesus as Christian god and Jesus as Jewish martyr. The poets to be considered—Zalman Shneour, Uri Tsvi Grinberg, and Leyb Kvitko—are representative of the wave of Yiddish modernism that dominated the early 1920s. Moreover, the three poems we shall examine are all highly indicative of a specific cultural moment: they were written in Berlin in 1922–23, which at that time was one of the centers of Jewish modernism (in Hebrew, Yiddish, and German), and modernism in general;[27] and the authors were Russian/Polish Yiddish poets, who were all grappling with the horrors of the Ukrainian pogroms that two of them (Grinberg and Kvitko) had experienced firsthand.

Zalman Shneour (1887–1959) was a well-known Hebrew and Yiddish poet and novelist, recognized as part of a triumvirate of great Hebrew poets of his generation, along with Chaim Nachman Bialik and Saul Tchernichowsky. He became known as the poet of Jewish heroism and resistance, adopting a strongly nationalistic perspective, in a way similar to Uri Tsvi Grinberg. He often showed an ambivalence toward Christians in his writing, stressing the tensions inherent in Jewish-Christian relationships, both ancient and contemporary. In this vein, Shneour wrote vociferously against the rising climate of anti-Semitism in Europe in the 1910s and 1920s. In one such work, the narrative poem "The Words of Don Henriquez"—which he wrote first in Hebrew as "Divrei Don Henriquez" (Berlin, 1922) and later expanded on in a Yiddish version, "Di verter fun Don Henriquez" (Paris, 1931)—Shneour portrays Jesus as a Jew appropriated by the Christians who now justify their oppression of other Jews in his name.

Set in the era of the Spanish Inquisition, the poem is narrated by a Marrano named Don Henriquez, who implores Jesus, whose crucified image he sees before him as he is about to be burned at the stake, not to trust his Christian worshipers, who will turn on him one day as they have on the rest of the Jews. Henriquez beseeches Jesus to come down from the cross and rejoin the Jews as their leading martyr and partner in pain and suffering. The quintessential emblems of Christianity—Jesus on the cross, the Madonna, and the bloody wounds of crucifixion—are transformed by Shneour into symbols of Jewish affliction. Indeed, in this poem we encounter nearly all of the motifs that appear in modern Jewish writing on Jesus: (1) Jesus as a long-lost Jewish brother; (2) Jesus separated from Christianity; (3) Jesus as an ideal Jewish martyr; (4) Christians depicted as violent oppressors of Jesus' people, along with a general deprecation of Christianity and Christian morality; (5) Jews depicted as suffering martyrs in Christ-like terms with Christian emblems of piety and martyrdom applied to Jewish victims; and (6) Jesus implicated in the Christians' treatment of the Jews in his name; as well as other permutations of these established themes.

For Shneour, Don Henriquez serves as a chronicler of Jewish history—a Wandering Jew—who can testify to all of the atrocities suffered by the Jewish people at the hands of Gentile (mostly Christian) leaders and nations. As we have already alluded to, employing the Wandering Jew figure as a narrator or witness of historical events had been established as a historiographic strategy in nineteenth-century Europe, and many twentieth-century Yiddish and Hebrew writers also incorporated this practice.[28] In his role as historical witness, Henriquez warns Jesus:

> Don't trust the Gentiles, oh, Jesus!
> Through hundreds of years of wandering
> I've fully recognized their holiness,
> I've compared their deeds to their words:
> Your compassion is as tasteless to them
> As straw in a tiger's mouth.[29]

Making use of the premise that Jesus has been absent from Jewish history since his crucifixion, Shneour's narrator sets out to inform Jesus of the hatred and violence that has been perpetrated against Jews in his name. In so doing, he depicts Christians throughout the centuries as barbaric pagans who have hunted and tortured Jews and other "infidels" in the name of religion and morality. Becoming Christians and adopting Jesus' teachings of compassion and love had not erased the intrinsic brutality and blood lust of the Gentile nations. Like much of Grinberg's work, Shneour's poem is laden with sentiments of Jewish nationalism and incorporates both strong feelings of solidarity with

Jesus as a fellow Jew and a fervent animosity toward Christians who have maltreated both Jesus and his people.

It is precisely this reclamation of Jesus as a Jew along with the assertion of the fundamental brutality of Christians that allows Don Henriquez to warn Jesus, rather ironically, that eventually Christians will persecute him in the same manner that they have long mistreated the rest of the Jews. To Don Henriquez's mind, it is only logical that as a Jew, Jesus will ultimately be forced to leave the refuge of the cross and share in the cruel fate of the Jewish people:

Don't trust the Gentiles, Jesus!
A day will soon come when
They will hunt and chase you, like a wild beast,
From peasant's huts and palaces,
From ships at sea and thrones,
They will tear your cross from the throats
Of children, women, and grandfathers,
Just as they now tear beards and mezuzahs
In the Jewish ghetto of Seville . . .

"Away from us you dirty little Jew!"
That's how they'll curse you, chasing you;
Just as they curse and chase us
Out of love for you . . .
"To the devil, to the fire, Marrano!"
This is the fate of us both
And you cannot avoid it:
Today—Don Henriquez, and tomorrow . . .
Our brother, the crucified Jew from Nazareth!" (278)

Here we see how the events of Jewish history, especially the Spanish Inquisition and the plight of the Marranos, are established as models for understanding Jesus; he is seen as a Marrano—a Jew posing as a Christian—who will be sent to the stake with the other Marranos once his true Jewish identity has been revealed. It is significant that the poem's two central protagonists—Don Henriquez and Jesus—are both cast as Marranos, a complex form of Jewish identity that constitutes a conflation of Jew and Christian and, more recently, has come to be understood as symbolic of modern, assimilated Jews in general. In this sense, the modern Jew as Marrano and Jesus, also a Marrano, have another common bond: they both represent a type of Jewish identity that does not fit into traditional categories of Jew or Christian.[30]

In Shneour's poetic vision, Christian anti-Semitism thoroughly discredits Christianity and the entire civilization it has founded. Moreover, the Jewish historical experience is presented as the quintessence of martyrdom and suffering, surpassing Golgotha and the crucifixion of Jesus. This reassessment of previously established typologies of suffering accomplishes two things: it allows the cluster of symbols associated with Jesus' crucifixion to be applied to Jews, and it subverts the basic tenets of Christian theology by demonstrating that Jesus' suffering mirrors the suffering of the Jewish nation, and is actually less significant than theirs. Christology thus becomes a way to understand Jewish history, not Jesus, who is simply one more "dirty little Jew" to be burned at the stake.

In drawing parallels between Jesus' suffering and that of the Jews, Shneour engages in what today might be called "comparative victimization." Throughout the poem Jesus' anguish is depicted as a microcosm of the Jewish experience, and the Jews are portrayed as "better martyrs" than Jesus. Shneour was not alone in making this point, and it must be understood as a polemical barb against the dominant Christian cultural paradigm (even though few if any Christians could read these works in the original), which upheld the martyrdom of Jesus as central while viewing Jewish suffering as peripheral. This theme became somewhat common among Jewish writers and was articulated boldly by the French Jewish writer Edmund Fleg in his *Jésus, raconté par le Juif errant* (Paris, 1933), in which he compares the suffering of Jesus on the cross to that of the Jewish thieves crucified beside him, and by extension to that of all Jewish victims of Gentile violence: "But he, the 'Son of God,' how long did he have to endure on the cross? Six hours. . . . And the sons of Israel, on his right, on his left, it is almost twenty centuries that they have been nailed to their crosses in his name."[31]

Shneour depicted Jesus' suffering in a sympathetic manner, yet he tempered it by comparing it to the historical plight of the Jews. In one

passage, after envisioning Jesus' abandonment by the Christians, Don
Henriquez informs him,

> You will remain all alone, god-Jesus!
> With your thin arms outstretched
> On your flimsy cross—
> You will limp along on stone streets,
> With your pierced feet;
> Just as we, your kin,
> Have limped for hundreds of years. (279)

The author offsets the sorrowful image of an emaciated, solitary Jesus
limping with his cross through the streets of Europe by asserting that
the Jews have been doing this for hundreds of years. Jesus' experience is
neither unique nor unusual.

In one remarkable passage, Don Henriquez foretells a scene in which
the icons of Jesus are expelled from churches, museums, and monaster-
ies throughout Europe, coming to life in a mass exodus that resembles
the Israelites' exodus from Egypt. This procession of icons/exiles winds
its way to the land of Israel, where it is greeted by a throng of Jewish
women. The women recognize in the procession not icons depicting
Jesus' passion, but rather all of Europe's Jewish martyrs throughout
history:

> And they will recognize
> In you and in your statues
> And in thousands of your gaudy icons:
> Victims of all libels
> And harsh decrees throughout the centuries.
> Each Jewish mother—her son,
> Each wife, her husband and father-in-law—
> Pinched with glowing tongs
> With tongues ripped out
> At the pillory in Gentile marketplaces.
> And sisters will recognize brothers—
> Butchered with axes in pogroms
> And buried alive in prisons without proper Jewish burial.
> And grandmothers will recognize
> With half-blind eyes, their grandchildren—

Burned as well-poisoners,
And as host desecrators and eaters
Of matzos made with blood.
And also me, today's victim
Of your boorish monks,
My wife and daughters will recognize.

And each Jewish woman will press to her broken heart
A picture, a sculpture, a statue, of her lost one,
Burnt, crucified, or broken on the wheel
And each one will be transformed into a living Madonna
Weeping for their children,
Who lie in their laps . . .
One immense line of pietàs
From Europe to the hills of Zion. (281)

These two stanzas sharpen the poem's biting condemnation of Christian brutality by presenting a painstaking account of Jewish victimization in medieval Christian Europe. Furthermore, Shneour boldly appropriates Christological symbolism in a striking way: all Jewish victims and survivors of European persecution are likened to Christian icons. All Jewish women are seen as Madonnas, and all Jewish men as crucified Christs. The prophetic vision of the in-gathering of the exiles to Zion is construed as a procession of pietàs. Shneour's use of these iconic images subverts the reigning Christian cultural paradigm in which they have traditionally wielded their symbolic significance and suggests that the power and holiness inherent in these Christian symbols are only valid when they are applied to Jews. Moreover, it provides him with a way to viscerally and graphically depict Jewish persecution and martyrdom that radically departs from more traditional forms of Jewish literature. While, as we have seen, Shneour was by no means the first Jewish poet to appropriate Christian symbolism, his bold use of this motif, combined with the historical sweep and anti-Christian tenor of the poem, make it one of the most jarring examples of this genre.

Despite his application of the symbols of the passion to Jewish victims of Christian violence, Shneour does accord a central place for the real, flesh and blood Jesus in this procession of exiled martyrs/icons: he is "the first martyr" who leads the exiles back home to the Holy Land, functioning as a new Moses. However, it is not as a redeemer like Moses that Jesus possesses any significance, but rather as a martyr. Earlier in the poem Don Henriquez declares to Jesus that

There is no martyr besides you!
No martyr in the name of God,
Besides Jesus—the pale Jew—
Crucified once upon a time at Golgotha. (276)

So, despite illustrating that the historical predicament of the Jews has been far worse that what Jesus experienced, the poem still extolls Jesus as the ideal Jewish martyr. But the author again challenges this status when he compares Jesus' martyrdom at Golgotha to that of Don Henriquez at the auto-da-fé in Seville. Shneour depicts Jesus as somehow less admirable than Don Henriquez because he called out to God during his crucifixion asking why God had forsaken him. On the contrary, Don Henriquez savors his opportunity to become a martyr in God's name:

Look, how beautiful my stake has become,
It sparkles like Solomon's throne:
The bright flame—as if purple,
Engulfs my naked flesh;
And my burning hair is my crown . . .
I will not groan as you did, Jesus:
"My God, why have you forsaken me . . .
The God of Jacob has chosen me
Above all other mortals.
I will glorify the Lord. (283)

Shneour was by no means alone in conceiving of Jesus' martyrdom as somehow lacking. In an essay entitled "My Religion and the Religion of Jesus," the American Reform rabbi Emil Hirsch advanced a similar perspective. Hirsch contrasts the dying words of the legendary Jewish martyr Rabbi Akiba with the dying words of Jesus. He shows that the former was more noble in his martyrdom, proclaiming his faith instead of accusing God of abandoning him. Hirsch concludes with the observation that "The Jews have died by the millions; they are dying now in Poland and Ukraine by hundreds of thousands; they are dying in Hungary simply because they are Jews and they die and don't cry out: 'God, why hast thou forsaken me?' but when the last hour has come they say: 'Shema Yisrael, Adonay Elohenu, Adonay Echad.' Amen. Amen."[32] Indeed, in the final stanza of Shneour's poem, Don Henriquez makes this same Jewish declaration of faith in God's unity and calls upon his "brother Jesus" to join him in so doing (284). Thus, we see that Jewish writers attempting somehow to return Jesus to the Jewish fold commonly display a deep ambivalence about what his place should be. In Shneour's poem, Jesus is simultaneously the leading Jewish martyr and an inferior one who has been sheltered from the hardships of Jewish history while on the cross.

At the same time that Shneour wrote his Hebrew version of "Don Henriquez" (1922), Uri Tsvi Grinberg published his Yiddish prose poem "Uri Tsvi farn tseylem INRI" ("Uri Tsvi in Front of the Cross INRI"), in which many similar themes are expressed. Appearing in the second issue of *Albatros* (November 1922) and sensationally typeset in the shape of a cross, this poem represents Grinberg's boldest endeavor to wrestle with the Jesus theme in his Yiddish poetry. It is especially striking for its appropriation of the symbols of Jesus' passion to emblematize Jewish catastrophe. The poem consists entirely of a monologue spoken by the narrator to his "brother Jesus" as he stands in front of him hanging on the cross. The narrator wonders why he himself does not join Jesus hanging on a cross at some rural crossroad. He implores Jesus to look at him—his brother—and see how much he suffers. Not only does the speaker establish an intimate relationship with his brother Jesus, but in many ways, he asserts that his own suffering, that of a "skin-and-bone Jew," surpasses that of Jesus, a recurrent theme in Grinberg's work, as it is in Shneour's "Don Henriquez," Manger's "Ballad of the Crucified and the Verminous Man," and other works. Yet, what sets this poem apart from earlier poems of Grinberg's in which personal or cosmic catastrophe is expressed through means of the cross is the explicit association between Jesus' passion and Jewish collective suffering. While this linkage certainly exists in earlier works of his, it is with "Uri Tsvi farn tseylem INRI" that Grinberg effectively "created a new mythology of Jesus from the nationalist Jewish perspective" in which Jesus functioned as a "symbol of Jewish suffering at the hands of the goyim; Jesus' crucifixion became the paradigm for crucifixions of Jews throughout the centuries."[33]

Unlike in his earlier poems, here Grinberg confronts the figure of the crucified Jesus with a powerful challenge to remember his own Jewishness and recognize the "primal Jewish pain" (*uryidn-vey*) of his fellow Jews, to which he, perched on his cross, seems oblivious. The narrator assails Jesus with questions about his past, asking him if he remembers the events of his lifetime in the land of Israel. Clearly, he does not, and the speaker proclaims that "thousands of church bells ringing, prayers directed to him, and the bloody Latin letters INRI over his brain," have forced him to forget his Jewish past.[34] Grinberg implies that the divine, Christian Christ has eclipsed the human, Jewish Jesus: his divinity has eclipsed his humanity. In the process, Jesus has become cut off from his own Jewish roots as well as from all of the Jewish suffering that has occurred since his crucifixion. Like Shneour's Don Henriquez, Grinberg's speaker assumes the responsibility of bearing witness to Jesus for nineteen hundred years of Jewish history. He rebukes Jesus for becoming mute and tranquil after so many years on the cross, not feeling the misery of the real world as the poetic speaker does: "you have forgotten everything. Your coagulated brain does not think."[35] Grinberg insinuates that since Jesus has been frozen on his cross, other Jews have become victims and martyrs in his place.

The latter sections of the poem contain a powerful lament for Jewish suffering, to which Jesus is oblivious, and a Zionist-oriented portrait of heroic Jewish pioneers in Palestine. The poem's narrator confronts Jesus: "Your congealed eyes don't see: at your feet: a heap of Jewish heads. Ripped prayer shawls. Tattered parchments. White canvas with blood specks . . . Primordial Jewish agony. Golgotha, brother, you don't see. Golgotha exists: all around. Pilate lives."[36] Toward the end of the poem the speaker exclaims, "You became mute, you have tranquility on the cross. Not I, not I."[37] Jesus is spared the agony that his fellow Jews have experienced during their long exile, and that the speaker experiences in the present. For Grinberg, Golgotha became symbolic of Jewish space in the Diaspora: wherever Jews live (and die) has become Golgotha. He depicts the figure of Jesus on the cross as a kind of altar to which Jewish martyrs are brought as sacrifices. Jesus has forgotten his Jewish past, made dumb by his tranquillity on the cross and the Christian praise of his divinity, while all around him Golgotha has become a graveyard for Jewish victims of Christian violence. Golgotha—the "place of the skulls"—is now a place of Jewish skulls, which are offered to Jesus in a macabre temple-like ritual.

One year later in Berlin, another prominent Yiddish modernist, Leyb Kvitko, depicted a Jewish Jesus, this time as a witness/survivor of a Ukrainian pogrom. Kvitko (1890–1952) was part of the Kiev group of Yiddish writers (associated with the journal *Eygns* along with Peretz Markish and Dovid Bergelson. He left Russia at the beginning of the 1920s for Germany, where he lived until 1925. It was there that in 1923 he published *1919*, a collection of poems lamenting the wave of pogroms that had recently taken place in Ukraine. In the foreword to *1919*, Kvitko claims that his book is more than just "poems about pogroms," which Kvitko himself witnessed in Uman in 1919; he describes the collection of poems as "moments on the thin edge of being and disappearing," alluding to their more metaphysical quality. He praises the soldiers who fought for the Revolution and the liberation it brought from the hated followers of the Ukrainian nationalist Petliura, who were responsible for the pogroms. Interestingly, Kvitko presents himself and the other Jews with him as passive witnesses to the pogroms—not as martyrs and not as resisters, but as witnesses. One of these witnesses is Jesus.

In Kvitko's poem "Eyns, a zundele, an unzers" (roughly translated as "A Son, One of Our Own"), he identifies Jesus, whose name does not appear in the poem, as a fellow Jew, who wanders from place to place, presumably after a pogrom, covered in blood, viewing Jewish suffering from a distance. The poem is reminiscent of Asch's "In a Carnival Night" in that Kvitko's Jesus also sympathizes with the suffering of the Jews, and even wants to take part in that suffering; he bitterly rejects those who worship him, and the concrete symbols of that worship. Kvitko portrays Jesus as a quintessential Jewish victim (another Wandering Jew) who walks about from place to place bloodied and beaten. What distinguishes him from other Jews is his outsider status; he views Jewish trials and tribulations "fun vaytns" ("from afar") and does not dare to come near. This reveals the ambivalence that often accompanies such depictions of Jesus: he is viewed as both insider and outsider, bloodied by anti-Jewish violence, yet somehow not a part of it.

However, Jesus' solidarity and sympathy for the plight of his fellow

Jews is unmistakable, "Our afflictions and patience [are] in his veins" asserts the Jewish speaker, and Jesus

> Looks gently from afar
> At each Jewish house
> And seeks out footprints
> Of Jewish children.[38]

Here, the author portrays Jesus directly confronting the horrors of contemporary Jewish life, rather than having them proclaimed to him by the poem's speaker as in Shneour's and Grinberg's works. Ziva Amishai-Maisels relates a similar phenomenon in the visual arts during this period, noting that "several Jewish artists reacted to the pogroms that accompanied and followed the [First World] War by portraying Christ as a Jew among Jews."[39] Among others, she cites a painting by the Galician Jewish painter Wilhelm Wachtel, *Christ in the Pogrom Quarter* (1920), which depicts Jesus walking through a shtetl after a pogrom. The painting is clearly a response to the pogroms in Ukraine from 1919 to 1921, like Kvitko's poem, and both incorporate the same central image: Jesus walking through a Jewish town to witness in person the devastation his fellow Jews have suffered at the hands of the Christians.[40] It is as if these writers and artists sought Jesus' confirmation, or perhaps validation, that, indeed, Jews did suffer to a degree unsurpassed even by him; theirs was a common fate.

As a way of further establishing Jesus' separation from Christianity and allegiance to his fellow Jews, Kvitko portrays him confronting his own images (icons and crucifixes) as he wanders on the rural paths and back roads (presumably in Ukraine). He stares at them as if in disbelief, and on occasion he "Tears down his own image, / Breaks it into little pieces / And throws it into the bloody slush."[41] Like Asch in "In a Carnival Night" before him, Kvitko employs this powerful image of Jesus forcefully rejecting his own worship. Indeed, this is a frequently recurring theme in the Jewish treatment of Jesus—separating the Jewish man, Jesus, from the Christian Christ. In the works of Asch, Leyvik, Kvitko, and other modern Yiddish writers, Jesus himself is commonly depicted as enforcing this distinction, disgusted by Christian claims of his divinity. Kvitko intensifies this theme in the last stanza of the poem in which Jesus bitterly rebukes the religious leaders of Christianity. This, too, was frequently a feature of the modern Jewish depiction of Jesus, as reclaiming Jesus as a Jew typically coincided with chastising Christian anti-Semitism and violence against Jews in the name of Jesus. In the last stanza of Kvitko's poem, Jesus castigates those who had worshiped him:

> And he stops
> In front of every priest's house,
> In front of the holy tents
> Of clergymen and monks—
> He makes crosses on the walls
> With silent gall
> With bitterness—
> He etches deep black shame crosses.[42]

Jesus uses the symbol that was intended to represent his own sacrificial death—the cross—but instead had come to embody the Christian persecution of his Jewish brothers and sisters, as a means of repudiating the Christian persecutors who have transformed it into a shameful symbol of hatred and violence (much like in Shapiro's story "The Cross").

For writers like Kvitko, Grinberg, and Shneour (and they were by no means alone), when confronted with the calamities of Jewish history, the Jewish Jesus had two options: he could remain on the cross and let "skin-and-bone Jews" assume his mantle as supreme martyr, or he could come down from his cross to join his fellow Jews as a witness and partner in their pain and suffering. In both cases, these poets make clear that the passion of Jesus is an appropriate paradigm for understanding Jewish history. We will now turn our attention to the aftermath of World War II and the Holocaust to see how Jewish writers and artists envisioned the place of Jesus and his relationship to his fellow Jewish victims in the wake of the most catastrophic experience of Jewish suffering.

Christ in the Ghetto:
Christological Responses to the Holocaust

In 1949, the German critic Theodor Adorno proclaimed that "after Auschwitz it is barbaric to write poetry."[43] For Adorno and many of his contemporaries, the horrors of the Holocaust were seen as "an obscene contradiction" to the aesthetic, lyrical nature of poetry.[44] In opposition to Adorno's stance, numerous Yiddish and Hebrew poets in Europe and America did begin to write poetry—even before the war had ended—that wrestled with the great tragedy of the Jews of Europe and the atrocities of the Nazi genocide, but many of them implicitly embraced the attitude that "after Auschwitz it is barbaric to write poetry that incorporates the figure of Jesus." Indeed, the realities of the Holocaust caused several prominent Yiddish writers and critics to stop seeing Jesus as an appropriate subject for Jewish literature and art, and to reject the crucifixion as a symbol of Jewish suffering. After the war and the revelation of the extent of the Nazi atrocities, poets such as Itzik Manger, Hey Leyvik, Uri Tsvi Grinberg, and others, who had boldly appropriated the figure of Jesus in their poetry before the war, "expunged the glowing references to Jesus and Gentiles from their earlier poetry," or, in Grinberg's case, refused to republish "any of his prewar poetry . . . until the late 1970s."[45] More generally, the cultural openness toward Jesus that had been the hallmark of the Jewish reclamation of Jesus since the beginning of the nineteenth century quickly faded in the wake of the Holocaust, only to seriously reemerge in the 1970s. Despite this widespread turn away from Jesus, a number of important Jewish writers and artists continued to portray him as a Jewish brother and depict Jewish victimization during the Holocaust in Christ-like terms; chief among them, and not without controversy, was Sholem Asch.

While Sholem Asch had continued to incorporate Christian motifs and sympathetic appraisals of Jesus in his writings in the years after "In a Carnival Night" was published (1909), his epic novel on the life of Jesus, *The Nazarene* (1939), was his first work to again elicit such serious controversy. Asch's empathetic presentation of the historical Jesus, whom he affectionately depicts as a wonder-working *rebbe* and pious Jewish patriot in his nearly seven-hundred-page novel, incited many harsh responses. By structuring his narrative as a recovery of historical eyewitness accounts of Jesus' life, such as the lost Gospel of Judas Iscariot—although fictional—Asch lent an air of authenticity and immediacy to his glowing account of Jesus' life and teachings.[46] Like the Crucifix Question debate of 1909, the controversy following the publication of the English translation of Asch's *The Nazarene*[47] in 1939—as well as Asch's subsequent "Christian" works in the 1940s, *The Apostle* (1943) and *Mary* (1949)—reflected the conflicting views in the Yiddish literary community regarding the figure of Jesus at the outset of World War II. An in-depth analysis of Asch's novel is beyond the scope of this book,[48] but a brief discussion of the various responses to it in the Yiddish press will help to illustrate that in the thirty years since the Crucifix Question this subject remained highly contentious, and that the two main perspectives on the matter had changed surprisingly little. The outbreak of World War II and the Nazi assault on Europe's Jews did change some writers' opinions regarding the appropriateness of Jesus imagery in Jewish literature and art, but the fundamental reasons for or against such opinions remained essentially the same; one's overall ideological orientation (and personal relationship to Asch) tended to dictate the assessment one gave in responding to *The Nazarene*.

Many in the Yiddish press echoed Ansky's basic sentiments as expressed during the *tseylem frage* controversy, arguing that Jesus could only symbolize Christianity and the Christian mistreatment of the Jews and therefore was off limits as a subject for a Yiddish writer, especially when European Christians were massacring Europe's Jews in greater numbers than ever before. Despite the fact that numerous Yiddish writers had been positively depicting Jesus for the past thirty years, many felt that Asch had gone beyond the pale with his tender portrayal of Jesus in *The Nazarene*.[49] Abraham Cahan, the influential editor of the daily Yiddish newspaper *Forverts* in New York, led the assault on Asch's work, refusing to serialize it in his paper—although he had serialized many of Asch's previous novels—and seeing it as a dangerous, pro-Christian tract. He wrote one article that asked: "Should There Be a New Question about Jesus Among Jews?" and, later, went as far as calling *The Nazarene* an "indescribable mistake, and . . . a disgusting stain on Yiddish literature."[50] A journalist for the *Forverts*, Chaim Lieberman, also bitterly condemned Asch's work, professing that Asch had "sinned a great sin against the Jewish people," and that Asch had written *The Nazarene* with the intention of converting Jews to Christianity.[51] Lieberman, a former secular Zionist and Yiddishist who had become fervently Orthodox in the 1930s, published several articles in the *Forverts* attacking Asch and *The Nazarene*, and went on to write an entire book—*Sholem Asch un kristentum* (*Sholem Asch and Christianity*, 1950)—in which he harshly decried Asch and repeated charges of his apostasy and missionary activities.[52] This hysterical tone was echoed by others in the Yiddish press, such as Ephraim Kaplan, an Orthodox writer for the *Morgen Zhurnal* (*Morning Journal*), who "condemned Asch for having written 'a shtik shmad-propoganda' [a piece of proselytizing propaganda]" and also contended that "*The Nazarene* is a stab in the back to Jewry in this terrible time,"[53] thereby suggesting that in the face of the war in Europe and the Nazi slaughter of the Jews, Asch's "praises" of Jesus were especially treacherous.

While Asch's critics—especially Cahan and the *Forverts*—may have been more vocal and prolific in their condemnation of Asch's novel, his defenders were just as numerous, if not more so. There were many who maintained that Asch's choice of subject was perfectly acceptable even if they found the book itself to be a literary failure. A writer for the socialist Zionist paper *Idisher kempfer* (*Jewish Fighter*) found it "ludicrous (*lekherlekh*) that the socialist *Forverts* considered Jesus to be a taboo subject."[54] Many others, including Hey Leyvik, also expressed their dismay and surprise that the *Forverts* would refuse to publish Asch's novel.[55] Melekh Ravitsh, in an essay reviewing Asch's subsequent novel, *The Apostle*, dismissed those would-be pious Jews (*frumakes*) who condemned Asch's *Nazarene*, claiming that it would cause scores of Jews to convert. He argued that, to the contrary, Asch only glorified the Jewish aspects of pristine Christianity and that, like *The Nazarene*, *The Apostle* could provide a foundation for a "new *yiddishkayt*."[56] In one of Shmuel Niger's several essays discussing *The Nazarene*, he defended Asch's book as a literary masterpiece, while at the same time explaining why many Jews had such a strong reaction to it. He noted that young Jews in the shtetl, when still traditionally pious, were afraid to even utter the name of Jesus, and how, as adults, they came to associate Jesus with two thousand years of Christian hatred, persecution, and prejudice.[57] Niger pointed out, astutely, that the controversy surrounding *The Nazarene* had little to do with the artistic-literary content of the book, and that the religio-cultural issues raised by it, and by Asch in his many interviews, were the main causes of controversy.[58]

Chaim Zhitlovsky (at the age of seventy-five) also took part in the torrid debate surrounding *The Nazarene*. In an article entitled "Our Brother, Jesus of Nazareth" ("Unzer bruder, Yeshu fun Notseres"), Zhitlovsky reiterated many of the same ideas about Jesus that he had raised in *Dos naye lebn* thirty-one years earlier. He asserted that *The Nazarene* did not offer any new revelations, but rather simply "illustrates" scenes from the New Testament, with a strong artistic style. In general, Zhitlovsky's review is not very favorable; he questions why Asch presents Jesus in such a supernatural light, retaining so much of the New Testament material, musing that maybe Asch was expressing his "true beliefs." He also claimed that Asch's situating Jesus in a Jewish context—showing him to be, for example, a *talmid chochim* (Jewish sage), a *rebbe*, and a Pharisee— was absolutely not new, citing both Geiger's and Graetz's historical writing as earlier examples of such a view. Nonetheless, Zhitlovsky argued that Asch's major contribution was his ability "to show the purely Jewish character of almost all of the Christian legends . . . and the purely Jewish source of Jesus' teachings."[59] Zhitlovsky repeated a claim similar to one he made in 1909, saying that the Jewish radical who has not left behind the age-old Jewish hatred toward Jesus had a lot to learn from Asch's novel. Not surprisingly, Zhitlovsky faulted Asch for overlooking the socialist nature of Jesus and the early Christian movement, and lamented that the author stressed the mystical, supernatural qualities of Jesus over his "down-to-earth" social reformer character and his universal humanism. Ultimately, Zhitlovsky still viewed Jesus as a "radical reformer of the human moral consciousness,"[60] and only criticized Asch's novel for casting him in a more transcendental light.

In the end, left-wing, secular Yiddish writers of a more internationalist or cosmopolitan orientation, like Zhitlovsky, were typically more open to Asch's depiction of Jesus—even against the backdrop of the Nazi persecution of European Jewry—than more ideologically conservative, and especially Orthodox, writers like Lieberman. Indeed, the Communist Yiddish paper in New York, *Morgen frayhayt* (*Morning Freedom*), became one of Asch's major supporters during the ongoing controversy surrounding his Christian novels, taking over the *Forverts*'s role as Asch's main employer and publisher, and seeing his works as advancing its own internationalist, antifascist agenda.[61] Clearly, such differing views of Jesus and his proper place in Jewish culture cannot simply be explained as a case of left-wing versus right-wing ideologies, since left-wing secularists like Manger and Leyvik also backed away from their earlier depictions of Jesus and use of Christian symbolism after the Holocaust (though Leyvik offered a sympathetic defense of Asch in the wake of the *Nazarene* controversy).

Despite all the controversy generated by *The Nazarene*, Asch revisited the Jesus theme four years later in a melodramatic story, "Kristos in geto" ("Christ in the Ghetto," 1943), which he wrote during the apex of the Nazi genocide against the Jews.[62] It is Asch's boldest fictional attempt to merge Jesus on the cross with real-life Jewish victims, and is also significant as one of the earliest literary responses to the Nazi atrocities of World War II.[63] Set in the Warsaw Ghetto, the action of Asch's story revolves around a group of traditional Jews who have been rounded up by Gestapo officers during their Rosh ha-Shanah prayer service and brought to a Catholic church. Once in the church, the Nazis order the Jews to desecrate the holy objects, including the Jesus figure on the cross. The rabbi refuses and is murdered by a Gestapo officer, and the Nazis proceed to desecrate the church themselves. Once everyone has left the church, the Jesus figure comes to life and assumes the form of the murdered rabbi lying at his feet. He then heads out into the ghetto streets and dissuades a Polish mob, which has been tricked by the Nazis into believing that the Jews wrecked their church, from seeking revenge by instilling love and compassion into their hearts. The story concludes with the Jesus/rabbi figure entering a Jewish house and greeting the residents there with the Yiddish/Hebrew greeting *shalom aleichem*. The basic plot of the story, while quite sensational, does not convey the full extent to which Asch attempts to portray a fundamental kinship between Jesus and the Jews.

As with so much of his fiction, Asch's underlying ideology shapes the thematics of his writing in a very direct way, making it possible to grasp his overarching ideological program by closely reading his stories and novels. Indeed, "Kristos in geto" reads like a point-by-point outline of Asch's basic thesis concerning Jewish-Christian reconciliation. The key ideological principles that Asch incorporated into the story are: (1) Jesus feeling deep sympathy for the suffering of Jewish victims; (2) the Jewish victims being depicted as exact images of Christ on the cross, sharing a physical resemblance as well as acting in a way that embodies Jesus' teachings of compassion such as loving one's enemies; (3) erasing the historical animosity between Jews and Jesus by exonerating Jesus of the violence Christians perpetrated in his name; (4) ecumenical overtones expressed as a desire for Jewish-Christian reconciliation, and a denial of Jewish complicity in killing Jesus; (5) the ultimate conflation of Jesus and real-life Jews, in the form of Jesus taking on the image of the murdered rabbi.

Asch's Jesus in this story is lifelike, tragic, and heroic. The narrator asserts that "the man that hangs on the cross appears to want to free himself" (231). At first the Jews refuse to raise their heads and look at the Jesus-figure—an example of the traditional taboo and fear that ruled Jewish perceptions of Jesus—but a few are compelled by their curiosity to look up at him. The narrator relates that "through their fingers they glanced at the Hebrew letters which shone forth from his head; however they quickly looked away, afraid that they would go blind" (232). Those Jews who manage to overcome their fear, even for a brief moment, encounter the essential Jewishness of Jesus, symbolized by the enigmatic "Hebrew letters" shining forth from his head (most likely the INRI tablet located above the head of Jesus on most crucifixes, which, occasionally, was written in three languages: Latin, Greek, and Aramaic). To be sure, this scene reveals one of Asch's central concerns: to bridge the gap between Jews and Jesus by demonstrating Jesus' *ur*-Jewishness. Asch concedes the deep aversion to Jesus felt by traditional Jews, and his core project is to overcome this perennial antipathy by portraying both Jesus and the Jews themselves in a different light.

The Nazi protagonists assume that, like them, the Jews consider Jesus their enemy, and will therefore happily follow their command to desecrate the church. It is significant that Asch emphasizes that the Nazis no longer see themselves as Christians, as this bolsters his belief that only errant or nominal Christians are guilty of anti-Semitism, not those who truly follow Jesus' teachings. The Jews refuse to desecrate the church, as the rabbi explains that despite ongoing accusations that the Jews killed Jesus, Judaism actually dictates tolerance and acceptance of

Christianity; this sentiment more than subtly conveys Asch's own ecumenical stance. The rabbi also pronounces that Jesus is not responsible for all the evil that Christians have done in his name (236), another key theme in Asch's thinking. In the story's climax, the main Gestapo officer tries to incite a Polish mob against the ghetto's Jews by enumerating a long list of anti-Semitic charges, and stressing the Jews' antipathy toward Jesus and Christianity. However, Jesus, looking like the rabbi, appeases the mob by preaching to them love, compassion, and tolerance. In Jesus' speech to the mob one can see Asch's attempt to assert his own version of Jesus' message to his followers, a message of universal brotherhood, compassion, and shared sorrow that would effectively end traditional Christian-Jewish acrimony. The Poles ultimately realize that since they are Christians—the Jews' partners in pain and suffering under the Nazis—they cannot shed the blood of their brothers.

Jesus' deep sympathy for his suffering Jewish brothers is established early on in the story. Immediately following the scene in which several Jews quickly glance at Jesus on the crucifix, the narrator conveys that Jesus himself is looking at them:

> However, while the Jews didn't look at the crucified one, the crucified one looked at them. It was as if the wooden figure hanging on the cross lifted, with one hand, his fallen head from his chest and turned his huge eyes to the imperiled Jews. The rainwater which washed his face formed two cracks creating the effect of two streams of teardrops cascading from his huge eye holes, and landing in his beard. With his one hand freed from the cross he pointed to the wound on his side. (232)

Jesus not only notices the Jewish captives in the church, he sheds tears for them while pointing at his own wounds, indicating the deep pain he feels at seeing their harrowing plight, or possibly suggesting that like him, the Jews carry their own stigmata, symbolizing their perpetual victimization and martyrdom. Again, when the rabbi is shot dead at his feet, Jesus expresses deeply felt sympathy. As the rabbi lies there, and the remaining Jews look at him, Jesus is depicted as "writhing on his cross in torment and grief, just like their rabbi on the steps behind him" (238). The narrator describes how Jesus points again with his free hand to the wound in his side; however, this time he "also pointed to the blood which flowed through the pierced *tallis* from the pierced heart of the rabbi, who was lying at the foot of the cross" (238). Here, Jesus makes an explicit connection between his wounds and the fresh blood flowing from the murdered rabbi.

From the moment he enters the narrative, the central Jewish protagonist—the rabbi Yudel Zilbershlag—is compared to the man on the cross; the narrator delineates their physical similarity as well as their shared inner qualities: "Like the figure on the cross, the Jew was also tall and thin, his face imprinted with the same expression of sorrow and compassion. However, in truth, the most amazing aspect of their resemblance was the look in their eyes: present in their eyes was not anger or bitterness, but heart-wrenching compassion for the state of man, who has fallen so low" (234). Just as Jesus felt only compassion for his tormentors, so, too, Yudel the rabbi harbors no hatred for his Nazi captors. Like Jesus, Yudel represents the ideal paradigm of compassion and forgiveness in the face of suffering and persecution. In Asch's vision, there is no room for feelings of revenge or contempt toward Jesus or one's Christian oppressors, contrary to much of the writing of Uri Tsvi Grinberg and Zalman Shneour. Unlike these other writers, Asch wanted to appropriate not only Jesus' crown of suffering for the Jews, but also his ethical principles of passivity and compassion. Asch's position implied that the Jews were like Jesus in life as well as in death. Thus, in death, the rabbi and Jesus are again shown to be identified. The rabbi urges the Jews to refuse the Nazis' orders to desecrate the church, even if it means paying with their lives. He beseeches them, "this is a proper time for great *kiddush ha-shem* [martyrdom]" (237), and immediately is shot dead by a Gestapo officer, falling at the foot of the cross.

Asch's depiction of Jesus' resurrection in "Kristos in geto" goes even further than that in "In a Carnival Night" in transforming him into a flesh-and-blood Jew. Once revived and descended from the cross, Jesus undresses the rabbi and puts on his entire outfit—a satin caftan and belt, shoes, a skullcap, a blue and white Jewish star armband, and a *tallis*. As Jesus picks up the bloodstained *tallis* he shakes it, causing the blood to miraculously disappear, then he wraps it around his own face, uttering the proper blessing, like any pious Jew. Once the *tallis* is on, the narrator comments that Jesus' face is transfigured to become exactly like that of the fallen rabbi—a pious countenance full of love and anguish. The similarities between Jesus and the rabbi now give way to their ultimate conflation: Jesus is resurrected as a contemporary Jew, a rabbi in the Warsaw Ghetto dressed in traditional garb. Instead of having Jesus use his miraculous power to revive the rabbi, Asch stages a scene in which the reader can watch as Jesus becomes a traditional Jew, step by step. Asch's vision of the modern-day Jesus as a Polish rabbi in the Warsaw Ghetto reflects both his understanding of the historical Jesus as a normative rabbinic figure and his perception of Jewish victims as Christ-like. For Asch, both the human Jesus—the rabbi from Nazareth—and the supernatural Jesus—the crucified "martyr of the ages"—are relevant.

While writers such as Grinberg, Leyvik, and Manger unequivocally abandoned such Christological images in light of the Nazi genocide of European Jewry, Asch continued to apply such an understanding to Jewish suffering. Nor, as we shall see, was he alone in expressing the Christ-like nature of contemporary Jewish martyrdom during the Holocaust.[64] Asch found the image matrix associated with Jesus' passion entirely appropriate in depicting scenes of even such extreme Jewish martyrdom. In a short nonfiction booklet written at the end of the war entitled *One Destiny: An Epistle to the Christians*, Asch recounted the horrors of life in the Warsaw Ghetto and described the liquidation of the ghetto's Jews in Christological terms:

> battalions of people dragged themselves across the streets of the ghetto, singing, praying, crying out to God with the same prayers which accompanied victims in former days on their way to the stakes of the Inquisition, the same outcry heard on the cross from him who gave his life to save the world, 'Eli, Eli, lama sabachtani?'—'My God, my God, why hast thou forsaken me?' That same cry was heard on the streets of Warsaw from hundreds of souls who, with their crosses, were being whipped on the way to Golgotha.[65]

Asch uses this imagery to convey his understanding of Jewish martyrdom as the blood heritage of all Jews—apostate and Hasid alike—and suffering as "the highest price exacted for one's faith."[66] In suffering, Asch sees all of the variegated types of modern Jews unified into the one, simple, primordial Jew, a folk typology that reflects the simple Jew of faith—the "psalm-Jew" (*tehillm yid*)—that Asch attempted to create in his fiction. Unlike Shneour and others, Asch does not see Jesus' martyrdom as tarnished because he cried out to God, asking why he was abandoned; indeed, he imagines the deaths of the Jews of the Warsaw Ghetto in the same terms. He reads all of Jewish history as a continual test of faith and call to martyrdom, modeled on Jesus' death on the cross at Golgotha. He understands "the Jew" as the suffering Christ, whose martyrdom will ultimately bring redemption to Israel, and to the world.

The avant-garde Yiddish poet Peretz Markish, who experienced World War II in the Soviet Union, was more critical than Asch in imagining Jesus' connection to Jewish tribulations during the war, although he, too, appropriated Christological imagery in depicting Jewish suffering. Markish had earlier included Christ-figures and Christian motifs in many of his apocalyptic poems from the 1920s, often depicting the stark contradiction between the historical Jewish Jesus and the Christian Christ, and containing a trenchant anti-Christian tone.[67] In his later work in response to World War II, Markish juxtaposed the Christ-like suffering of the Jews to the Christian Christ's seeming indifference.

Markish's *Milkhome* (*War*) is a two-volume cycle of poems containing 162 chapters, which constitutes Markish's poetic narrative response to the experience of World War II. It was first published in Moscow in 1948, though Markish had begun writing the poems during the war itself and continued after the war ended. *Milkhome* chronicles the war from beginning to end, painting a wide vista of epic scope, and focusing particularly, though not exclusively, on the tragic plight of the Jews. Markish does not present one continuous narrative, but rather a series of vignettes or scenes that show the variety of situations and characters encountered during the war, with the thread joining it all together being the suffering of war and the evil of the Germans.

He depicts a wide array of Jewish characters that represent several themes, such as heroism, resistance, martyrdom, and sacrifice. One of Markish's central characters is Gur Aryeh, a kind of Wandering Jew figure who embodies the eternal suffering, martyrdom, and self-sacrifice of the Jews through his own bitterly tragic wartime experiences. He also functions as a kind of spokesperson who addresses the world and expresses the collective pain of the Jewish nation. (His name itself is symbolic of the Jewish people—the tribe of Judah—as in Gen. 49:9, where Jacob blesses his children: "Judah is a lion's cub [*gur aryeh*]." Ironically this implies physical strength and prowess, unlike Markish's Gur Aryeh, whose strength is mainly spiritual.) The Yiddish literary critic Nakhman Mayzel claims that Gur Aryeh is the archetypal victim of the most brutal atrocities at the hands of the enemy, who survives and is able to confront his enemy face to face and proclaim the eternity of Israel.[68] In one section, Gur Aryeh crawls out of the mass killing pits in Babi Yar, Ukraine, where thousands of Jews were slaughtered, and wanders through the forest to the hut of a peasant. There he sees the figure of Jesus on a cross on the wall of the house, and proceeds to address him as if in a dreamy trance in the poem "A bagegenish mit dem gekreytsten" ("An Encounter with the Crucified").

The poem opens with Gur Aryeh approaching a peasant's hut in the woods after escaping the death pit in Babi Yar and collapsing at the door. He is half-naked and flecked with blood. The peasant is taken aback, but invites him in, asking him if he has "come from the pit," which implies that like Jesus, Gur Aryeh had been resurrected from the dead.[69] As Gur Aryeh enters the hut, dazed and feverish, he catches sight of the crucifix on the wall and notices that "Yoyzl peered at him from his crucifix in the corner." Like Asch's Jesus in the Warsaw church, Markish's "Yoyzl" also ponders the Jewish victim standing before him. As Gur Aryeh contemplates the figure on the crucifix, with oil from a hanging lamp falling on it, seemingly "flowing like fresh blood," he moves toward it while relating that the "crucifixion in his [own] blood glimmers and disappears." It appears to Gur Aryeh that "the two of them are coming toward each other, / As each one recognizes the other's wounds."[70] Gur Aryeh wonders if Jesus has also come from the killing pits. Thus, in this first encounter Gur Aryeh relates to Jesus as a kindred spirit: both are covered in blood, bearing wounds from their persecutors; both have felt the torment of crucifixion—whether literally or symbolically. Gur Aryeh assumes that Jesus must be a Jewish refugee, like himself, who has escaped the Nazi massacres, and sought shelter in the peasant's home.

However, in the following stanza, Gur Aryeh's sympathetic attitude toward Jesus shifts dramatically. He begins to address the "crucified man" with a litany of accusations and demands, regarding him as one who has ceased to be a fellow Jewish victim. He asks Jesus why he is not suffering along with the Jews in the ghetto, and calls on Jesus to go to the mass graves, where the putrid stench of rotting corpses has forced even animals to run from the forest. He implores Jesus to renounce his own salvific powers:

> Go crucified man, go!
> And let them know in the ghetto,
> That no one ascends to heaven from the cross,
> You, yourself are in hiding in the hut of a peasant,
> Who still doesn't know,
> That the world is expiring in blood on your account,
> You have better served the executioner with your redemption,
> Divine messenger, than the liberators![71]

This harsh indictment of Jesus' moral culpability is a recurring theme among Jewish writers; he is seen as a fellow Jew who has betrayed his people by allowing himself to be made into a Gentile god. Markish underscores the bitter irony of the fact that Jesus, the reputed Christian savior, is unable, or unwilling, to save his own people from their brutal fate, and, moreover, is in some way responsible for the murderous actions of his followers. In this formulation, it is the Jews who have the moral high ground because of their endless martyrdom and selfless sacrifice, and therefore they usurp Jesus' role as the Christ: the epitome of suffering and martyrdom. Markish articulates this stance in the next section of the *poema*, as Gur Aryeh continues to chastise Jesus. Now addressing him as "Nazarite" (*nozer*), Gur Aryeh asks Jesus, "What good has come, *nozer*, for your crucified hide? / For turning the other cheek? / For the contrived story made up after your death?"[72] With these questions Markish's protagonist condemns the core legends and ethics of Christianity as, at best, futile and, at worst, pernicious.

Gur Aryeh, as the Eternal Jew, captures Jesus' crown of suffering; he is the one who is resurrected from the pit of death; he is the one who bears the suffering of his entire people; he is the one who is persecuted falsely and fated to die the martyr's death. This transference of the crown of suffering is alluded to in the poem when Gur Aryeh implores Jesus to remove his crown of thorns and kick it in the dust. Throughout the poem Gur Aryeh implies that Jesus is not worthy to wear this crown; Gur Aryeh and the "crucified children" in the ghetto are more holy, and therefore more worthy. At one point Gur Aryeh exclaims to Jesus, "Go to the ghetto and knock on every door, / You will meet a limitless amount of crucified children, / Who are holier and purer than you, *nozer!*"[73] As spokesman for the Jewish nation, Gur Aryeh proclaims to Jesus, and by extension to the Christians who worship him, that today's Jews are the crucified ones, the true victims of mankind, not Jesus who hides in a peasant's hut. Like Shneour, Grinberg, and Kvitko in the early 1920s, writing in response to the Ukrainian pogroms, Markish articulates the suffering of Jewish victims of World War II in Christological terms while powerfully indicting their Christian tormentors. Moreover, he deposes Jesus from his throne of suffering in favor of the Jewish children in the Nazi ghettos whom he sees as "holier and purer" than Jesus.

In this sense, the Yiddish literary depiction of the passion of Jewish history shares the basic premises of the Reform Jewish rabbis of the nineteenth and early twentieth centuries: the Jewish people, throughout history and at present, are the true "man of sorrows," the Christ of the nations. Throughout these works, Jesus is simultaneously idealized as a symbol of Jewish martyrdom and reviled as the emblem of the Christian persecutors of the Jews; again, this duality of Jesus as Jewish martyr and Christian god is a source of profound ambivalence and tension for the Jewish writers who engage him. In a larger context, this represents the ambivalence these writers felt for the greater Western society they were living in. On the one hand, they were Jews who fervently embraced the extrinsic cultural and intellectual traditions of the Gentile world, while on the other hand, they were fiercely proud, at times nationalist, Jews committed to creating a vibrant, modern Jewish culture. When this Jewish culture, and Jews themselves, became threatened by the violence and persecution of the Christian world, in the form of anti-Semitic discrimination, pogroms, and ultimately genocide, these Jews appropriated some of the most powerful symbols of the Christian West—Jesus and the crucifixion—to represent their own national tragedy.

Five The Artist Crucified

> I run upstairs
> To my dry brushes
> And am crucified like Christ
> Fixed with nails to the easel
> > —Marc Chagall

Painting the Jewish Jesus

As I have argued throughout this book, the phenomenon of Jews reclaiming the figure of Jesus and all of the rich symbols related to him has permeated all forms of modern Jewish culture, from theology to historiography, and from poetry and literature to the visual arts. Possibly the most striking example of this phenomenon is the recurring use of Jesus-figures and Christian motifs by a number of important Jewish artists, chief among them Marc Chagall (1887–1985). In many ways, more than all of the other genres of Jewish culture I have focused on up until this point, modern Jewish art posed a radical challenge to traditional forms of Jewish culture because of its bold new use of the visual image and pictorial representation of human forms, as well as its embrace of Western forms and genres of the plastic arts. Yet, as with much of the Yiddish modernist poetry and literature we have examined thus far, what made modern Jewish visual art (especially modernist art) so unique was its creative combination of traditional Jewish images, motifs, and artistic genres with Western (especially Christian) ones. Perhaps the most noteworthy of such combinations is the adoption of the Christ-figure, the crucifixion, and other traditional motifs of Christian art, both religious and secular, by modern Jewish artists, who often presented these traditionally Christian images in markedly Jewish terms. Like the Jewish historians, writers, and poets discussed above, Jewish artists in the nineteenth century began to reclaim the figure of Jesus as part of an ideological challenge to the dominant Christian culture, in an effort to recast him and the symbols associated with him as intrinsically Jewish. Whether seeing Jesus as an important figure in Jewish history, or symbolic of Jewish martyrdom through the ages, Jewish artists incorporated Jesus-figures in a variety of significant ways, effectively creating a subgenre of modern Jewish art: the Jewish Jesus.

Here I focus particularly on the fascination of one artist—Marc Chagall—with the figure of Jesus in order to shed light on the complexity of this phenomenon and explore its myriad manifestations. Chagall's status as the quintessential Jewish modernist artist of the twentieth century, closely connected to a number of the Yiddish writers who inscribed Jesus into Jewish culture (such as Sholem Asch), renders him an exemplary subject for seeing how and why a Jewish Jesus was created in the visual arts. Chagall's Jewish Jesus, in fact, moved beyond the Jewish world so that many know him not only as *the* modern Jewish painter, but also as *the* modern painter of Jesus. Although this is often seen as paradoxical, by situating Chagall within the larger trend of the appropriation of Jesus as a key aspect of constructing modern Jewish culture, his position as the leading Jewish painter of the twentieth century need not be seen as at odds with his creation of more than one hundred paintings and sketches featuring Jesus-figures and images of the crucifixion. More than sharing in the fascination with the figure of Jesus that so preoccupied contemporary Yiddish modernists, Chagall also tapped into a tradition within the Jewish visual arts of depicting the Jewish Jesus that went back to the late nineteenth century.

While the *tseylem frage* was raging on the pages of *Dos naye lebn* in New York in 1909, Chagall executed his first crucifixion sketch (fig. 1, 1908–9), which later became the study for his painting *Golgotha* (fig. 2) of 1912, completed while he was living in Paris. This early drawing reflects the influence of the Russian Orthodox iconic tradition on the young Chagall, who was studying in St. Petersburg during these years and was exposed to many works of Russian church art. Chagall's crucifixion drawing incorporated many of the standard motifs of traditional Russian Orthodox icons, from the inclusion of Mary and John at the foot of the cross to their attire, the stylized halos, the nails and bleeding of Christ, and the skull at the base of the cross signifying Golgotha as the "place of the skull."[1] In different preliminary sketches for *Golgotha*, Chagall's original crucifixion scene underwent some serious stylistic as well as thematic changes. Many of the iconic elements were eliminated or modified, especially the figures at the foot of the cross, who, as Amishai-Maisels observes, "gradually become a Jewish couple!" which Chagall later claimed to be his own parents.[2] In some pencil sketches the INRI at the top of the cross was replaced with a Hebrew inscription that, though blurred, seems to spell out "MARC" and may underscore the acute personal identification Chagall felt with the crucified Jesus.[3]

This demonstrates both the Judaization and the personalization of Russian themes and styles in general, and the crucifixion in particular, in Chagall's work. Despite the fact that Chagall was influenced by the Russian iconic art of his surrounding environment, he goes from mimicking that genre to transforming it into something distinctive: a personal, Russian-Jewish, crucifixion scene. Chagall's earliest finished work on this theme, *Golgotha*, originally called *Dedicated to Christ*, is more abstract than his earlier sketches. Cubist and geometric patterns in the painting fix the cross as the central, linking structural element that places and connects all the other figures in the painting; it is the aesthetic and structural anchor of the piece. Was this purely an aesthetic statement then, or could it be seen as a political or theological-spiritual one? Why had this young Jewish artist from Vitebsk[4] become interested with Jesus and the cross at this early stage in his career? And why did the crucifixion continue to be one of the predominant images in Chagall's later works as well? In other words, what led a young, aspiring Jewish artist, from a Hasidic family in the Jewish heartland of tsarist Russia, to adopt, and ultimately transform, the figure at the heart of Christianity and, moreover, the central image of Western art through the ages, into a major Jewish icon?

As we have established in the preceding chapters, Jewish modernists shared freely in the symbolism of the Western (secular Christian) canon, even when their works were imbued with unambiguously Jewish themes and concerns. This phenomenon of Jewish writers and artists partaking in the culture of the West while writing in Jewish languages or painting Jewish symbols and motifs reveals the hybrid nature of modern secular Jewish culture, and must be further considered in order to understand the allure of the figure of Jesus and the crucifixion for Jewish modernists such as Chagall. In looking at Chagall's early artistic style, especially around the period of his *Golgotha*, one sees a "convincing synthesis between East and West, between Jewish life experience, Jewish and Russian folk art and contemporary Western art."[5] This blending of cultural traditions and predilection for a fusion of disparate sources was fundamental to Chagall's artistic expression as well as being a central part of the creative discourse of other leaders of the modern Jewish revolution, especially modernist Yiddish and Hebrew writers.[6] Similarly, Chagall and other Jewish modernist painters around that time tended to incorporate freely and indiscriminately various styles, which often resulted in a virtual hodgepodge of images and motifs. Chagall's painting in these early years of his career resists easy classification and cannot be seen as purely cubist or expressionist or anything else. In a discussion of some of the leading modernist Jewish artists working in Poland immediately after World War I, including Marek Shvarts, Yankl Adler, Yitzkhok Broyner, and Henokh Bartshinski (who were all heavily influenced by Chagall), Seth Wolitz asserts that they "must be understood as rallying around the contemporary isms."[7] They eagerly employed various modernist trends without necessarily associating themselves with one rather than the other. Some of them, such as Shvarts and Bartshinski, under the influence of the apocalyptic poetry of their contemporaries Grinberg and Ravitsh, also began to "exploit the expressionist Christological theme."[8]

Avram Kampf suggests that Chagall's use of the image of the crucified figure in his *Golgotha* "is a result of Chagall's migration to the West and the reevaluation by Jewish artists and men of letters of their attitude towards the figure of Christ. Like many of the younger generation around the turn of the century, Chagall was powerfully attracted by the light which shone from the West."[9] He adds that these young Jewish artists like Chagall "portray Christ, venerated by the outside world, as a brother, a fellow artist, a performer of miracles."[10] Thus, Kampf posits that a direct link can be observed between the Jewish artists' zealous embrace of new forms and styles, especially Western European ones, and their preoccupation with the images of Jesus and the cross. In this light, Chagall's *Golgotha* embodies "much of the tension and conflict which the Enlightenment and the processes behind it brought into the Jewish community."[11] This implies that the iconography, symbols, and forms employed by Chagall in this painting somehow reflect the Enlightenment struggle to break "out of the ghetto" of traditional Jewish culture and society and find a creative home in the surrounding European culture. According to Kampf then, for Chagall and other modern Jewish artists and writers, their interest in Christian images was an essential part of the process of cultural assimilation.

This interpretation, however, tells only part of the story, as this process was far more complex than Kampf suggests. While painting or writing about Jesus was absolutely part of the Jewish artist's rite of passage into modern European culture, the meaning the Christ-figure took on in his work reflected the evolving process of the artist asserting his unique Jewish vision of European culture and its artistic traditions as well. In a letter from 1949 in which Chagall discusses his ongoing fascination with the figure of Christ, he reveals some of the underlying factors that motivated his painting of *Golgotha*: "The symbolical figure of Christ was always very near to me, and I was determined to bring it out of my young heart. I wanted to show Christ as an innocent child. Now I see him otherwise. . . . When I painted this picture in Paris, I was trying to free myself psychologically and plastically from the conception of the icon painters and from Russian art in general."[12]

This confession not only demonstrates the centrality of the Christ-figure in Chagall's artistic imagination, but also uncovers the tension Chagall experienced regarding his place in the Russian artistic tradition and his struggle to break free from it. This struggle to set oneself free from an established and possibly constraining tradition, be it in literature or the visual arts, is not necessarily unique, but in the case of Chagall and other Jewish artists it carried a heightened significance. For the Jewish artist it was often necessary to embrace aesthetic forms and genres from non-Jewish culture when there was no true avenue in Jewish culture for a certain type of artistic expression. However, the desire to move beyond mere mimicry of non-Jewish forms and styles in order to create a highly personal or, in some cases, distinctly Jewish, modern style also propelled these artists. This process could often be multilayered, as with Chagall himself, who initially turned from the Russian traditions that had originally inspired him to Western European influences such as cubism, before arriving at his own distinctive style.

It is important to keep in mind that, especially in the generation preceding Chagall, Jewish visual artists had no choice but to adopt Western styles and forms in creating their art. As a result of the Jewish prohibition against creating "graven images," most forms of visual art had traditionally been underdeveloped (if not altogether nonexistent) in Jewish society, especially in Eastern Europe.[13] Therefore, for the modern Jew to turn toward sculpting or the painting of human images was seen as an a priori radical act, more so than pursuing secular forms of Jewish literature. It was only in the wake of the Haskalah and with the onset of secularization in the nineteenth century that individual Jews began to take up the plastic arts as a serious vocation. Jews who chose to pursue the visual arts were often rapidly excluded from traditional Jewish culture, and typically had to hone their craft in predominantly non-Jewish settings, studying in various European art schools or with non-Jewish artists.[14] Indeed, one of the earliest groups of modern Jewish artists in nineteenth-century Germany was known as the Nazarenes, and consisted mostly of Jewish converts to Christianity who "tried to revive German Christian art."[15] Even though modern Jewish writers were, typically, enlightened intellectuals who sharply criticized traditional Jewish life, their milieu and reading audience remained largely traditional Jews. For Jewish artists this was not necessarily the case, as the medium of their art allowed their audience to be much wider, including the non-Jewish community. Also, unlike the modern Jewish author, the Jewish artist had fewer premodern Jewish traditions on which to draw in creating his art, making it more necessary and understandable that he would turn to Western models both for images and inspiration. Often chief among these models were artistic representations of Jesus and the crucifixion.

The late nineteenth-century Russian Jewish artist Mark Antokolsky (1843–1902), who was the first prominent Jewish sculptor to emerge from Eastern Europe, epitomizes the knotty predicament of the modern Jewish artist.[16] In the life and art of Antokolsky we see the complicated negotiations artists like him had to perform between Jewish and Christian, traditional and modern modes of artistic expression and identification. Born in Vilna in 1843, Antokolsky subscribed whole-heartedly to the ideals of the Haskalah, and identified himself as an enlightened Jew. He changed his name from Mordechai to Marcus, wrote an autobiography (the quintessential act of the nineteenth-century Russian *maskil*) and moved to St. Petersburg to pursue a career in sculpting.[17] His choice of sculpture as an artistic medium as well as of images to sculpt drove a wedge between him and the Jewish community. Even though he maintained an emphatically positive Jewish identity and continued to be traditionally observant, many Jewish writers harshly rebuked him for his artistic works, and "he was even accused of treason to the national ideals of the Jewish people."[18] While Antokolsky famously incorporated many Jewish themes in his art, some of his earliest works were copies of Christian icons and of New Testament images produced by Western artists, as well as commissioned crucifixes.

Antokolsky's first "original Jesus" was his 1873 sculpture *Ecce Homo* or *Christ before the People* (fig. 3).[19] In *Ecce Homo*, Antokolsky depicts Jesus with stereotypical Jewish (Semitic) facial features, side curls (*payot*), a skullcap, and an ancient Jewish costume.[20] Instead of establishing himself as an artist working fully within the Western tradition by sculpting his first original Christ-figure, Antokolsky boldly alienated himself from both Jews and Christians by distinctly sculpting Jesus as a Jew. In a letter written while he was still working on *Ecce Homo*, Antokolsky anticipated the rebuke he would encounter from Jews as well as Christians, "I imagine to myself how Jews and Christians alike will rise against me. Jews will probably say, 'How is it that he made Christ?' And Christians will say 'What kind of Christ did he make?'"[21] For Antokolsky, Jesus was a powerful Jewish figure who brought a great spiritual message to the Jewish people, a message that had been misinterpreted and corrupted by his Gentile followers through their age-old persecution of Jesus' own people, the Jews. In this spirit, Antokolsky conceived of and portrayed Jesus as a "purely Jewish type,"[22] partly as a declaration to his Christian audience that their maltreatment of Jesus' Jewish brothers was unjust. In creating something radically new—a sculpture of Jesus the Jew made by a Jewish artist—Antokolsky professed to be reclaiming something that he considered to be an integral part of the Jewish national patrimony and historical birthright. Thus, Jewish works of art such as Antokolsky's that incorporated Judaized images of Jesus "must be read as operating somewhere in between resistant affirmation of cultural specificity and total accommodation to the host culture."[23] In other words, Antokolsky's *Ecce Homo* was, to use Homi Bhabha's phrase, an "in-between space" that served to create a new Jewish cultural self-definition, and which incorporated the majority Christian and minority Jewish culture, while simultaneously rebelling against both of them.[24]

Antokolsky was not alone in such endeavors, as other Jewish artists of that time were also creating new forms of Jewish visual art, including images of the Jewish Jesus. The Polish Jewish artist Maurycy Gottlieb (1856–79) closely followed in the footsteps of Antokolsky, depicting Jesus as unmistakably Jewish in two paintings—*Jesus before His Judges* (1877) and *Jesus Preaching* (1878–79).[25] Gottlieb considered himself an enlightened Jew who had left the ghetto behind, transforming himself into an emancipated "Polish patriot."[26] In one painting, Gottlieb even went as far as portraying himself wearing Polish national costume, revealing the strong urge to become integrated in society at large, an urge that often dominated the thoughts and actions of Russian/Polish *maskilim* in the nineteenth century. For Gottlieb, there was no better way to integrate himself amongst the Polish people—who saw themselves as the Christ of the nations—than to include images of Jesus in his art. However, by painting Jesus in traditional Jewish garb, Gottlieb was explicitly rejecting the Polish image of Christ in favor of the Jewish Jesus. His own enlightened beliefs and artistic vocation estranged him from traditional Judaism and Jewish culture, but his persistent Jewish self-identification also alienated him from the Polish culture to which he aspired; anti-Semitic elements within Polish society made it nearly impossible for him to assimilate as he sought. He realized he would never be accepted as a true Polish patriot. In this light, Gottlieb's portrayal of the Jewish Jesus contained an apologetic, if not polemical, component typical of so many of the modern Jewish attempts at portraying Jesus, such as Geiger's and Graetz's writings (the latter of which both Antokolsky and Gottlieb were likely familiar with). In a letter written in 1878 Gottlieb hints at what he was attempting to accomplish

with his Jesus paintings: "How much I would like . . . to make peace
between Poles and Jews, for the history of both people is one of pain
and suffering."[27]

By asserting the Jewishness of Jesus in such visually striking terms,
Gottlieb was actually undertaking a far more complex process of assimilation than is usually recognized. While assimilation usually involves erasing all outer signs (if not inner ones as well) of the minority
Self in order to become part of the majority Other, Gottlieb's Jesus
and, for that matter, most of the images of the Jewish Jesus created by
Jews in the modern period were meant to inscribe the minority Self by
locating it at the center of the majority Other. The work of Gottlieb
as well as other Jewish artists who emphasized the Jewishness of Jesus
attested to the paradoxical plight of the modern Jew vis-à-vis the dominant Western culture. Modern enlightened Jews were frequently unable
to achieve full acceptance in Western society and culture, even when
fully assimilating its norms, if they maintained any form of positive
Jewish self-identification. Consequently, in the field of art and literature
many enlightened Jews went from mimicking the norms of the dominant culture, which perpetuated their marginal status, to transforming
these norms into something distinctively Jewish: in this case, the Jewish Jesus.[28]

Another contemporary of Antokolsky's added a new dimension to
the Jewish depiction of Jesus in modern art. The American Jewish
sculptor Moses Ezekiel (1844–1917), who, like Antokolsky, spent much
of his life in Rome, sculpted a scene of the crucifixion, which neither
Antokolsky nor Gottlieb had done—limiting themselves to images of
Jesus before the crucifixion—and explicitly identified the crucified Jesus with the Jews. The image was a reworking of a piece, *Israel, or the
Wandering Jew*, which he had sculpted as an art student in Berlin in
1873. This included a crucifixion scene along with other biblical images
such as Moses and David. The Wandering Jew occupied the center of
the relief, with the crucified figure off to the side.[29] The Jesus-figure
on his cross is depicted as springing from the spilled blood of the last
king of Israel, who is heaped at the feet of the crucified one. As in Jewish theological writings from the late nineteenth century, especially in
Reform circles, the Wandering Jew is portrayed as a counterpoint to

Christ; he, as the representative of Israel as a whole, is the historical suffering servant, the witness to God's unity and the eternal covenant with Israel.

In 1903, in the aftermath of the Kishinev pogroms in Russia, which elicited much protest and artistic response from the Jewish community in America, Ezekiel reworked his sculpture, renaming it simply *Israel*. In the new sculpture, he repositioned the crucified figure to the center, and explicitly depicted him as Jewish with his hands raised as if to perform the priestly benediction and his circumcised penis visible under his loin cloth; Jesus and the Wandering Jew gaze at each other in the sculpture, and the word "Israel" is inscribed below the crucifixion, implying "that Israel is Christ crucified."[30] Ezekiel's 1903 sculpture was one of the first Jewish works of art to depict the crucifixion in full, rather than depicting only the bust of Christ on the cross or Jesus preaching, and was therefore quite controversial, and not warmly received in the Jewish community in New York.[31] Amishai-Maisels claims that Ezekiel's *Israel* served as a prototype for later Jewish artists' depictions of the crucifixion and that its "reproduction in *Ost und West* had a profound effect on Chagall and other twentieth-century Jewish artists."[32] Indeed, Ezekiel was one of the first Jewish visual artists to explicitly link the crucifixion with historical Jewish suffering.[33]

In the same year as Ezekiel's *Israel* appeared, Ephraim Moses Lilien (1874–1925), a Galician-born illustrator and printmaker, combined Christological imagery with more traditional Jewish martyrological symbolism in his print *Dedicated to the Martyrs of Kishinev* (1903, fig. 4). Also created in response to the Kishinev pogroms of 1903 (just as many of the poems discussed in the previous chapters were written in response to the pogroms of 1919–21), Lilien's picture draws on the image of medieval Jews sacrificed at the stake, an image that was commonly associated with the Akedah motif in the Jewish cultural consciousness. The Akedah motif is further enhanced by the presence of the angel, who is bestowing the "kiss of death" on the martyr's forehead. Lilien also subtly incorporates Christological motifs by depicting the angel's wings perpendicular to the body of the martyr, creating the suggestion of a cross. In addition, he includes a moon-like halo over the martyr's head, as well as thorns that adorn the frame of the picture, alluding to

Jesus' crown of thorns. David Roskies persuasively asserts that "this sentimental, syncretistic approach to Jewish catastrophe went hand in glove with the idealistic appropriation of Jesus."[34] In this way, Lilien created a potent visual symbol of contemporary Jewish martyrdom by blending together traditional Jewish and Christian concepts and images.[35]

The power of such visual syncretism was not lost on Marc Chagall, who followed in the footsteps of these Jewish artists, but went even further in his use of crucifixion imagery and the figure of the crucified Christ. His use of the cross and crucifixion motifs ranged from intensely personal and autobiographical, to particularistically Jewish, to broadly humanistic and universalist, sometimes all in the same work (e.g., *Golgotha* and *White Crucifixion*). The tension between these various modes of discourse epitomizes the struggles that plagued Jewish modernist culture and, at times, even seems to be one of its defining characteristics. Regarding the tension between the Jewish and the universal content of Jewish art, Chagall stated that "if a painter is Jewish and paints life, how can there help being Jewish elements in his work! But if he is a good painter, there will be more than that. The Jewish element will be there but his art will tend to approach the universal."[36] The combination of the personal, the Jewish (particularist), and the Christian (European/universal) are seen as necessary for a Jewish artist to make his work universally valid.

This certainly rings true for a visual artist like Chagall, but nonetheless, it was also a serious concern for Yiddish writers who included universal, European, and Christian elements in their writing, not in order to reach a universal audience, but in order to transform themselves and their Jewish reading audience into a more universalist one. As Yiddish modernists often conceived of things European or Western as being "universal," Western secular humanism in Yiddish was often the outcome of their cultural creativity; the question of Jewish content or essence was always a troubling one. For several of the early Soviet Yiddish critics (1918–24), "modern Yiddish verse received critical acclaim in direct proportion to the absence of Jewish consciousness. Universality for these critics meant the assimilation of European culture and the ignoring of Jewish ethos and ethnos."[37] However, a large number, if not the majority, of these Yiddish modernists aspired to "fus[e] the particular with the universal,"[38] resulting in a new Jewish literary and cultural discourse with radically expanded boundaries and forms. Chagall himself was an integral figure in the Soviet Yiddish modernist scene of those years—he lived in Russia until 1922—contributing illustrations to several Yiddish literary publications and creating artwork for the Jewish theater in Moscow as well.[39]

In an analysis of Chagall's *The Falling Angel* of 1947 (fig. 5), which depicts certain traditional Jewish figures like an old Jewish man holding a Torah alongside Christian figures like a Madonna and Child and Christ on the cross, Ingo Walther and Rainer Metzger assert that Chagall's "Jewish vision, his personal life-story, and motifs of Christian redemption are incorporated into a programmatic statement that sums up Chagall's entire oeuvre."[40] Moreover, they claim that the combination of these diverse images "represent[s] Chagall's unceasing endeavor to locate one single, truthful, universally valid visual formula."[41] The continuous quest for a universal syncretism allowed Chagall to aesthetically reconcile the Torah and the cross, just as Ansky had charged Zhitlovsky and Asch with doing in 1909. This search for the universal, which unquestionably animated Chagall, also precipitated the need for new images and archetypes, which he as a modern artist could employ in creating this universal vision.

As we have noted in the previous chapters, in order to create a vibrant vocabulary for modern secular culture, traditional symbols and concepts were reinterpreted and invested with new meanings and associations. Thus, Chagall's interpretive use of traditional symbols is important to consider here. Franz Meyer (the definitive Chagall scholar, and his son-in-law) claims that "when Chagall takes over an accepted symbol he is determined to 'shatter' the significational context which has hitherto sustained that symbol."[42] For Chagall, this often meant combining Jewish, Christian, autobiographical, European modernist, and Russian iconic sources in creating a wholly new visual form. It also involved exploding and subverting older forms in an attempt to create new ones. I agree with those who argue that Chagall was interested in the Jesus-figure and the crucifixion as universal symbols, and claim that Chagall always strove for the universal over the particular.[43] In this same way, the cross became the quintessential symbol of universal suffering and the ultimate emblem of modernist angst for numerous avant-garde Yiddish writers as well. However, Chagall, more than most of his contemporaries, also utilized the image of the crucifixion in depicting the collective Jewish experience, and in highly individualized, autobiographical terms, sometimes even portraying himself as the man (or child) on the cross.

By briefly surveying several critical analyses of Chagall's *Golgotha*, as well as some of the artist's own comments on it, we can observe some of the many different elements—personal, Jewish, universal—at work in the painting. In later comments, Chagall saw his 1912 painting as the "first in a series of Golgothas or Crucifixions," and he reveals that as early as 1908 he began to conceive of Jesus as the ideal symbol of Jewish martyrdom, both ancient and contemporary: "For me, Christ has always symbolized the true type of Jewish martyr. That is how I understood him in 1908 when I used this figure for the first time. . . . It was under the influence of the pogroms."[44] Some critics have endorsed Chagall's declaration, claiming that his *Golgotha* depicts Jesus as a symbol of Jewish martyrdom, and that the Jesus-figure of the painting has "twisted facial features bearing the marks of a martyred Jew" while the figures at the foot of the cross represent "typical bearded, cap-wearing shtetl-Jews."[45] Amishai-Maisels concurs, at least in part, claiming that *Golgotha* is in some way an artistic response to the anti-Semitism Chagall encountered growing up in Russia, including a pogrom he witnessed in Vitebsk. She sees the Christ-figure of the painting as being mourned by his Jewish parents, substantiating her claim that this painting was a response to Jewish suffering, personal and collective. She further contends that Chagall's *Golgotha* "has always been interpreted as a highly personal statement,"[46] and she cites artistic precedents for his personal identification with Jesus, such as Gauguin's *Self-Portrait as Christ at Gethsemane* (1889).

However, others claim that the crucified child at the heart of the painting is "too vague, too abstract to symbolize either a crucified Christ (theologically) or a martyred Jew (historically)."[47] In fact, some critics argue that this figure should not be seen explicitly as Christ, but as the universal, innocent child who suffers on account of the world's cruelty.[48]

In a sense then, Chagall had already expropriated the image of the suffering Christ by 1912 in an attempt to create a new visual archetype of suffering. Susan Compton also endorses this view, arguing that Chagall, under the influence of the Russian poet V. Ivanov, attempted to transform the historically specific symbol of the crucifixion into a more general one. She writes: "[T]he moment of reconciliation between God and man, ascribed by Christians to the crucifixion of Jesus, could have been adopted in this picture as a schema for encompassing all myths of a suffering god. The artist has generalized the concept (embodied in its more usual form in his drawing) and replaced the figure by that of a child, flanked by magical-looking personages."[49] Chagall himself commented that "only a child had its place on the cross, and that was enough for me," and explained that "in the exact sense there was no cross but a blue child in the air. The cross interested me less."[50] Once he had rendered the cross as such an abstract symbol, Chagall was no longer limited in how he depicted it or in what meaning he attached to it.[51]

In *Golgotha* many of the traditional iconic motifs present in Chagall's earlier sketches were eliminated or significantly altered: the skull is gone, as are the nails, bleeding, and inscription on the cross, and the cross itself has almost vanished. The image of the crucified one is also highly unconventional. Supporting an autobiographical understanding of the painting, Chagall stated in 1950 that "when I painted Christ's parents I was thinking of my own parents. The bearded man is the child's father. He is my father."[52] It has been suggested that Chagall painted himself as the child on the cross, visually representing the episode of his own birth, which he writes about in the opening pages of his memoir *My Life*, where he claims that he was born dead, and later came to life.[53] In this light, for Chagall, *Golgotha* was a depiction of his passage from the realm of the dead into the realm of the living with the open arms of his parents and the breast of his mother waiting to greet him.[54] It is Chagall's own personal resurrection scene, his coming to life at the time of his birth. All of these competing theories as to the significance of the crucifixion theme in Chagall's *Golgotha*—Jewish martyr, suffering child, the resurrected infant Chagall—bear witness to the multiplicity of meanings that the artist could ascribe to this powerful image. Like the poet Itzik Manger, Chagall shattered the significational context of the cross, establishing it as a visual metaphor with myriad meanings; it could be at once a universal, a Jewish, and a personal symbol. Indeed, in the more than one hundred of his paintings that incorporate the crucifixion motif, Chagall freely blends these three components in transforming the crucifixion into a new visual archetype.

Chagall and/on the Cross

Surprisingly, after his *Golgotha* of 1912 Chagall did not incorporate the crucifixion motif in his work for approximately twenty-five years.[55] While numerous Yiddish writers turned to the figure of Jesus and the image matrix associated with his passion during the tumultuous years of the First World War and the Russian Revolution, especially in response to the bloody pogroms in Ukraine, Chagall only returned to the crucifixion theme at the outset of World War II. Beginning with *White Crucifixion* (1938), he created a series of paintings in which the man on the cross was depicted as a quintessentially Jewish martyr, as well as numerous paintings in which the crucified Jesus represented the horrors of war in general. Also in 1938, Chagall composed a Yiddish poem, "My Tears" ("Mayne trern"), in which he expresses his own personal mood of sorrow by resorting to images of the cross:

> I carry my cross every day,
> I am led by the hand and driven on,
> Night darkens around me,
> Have you abandoned me, my God? Why?[56]

Like Jesus, the poetic "I" in Chagall's poem bears the burden of the cross and feels abandoned by his God. In the same poem, he also addresses the problem of how to paint the world around him, asking God whether he should paint what is in his heart, or "cities that burn, brothers who flee,"[57] images that Chagall depicted in numerous paintings during the war years. This poetic musing suggests the struggle Chagall must have faced between the personal and the national forces in his work: what was "in his heart" over against "brothers who flee." Indeed, besides depicting scenes of collective Jewish suffering on a grand scale, Chagall created several landscapes reflecting his own individual plight and personal pain, frequently expressed in Christological terms. Beginning in 1940 Chagall produced numerous paintings that depict a painter (sometimes bearing a resemblance to Chagall) as the crucified one, or related to the figure of Jesus in a highly intimate way. By examining some of these works, we can see how Chagall's sense of his artistic self was bound up in his understanding of the crucified Christ.

In 1940 Chagall completed *The Painter Crucified* (fig. 6) as part of a series of four self-portraits spanning the years 1938–40. Meyer identifies in these paintings one of Chagall's major motifs—the self-portrait at the easel—and claims that in *The Painter Crucified* the Christ-figure

> is personalized as the symbol of the intensification and deepening of the pain of every single individual, represented as the pain felt by the painter himself through his sympathy with the fate of his nation and the horrors of war, and at the same time the symbol of the pain inherent in artistic creation. In fact, since then Chagall has always had a more intense perception of the ambivalence of creation as such. Though it brings joy and satisfaction, it always involves dedication and self-sacrifice.[58]

This analysis alludes to the same sort of sentiments reflected in Chagall's poem of 1938; the artist conceives of himself as a suffering servant who represents the anguish of his nation while simultaneously expressing his own inner moods, which occasionally results in a conflict of obligations.

In *The Painter Crucified*, the central image of the artist/Jesus crucified on a simple wooden cross alongside his easel does not appear to resemble Chagall, precluding an explicitly autobiographical interpretation of the painting. Nor, with its short black mustache, beard and hair, and wide-open eyes, does it invoke the classical Western Jesus, but rather the Byzantine Christ, which became one of the standard "Christ-faces" in Chagall's paintings from that period on.[59] His right arm is free and reaches for a brush from his palette by his side (yet there is another right arm, although fainter, that remains on the cross), while the left side of his body is fastened to the cross, suggesting that the artist is part captive, part free man. Yet, his freedom only comes after a struggle to liberate himself from the cross, which symbolizes the enormous burdens and responsibilities inherent in artistic creation. Above the painter/Christ are two hands coming out of the sky, seemingly God's hands blessing the figure directly below in the manner of the traditional priestly benediction. This implies that the artist—like the High Priest—is God's anointed intermediary on earth, an idea similar to the conception of the poet as prophet expressed by Uri Tsvi Grinberg and other Yiddish modernist poets. There is also an inverted row of houses directly above the woman-cow figure, possibly introducing the element of national tragedy that so pervades Chagall's paintings during this period (1938–44). Although the image is faint here, it reminds the viewer of the tableau of overturned, burning houses in Chagall's *White Crucifixion* where they clearly represent the initial destruction of Jewish communal life in Europe. However, in *The Painter Crucified*, Chagall foregrounds the suffering of the individual artist rather than focusing on the plight of the nation. On the easel is an Entombment painting, which in traditional Christian art depicts the scene of Jesus' burial, suggesting that while the historical Jesus is dead and buried, others—like the artist himself—now sacrifice themselves and suffer in the same fashion that Jesus once did.[60] Chagall appropriated the power of the crucifixion image to convey the artist's sense of self-sacrifice. This should not be understood necessarily as a religious or spiritual identification with Christ and his suffering, but rather as an individualized application of a universal theme: the artist expresses his subjective condition by employing the visual symbolism of Christ's passion.[61]

In another of his self-portraits from 1940 Chagall composed a very different type of crucifixion scene. His *The Painter and Christ* (1940, fig. 7) depicts the artist—this time in Chagall's likeness—with palette in hand, sitting in front of a painting of a crucified figure and a Wandering Jew. Unlike most of Chagall's crucifixion paintings, which are filled with a plethora of images, the canvas within this self-portrait is relatively bare, containing only the crucified figure on his cross with a ladder leaning against it, and the old, hunched Jew with his cane off to the side. The man on the cross bears little resemblance to traditional Christian depictions of Jesus (Western or Eastern); he has a rounded face and slanted eyes, hinting at Chagall's affinity for cubism, which render him stereotypically Asian, while the *tallis* (prayer shawl) covering his loins denotes his Jewishness.

Significantly, the artist is turned away from his painting with his hand cupped next to his face, a sign that he is purposely averting his gaze from the images on his canvas. This turning away suggests the ambivalence Chagall may have felt in painting crucifixion images, especially when he combined them, as he does here, with archetypically Jewish figures like the Wandering Jew. This ambivalence might imply that Chagall felt somewhat guilty about portraying Jesus-figures or, possibly, that he feared the repercussions of inscribing them into his newly created cache of Jewish iconographic types, especially in the midst of the Nazi onslaught against the Jews of Europe. The very title of the painting suggests that Chagall is somehow more connected to the image of Christ in the foreground than to the Wandering Jew in the background; they are kindred spirits in suffering.

In *Descent from the Cross* (1941, fig. 8), Chagall adapted a traditional Western iconographical genre by incorporating some of his stock images and inserting an autobiographical touch—placing a fragment of his own name (Marc Ch . . .) on the INRI tablet—which, as Meyer suggests, "makes the reference to his own, in the artistic sense vicarious, suffering still more explicit."[62] Chagall transformed the traditional scene of Jesus being taken down from the cross into a distinctly personalized and Judaized one. He depicts a carnivalesque bird-headed man removing the Jesus figure—again adorned with a *tallis* on his loins—from the cross with the help of a woman who holds his arm; while Chagall often painted animal-headed figures, this image compellingly evokes the well-known *Birds' Head Haggadah* (ca. 1300), and is thereby linked to premodern forms of Jewish art. Furthermore, the Jewish figures in traditional attire at the foot of the cross and the capsized houses on either side add elements of contemporary Jewish life to the painting. The figure who significantly alters and personalizes the scene is the angel approaching the Jesus/artist figure with a brush and palette in hand, again conflating the figure of Jesus with that of the artist himself—already identified as Chagall (Marc Ch . . .).

While in *The Painter Crucified* of the previous year the artist on the cross was able to reach his palette and brushes, and presumably paint the picture that stands on his easel, the implication here is that only when freed from the restrictions of the cross and its suffering can the artist resume his painting with the help of the angel. This rescuing angel also evokes the binding of Isaac in which the angel provides the means of Isaac's redemption by staying Abraham's hand before he can sacrifice his son.[63] In 1950 and 1959 Chagall returned to this theme with two new paintings entitled *Descent from the Cross*, each one with the image of Chagall the artist in the corner of the painting—not on the cross—watching the scene unfold. Chagall painted the first *Descent from the Cross* of 1941 shortly after fleeing France for America, so his own individual experience of the war reflected that of the Jewish collective experience: he himself had become one of the "brothers who flee." Thus, his conflict between painting what was "in his heart" and "cities that burn" was momentarily resolved. The timing of the painting, coming immediately after Chagall's escape from the war in Europe, also suggests that this experience amounted to Chagall's own metaphoric "descent from the cross" as he had so narrowly averted being caught in the impending Nazi "crucifixion" of the Jews.

In *The Soul of the City* (1945, fig. 9), painted in America at the end of the war, Chagall utilized the symbolism of the crucifixion in portraying a very personalized, tragic scene. He employed the motif of the artist at his easel, with the Janus-faced artist (who resembles Chagall) pointing triumphantly to the crucifixion scene painted on the easel. His green, second face looks at a white angel/bride figure (possibly a reference to Chagall's wife Bella, who had died the year before), who swirls and floats like a comet out of a red Torah scroll suspended in the air below two lions bearing the tablets of the Law. The face of the specter/Bella is staring at the three candles in the lower corner of the painting. The background for these figures is a deserted gray village scene, much sparer and more somber than typical in Chagall's earlier village scenes. The man on the cross has a unique look, not bearing any resemblance to Chagall's earlier Jesus-figures or incorporating traditional elements of crucifixion scenes. His legs are twisted and his face is clean-shaven, with short brown hair. His facial expression is ambiguous and there is very little detail on the face. He seems to be smiling slightly, and it is impossible to tell whether his eyes are open or closed.

It is as if Chagall wanted to depict a generic human form on the cross (yet once more wearing a *tallis* for a loincloth, marking his Jewishness), again distancing his painting from traditional Christian and artistic uses of the crucifixion. The artist's mourning and longing for his dead wife, who floats nearby but is beyond his grasp, is articulated by his painting of the crucifixion, invoking not the pain of Christ or universal suffering, but Chagall's own personal grief. According to Meyer this painting was based on a sketch that Chagall made in 1940 as part of his series of self-portraits at the easel, which included *The Painter and Christ* and *The Painter Crucified*.[64] Unlike in *The Painter and Christ*, however, here the artist gestures proudly at the crucifixion he has executed on his canvas. Yet, signs of his ambivalence remain, as indicated by the artist's second head, which turns away from the painting on the easel.

In yet another self-portrait done two years later, *Self-Portrait with Wall Clock* (1947, fig. 10), the artist—half man, half animal—paints a sensuous scene of a bride in white nestled against a green-tinted Jesus-figure standing with arms outstretched in the crucifixion pose, although the cross itself is barely visible. The bride has her hand clasped over Jesus' heart as he stands, eyes closed, with a slight grimace on his otherwise serene face. A partially obscured rooster is above the two lovers, and a candelabra with three crooked candles appears at the bottom corner of the scene, with a distant village lightly sketched in the background. Outside the canvas, the red animal head and the blue human head both stare inexpressively at their creation while a floating clock with two blue, angelic, wing-like arms protruding seems to bless the whole scene. This painting, even more than *The Soul of the City*, imparts a personal, emotional landscape, equal parts love and longing, as the crucified figure is unable to return the affection of the bride and the artist looks upon his creation with detachment and a faint sense of sadness. By calling this painting a self-portrait Chagall once again articulates his affinity with Jesus, the would-be lover he depicts on the canvas; he seems to identify equally with both the artist and the crucified one. The fact that images of chaos and destruction from the recently concluded war are absent from the painting attests to the gradual personalization of the Christ-motif in Chagall's postwar paintings in which Jesus functions as "a symbol both of the artist and of the suffering of humanity in general and not only of the martyred Jew."[65]

With his *In Front of the Picture* (1968–71, fig. 11), Chagall once again returned to the theme of the artist at his easel, combining certain characteristic images of his in a radically new way. This time the painter is an animal-headed man while a figure resembling Chagall himself is the model crucified to a cross on the easel. The writing (in Hebrew letters) at the top of the cross spells out "Chagall" and the two figures to the left of the cross are depictions of his parents. Stock Chagall images like brides and angels also appear in this picture, but, in another new turn, Chagall's face appears behind the bride to the left of the easel, and in the sky above with two big, white hands cradling it. A calm village scene is vaguely delineated in the background at the foot of the cross. The wooden bar of the easel creeps out over the top of the painting, appearing to be a continuation of the cross on the canvas. Yet, despite the somber gray tones and the use of the crucifixion motif, there are no explicit scenes of external tragedy or suffering surrounding the central image of Chagall on the cross; this painting has the feel of autobiographic reflection—Chagall was over eighty when he painted it—with no explicit national allusions. The crucified Chagall figure is bending his left hand back in order to clasp his chest, immediately over his heart, alluding to the internal emotional nature of this entire scene.

This crucifixion has none of the traditional iconic traces or sweeping tableaus of Jewish history that frequent Chagall's other crucifixion paintings. *In Front of the Picture* reveals how Chagall had managed to appropriate the symbolism of the cross in order to create a richly personal scene that expresses the artist's inner feelings and reminiscences. It is extremely difficult to distinguish between personal and national images when assessing Chagall's oeuvre, yet given the paintings we have briefly examined here, we can see the importance of the crucifixion motif for Chagall in establishing a personal sphere in his work—in conveying what was "in his heart." For Chagall, the image of Jesus on the cross and the symbolism of his passion became a symbol of self-understanding.

Figure 1. Marc Chagall, *Crucifixion*, ca. 1908. Pen on paper.

Figure 2. Marc Chagall, *Golgotha* (*Dedicated to Christ*), 1912. Oil on canvas.
©2006 Artists Rights Society (ARS), New York / ADAGP, Paris (photo: Art
Resource, NY).

Figure 3. Mark Antokolsky, *Ecce Homo*, 1873. Tretyakov Gallery, Moscow.

Figure 4. Ephraim Moses Lilien, *Dedicated to the Martyrs of Kishinev*, 1903.
From Maxim Gorki's *Zbornik*.

Figure 5. Marc Chagall, *The Falling Angel*, 1923–33–47. Oil on canvas. ©2006
Artists Rights Society (ARS), New York / ADAGP, Paris.

Figure 6. Marc Chagall, *The Painter Crucified*, 1940. Gouache on paper.
©2006 Artists Rights Society (ARS), New York / ADAGP, Paris.

Figure 7. Marc Chagall, *The Painter and Christ*, 1940. Gouache on paper.
©2006 Artists Rights Society (ARS), New York / ADAGP, Paris.

Figure 8. Marc Chagall, *Descent from the Cross*, 1941. Gouache on paper.
©2006 Artists Rights Society (ARS), New York / ADAGP, Paris.

Figure 9. Marc Chagall. *The Soul of the City*, 1945. Oil on canvas. ©2006 Artists Rights Society (ARS), New York / ADAGP, Paris.

Figure 10. Marc Chagall, *Self-Portrait with Wall Clock*, 1947. Oil on canvas.
©2006 Artists Rights Society (ARS), New York / ADAGP, Paris.

Figure 11. Marc Chagall, *In Front of the Picture*, 1968–71. Oil on canvas.
©2006 Artists Rights Society (ARS), New York / ADAGP, Paris.

Figure 12. Marc Chagall, *White Crucifixion*, 1938. Oil on canvas.
©2006 Artists Rights Society (ARS), New York / ADAGP, Paris.

Figure 13. Marc Chagall, *Exodus*, 1952–66. Oil on canvas. ©2006 Artists Rights Society (ARS), New York / ADAGP, Paris (photo: Art Resource, NY).

Figure 14. Marc Chagall, *The Martyr*, 1940–41. Oil on canvas. ©2006 Artists Rights Society (ARS), New York / ADAGP, Paris.

Figure 15. Marc Chagall, *Yellow Crucifixion*, 1943. Oil on canvas.
©2006 Artists Rights Society (ARS), New York / ADAGP, Paris
(photo: Art Resource, NY).

Figure 16. Marc Chagall, *The Crucified*, 1944. Gouache on paper.
©2006 Artists Rights Society (ARS), New York / ADAGP, Paris.

Crucifixion as Jewish Catastrophe

Chagall's personal identification with the crucifixion and autobiographical application of this image were counterbalanced by a more overtly national-historical usage of this theme. His series of crucifixion paintings and sketches from 1938 to 1944 also graphically incorporated a Christological depiction of Jewish suffering during the war that explicitly identified the image matrix of Christ's passion with the contemporary victimization of Europe's Jews. During this period Chagall produced approximately ten such crucifixion pieces, in which the national and political context is foregrounded over Chagall's personal identification with the crucified.[66] The first and ultimately best known of these crucifixion paintings is Chagall's *White Crucifixion* (1938, fig. 12), which is significant for a number of reasons: it is Chagall's first crucifixion painting in twenty-five years (with one exception); it is his first explicit depiction of a markedly Jewish Jesus, with a *tallis* as his loincloth and the Aramaic inscription "Jesus the Nazarene, King of the Jews" below the more common Latin INRI;[67] it is also his first in what would become a long cycle of paintings in which he employs a crucifixion scene as part of his depiction of Jewish victimization during World War II. In fact, this painting should be seen as initiating a specific subgenre of Chagall's work, the Jewish catastrophe scene, in which several stock images are typically depicted: the Wandering Jew, a man fleeing with a Torah, a mother with a child in her arms on the run, a shtetl burning, desecrated Torah scrolls, a throng of Jewish refugees, and a man (or men) on the cross.[68]

White Crucifixion, like several of Chagall's subsequent crucifixion/ Jewish catastrophe paintings, has an explicit narrative component, relating a number of contemporary episodes of anti-Jewish persecution and wartime tragedy. Amishai-Maisels has attempted to match several of Chagall's crucifixion paintings to specific events in the course of World War II, in some cases more persuasively than in others.[69] However, for our purposes, we will focus primarily on the symbolic significance of these works rather than the particular historical events that might have inspired them, though it is important to acknowledge that they are most likely inspired by such contemporary events. Just as much of the

Yiddish literature that incorporated the crucifixion motif came in the wake of various pogroms, Chagall's works must be seen as an artistic response to contemporary acts of violence perpetrated (by Christians) against Jews.

Most often, the crucified figure at the center of Chagall's *White Crucifixion* is understood as symbolizing the suffering Jews depicted all around him. Yet, the Jesus-figure located in a shaft of white light in the middle of the painting is effectively insulated from the Jewish victims that surround him; he is passive and calm on his cross, eyes shut, seemingly oblivious to the adjacent tableau of destruction and despair. The Jewish victims also seem unaware of the crucified figure; none look directly at him, and their situation is thoroughly unaffected by his presence. This complicates the notion that Chagall intended Jesus to serve here as an emblem of Jewish suffering. Other works of Chagall's, such as *Exodus* (1952–66, fig. 13), depict Jesus as more emblematic of the nation as a whole. In that painting, the crucified Jesus looms above a mob of Jewish refugees, a totemic mascot of sorts in this contemporary reenactment of the Exodus of the Israelites from Egypt. Moses is no longer the leader; he is located at the periphery of the scene—Ten Commandments in hand—while Jesus occupies the center, embracing his nation, leading them on their journey (whether this is a journey into the Promised Land or into exile is open to question). His eyes are still closed, but his location at the center of the throng implies his solidarity with his fellow Jews, unlike the sequestered Jesus of *White Crucifixion*, who, despite being the focal point of the painting, appears detached from the catastrophe of his people going on around him.

This ambiguity surrounding the nature and function of the Jesus-figure at the center of *White Crucifixion* is intensified by the four characters floating above his head. Often referred to as biblical patriarchs and a matriarch, although there is no conclusive visual evidence to support this claim, these figures seem to be suggesting with their hand gestures the saying "See no evil, speak no evil, hear no evil." This would imply that the Jesus-figure, possibly representative of Christians rather than Jews, has failed in his responsibilities as a witness to these calamitous events by seeing, saying, and hearing nothing. Susan Compton offers a similar interpretation: "Looking at this figure, who radiates a quietness and peace superlative in twentieth-century art, one has to ask with any Jew, why are Christians watching while the world kills Jews?"[70] Yet, it also seems plausible to read these figures' gestures as a form of lament, a crying out to the heavens for the tragedy transpiring below on earth. They could just as easily be bemoaning the plight of all the victims, including the man on the cross, thereby asserting the common fate of Jesus and the Jews. Is this crucified Jesus, then, an emblem of his suffering people, a reminder of Christian indifference to Jewish persecution, or a universal symbol of martyrdom and man's inhumanity to man?

Chagall himself provided possible answers to this question. In 1957 he proclaimed that for him, painting the figure of Jesus was "an expression of the human, Jewish sadness and pain which Jesus personifies. . . . Perhaps I could have painted another Jewish prophet, but after two thousand years mankind has become attached to the figure of Jesus. For me, a Jew, it is much easier and, moreover, a matter of course, thus to express to the world the artistic truth of our pain and mood."[71]

This explanation implies that Chagall turned to the image of the crucifixion as an expedient means of conveying to mankind—which seems to imply the Christian world—the pain of the Jews. Yet, in a later interview in the 1970s, Chagall expands on his reasons for using the crucifixion as one of his stock images, offering more intrinsically Jewish motivations. He strikes a more apologetic tone—possibly the result of being interviewed by a Yiddish paper, and wanting fellow Jews to better understand his motives—reiterating the Jewishness of his own worldview and conception of Jesus. He states: "My God is the Jewish God, the God of our fathers. My holy book is the Bible. In my fantasy 'Christ' is only our Jewish martyr, with his Jewish mother, surrounded by our Jewish prophets. . . . My Christ as I depict him, is always the type of the Jewish martyr, in pogroms and in our other troubles, and not otherwise. I believe that the world understands me."[72] Again, we witness the tension, even in the artist's own mind, between the universal-human and the Jewish meaning of such imagery.[73]

Despite such explanations, Chagall's critics typically downplayed the explicit Jewishness of his World War II crucifixion scenes, seeing this work, rather, as indicative of Chagall's universal humanism.

For example, in commenting on *Golgotha*, *White Crucifixion*, and *The Martyr* (1940–41), one critic asserts that "no other painter before Chagall had imparted such a meaning to the Crucifixion, which, with his conception, becomes the basis for a universal humanist syncretism."[74] Another critic, commenting on Chagall's *Exodus*, asserts that "the importance that the image of Christ acquires in Chagall's iconography reveals the universal scope of his religious thinking."[75] A third author, commenting on *White Crucifixion*, proposes that "in the figure of Christ on the cross, symbolizing the Passion of the prophet of the Jews and the death of the Christian God who took on the form of a man, Chagall located a universal emblem for the sufferings of his time."[76] This same author also suggests that Chagall's Jesus in *White Crucifixion* retains his redemptive, Christian connotation: "All trace of his suffering is gone, and worship of his centuries-old authority is seen as a path of hope amid the traumatic events of the present day. Belief in him, so Chagall says, can move the mountains of despair."[77] This clearly Christocentric reading ignores the prevailing image structure of the painting. Rather than "moving the mountains of despair" the Jesus of *White Crucifixion* appears utterly powerless, unable to abate the landscape of Jewish suffering that practically engulfs him.

This commentary also highlights the complex nature of the challenge to fully comprehend the meaning and significance of a Jewish Jesus in a visual medium that addresses both a Jewish and a Christian audience. In other words, how do Christians, and Jews for that matter, respond when a Jewish artist (re)claims Christian iconography and symbolism for Jewish purposes? The easiest solution is to understand this as an attempt at universalizing these symbols, making them valid and applicable to all who wish to share in the power and depth of their meaning, without necessarily adopting a Christian worldview (especially since many secular Christians also used these images without actually accepting their traditional religious meanings). It appears to be much more difficult for Christians especially to recognize this move as an explicit Judaization of these Christian symbols, because this presents an overt challenge to the exalted place these symbols hold as archetypes in the Christian cultural canon. This sort of refiguration also tended to disturb Jews. The reason that Asch and Chagall frequently elicited such controversy within the Jewish community because of their so-called Christological works stems from the transgressive nature of importing Christian archetypes—even if they were originally based on Jewish concepts or texts—into the Jewish cultural consciousness, especially when, in many cases, the distinction between Christian and Jewish becomes utterly blurred.

Like Asch, who depicted Jesus coming to life in the form of a Polish rabbi in the Warsaw Ghetto, Chagall also frequently blurred the distinction between the historical, crucified Jesus, and contemporary Jews. In three of his crucifixion paintings from this period (*The Martyr*, *Yellow Crucifixion*, and *The Crucified*), Chagall rather unambiguously portrays contemporary Jews hanging on the cross and not the figure of Jesus himself. This sharpens the symbolic meaning of these paintings, utilizing the image of the crucifixion to explicitly articulate the modern Jewish experience. In fact, *The Martyr* (1940–41, fig. 14), although it shares many of the same features as Chagall's other wartime crucifixions, is not technically a crucifixion scene at all. The panting's central figure is that of a cap-wearing Russian Jew who is tied to a stake, invoking the same medieval Jewish tradition of martyrdom that Lilien's *Dedicated to the Martyrs of Kishinev* does. His body is wrapped in a *tallis*, similar to Chagall's more overt Jesus-figures, except for the fact that here it is more than just a loincloth as it covers most of his torso as well. There are bloody wounds on the martyr's feet, suggesting Jesus' stigmata, and he is mourned by a bride who stands at his feet, an allusion to Mary Magdalene mourning at the feet of Jesus on the cross. Yet, here the Christian images end.

Unlike the Jesus-figure in *White Crucifixion*, who is blonder and resembles a more classical, iconographic rendering of Jesus, and is located in a shaft of white light—a no-man's land of sorts—this martyr is firmly located at the heart of the shtetl, most likely Chagall's own Vitebsk, which is going up in flames. Moreover, two animals linked in Jewish tradition to purification and vicarious sacrifice float near the martyr's head: the red heifer and the rooster. The red heifer is the animal whose ashes were used in the ritual purification of those who had become defiled by touching a corpse (Numbers 19). This animal played an integral role in the workings of the sacrificial cult of the Temple, and the ritual ceased shortly after the destruction of the Second Temple. The rooster (or hen) is the animal used for the ceremony known as *kapparot* or *shlogen kapores* in Yiddish. This is a custom practiced on the day before Yom Kippur in which the sins of a person are symbolically transferred to a fowl; the bird is swung around the head three times while reciting the formula: "This is my substitute, my vicarious offering, my atonement," and then it is slaughtered and donated to the poor. Chagall would have been well aware of both rituals as the former, though defunct, was discussed in depth in the Talmud (in the tractate Parah ["Heifer"]) and in the annual cycle of the reading of the Torah, and the latter was still practiced widely by East European Jews during Chagall's lifetime. Thus, by including these two sacrificial animals in such close proximity to the martyr on the stake, Chagall imbued the whole scene with the Jewish concept of vicarious atonement, thereby re-Judaizing the more typical Christological understanding of this type of martyrdom. As in much of Asch's work, Chagall conflates Jewish and Christian images of martyrdom and vicarious sacrifice: the allusion to Christ on the cross is combined with recollections of medieval Jewish martyrs, and Jewish rites of expiation—themselves reconfigured in Christianity.

Chagall's *Yellow Crucifixion* (1943, fig. 15) is commonly seen as a slight variation on his earlier *White Crucifixion*, yet there are several crucial differences that serve to demonstrate the gradual evolution in Chagall's depiction of the Jewish Jesus on the cross and his relation to Jews in general. As in *The Martyr*, the visage of the crucified victim in *Yellow Crucifixion* is more stereotypically Jewish than in *White Crucifixion*: his hair is dark and wavy. Further establishing his Jewishness—and his traditional piety—the crucified figure's head and left arm are adorned with *tefillin*, and an open Torah scroll hovers to his right, partially obscuring his arm. Also, noticeably absent is the INRI tablet identifying the crucified man as Jesus of Nazareth. Is this, then, the historical Jesus, or simply one more crucified Jew? Two other images further suggest the intrinsically Jewish framework for understanding the sacrifice/martyrdom that the picture depicts: the angel blowing a shofar (ram's horn) immediately beneath the Torah scroll, and the faintly rendered rooster located behind the crucified's head. The angel by itself suggests the Akedah scene, while the addition of the shofar and the rooster alludes once again to Yom Kippur and the concept of a vicarious sacrifice. The shofar, in addition to being blown at the conclusion of the Yom Kippur liturgy, is also traditionally associated with the coming of the Messiah. This adds an apocalyptic element to the painting and suggests the redemptive nature of suffering.[78]

Moreover, in a sketch for Chagall's *Yellow Crucifixion* from 1942, the artist included several more explicit allusions to the Akedah next to his central image of Jesus on the cross. The images located on the open Torah scroll alongside the crucified Jesus—a hand holding a large knife surrounded by five supine bodies lying beside it—evoke the Akedah. Strengthening this allusion is the ram hanging on the cross beside Jesus, and the two figures—a man wrapped in a prayer shawl, or possibly a shroud, and a young man or boy upside down behind him—suggesting Abraham and Isaac.[79] Chagall's inclusion of these images in a crucifixion sketch, even though they are absent from the finished painting, reflects the view that both the Akedah and the crucifixion are fitting visual symbols of Jewish affliction. Far from being a theologian, Chagall was utilizing powerfully rooted Jewish symbols along with the crucifixion—which he and others established as a Jewish symbol—as part of his quest to find a meaningful visual representation of the plight of Europe's Jews during World War II.

In *Yellow Crucifixion* Chagall more saliently depicts the connection between the pious Jew on the cross and the suffering Jewish masses around him than he did in *White Crucifixion*. There is no shaft of heavenly light separating the crucified from the tableau of Jewish troubles shown all around him; his feet nearly touch the street of the shtetl whose houses are in flames, and a group of Jewish refugees, led by the Wandering Jew with a pack on his back, floats in the air right beside him. An old Jewish man holds the ladder at the foot of the cross with one hand apparently pointing at the crucified, suggesting that ascending and descending the martyr's cross was a continual act, not just one isolated event; the link between those on the ground and the one on the cross remains open. Whether the historical Jesus or an ordinary modern Jew, the man on the cross embodies the ongoing suffering of the entire Jewish people (with the artist himself nowhere to be seen). In discussing the symbolic meaning of Chagall's work, the Israeli critic

Isaiah Avrekh raises the question of why Chagall uses a Jewish figure in *tallis* and *tefillin* as a symbol for the crucified. He suggests that Chagall's answer to this query would be thus: "Are they, the Christians, the crucified ones? Do people stick nails in their flesh? We [Jews] have been crucified for two thousand years, day after day, hour after hour, everywhere, in every country. Wherever one is tortured, it is a Jew in *tefillin*. Indeed then, the first crucified one was also a Jew."[80] Avrekh articulates the sense that because of the Jews' history of persecution and martyrdom it is only natural that the crucifixion should serve as a Jewish symbol of suffering, and that the man on the cross should be depicted as a stereotypical Jew. This implies that for Chagall, as for many of the Yiddish modernists, the crucifixion was a uniquely Jewish symbol, and its use by Jewish artists or writers did not constitute Jewish assimilation of Christian themes, but a reclamation of inherently Jewish ones.

In his painting *The Crucified* (1944, fig. 16), Chagall most definitively depicts the fate of Europe's Jews in such Christological terms. Here, it is modern-day Jews dressed in traditional East European garb who are shown hanging on crosses in the desolate, snow-covered streets of the shtetl. Alongside them, corpses line the street; there are no mobs of refugees fleeing the scene. The lone survivor is a man sitting on top of a house clutching a Torah scroll as he surveys the utter decimation of the shtetl. Perhaps this is the artist, Chagall himself, in his role as witness to the destruction of the Jewish heartland of Eastern Europe. With this painting Chagall achieves a transformation from the Jewish Jesus to crucified Jews, and as Rotermund observes, "the crucifixion becomes the symbol for the immeasurable suffering the Jews have endured in our time. Here the crucified [are] understood as the suffering servant of God mentioned in Isaiah 53; not, as according to Christian theology, one single man, but rather, the Jewish nation itself."[81] Unlike in *Yellow Crucifixion*, there is no ambiguity in *The Crucified* as to who now hangs on the cross: the historical Jesus has been completely replaced by contemporary "skin-and-bone" Jews. While after the war Chagall returned to more historical as well as more personalized images of Jesus, this last of his wartime crucifixions became the definitive illustration of his conceptualization of the crucifixion as *the* archetypal visual symbol of Jewish suffering.

Chagall was by no means the only Jewish artist to incorporate the crucifixion motif significantly in response to the atrocities suffered by the Jews of Europe during World War II. Ziva Amishai-Maisels has masterfully shown that a number of prominent Jewish painters and sculptors such as Max Band (1900–1974), Mane Katz (1894–1962), and Abraham Rattner (1895–1978), to name but a few, employed Christ and crucifixion motifs in addressing the plight of the Jews during the war.[82] In many of these works, the artists, like Chagall, depict contemporary Jewish victims in Christ-like terms, or portray the historical Jesus as markedly Jewish. Moreover, since the 1930s and even earlier, non-Jewish artists in Europe had begun to use the symbols of the crucifixion as representative of all victims of fascism and the Nazis, both Jews and non-Jews.[83] In most of these cases however, the Jewishness of the Christ-figures was not typically emphasized, or it was overlooked altogether. Even some Jewish artists, such as Rattner, an American painter who featured the crucifixion prominently in his works of the 1930s and 1940s, did not explicitly identify their Christ-figures as Jewish, instead choosing more universal images to represent the suffering of the victims of the Nazis.[84] However, despite this widespread adoption of the crucifixion as part of an artistic response to the Holocaust and the crimes of fascism, it is only in the work of Marc Chagall—both during the war and long after— that the crucifixion is wholly transformed into a central Jewish icon. No other Jewish artist went as far as Chagall in inscribing the figure of Jesus and the crucifixion into the canon of modern Jewish culture.

Epilogue

The Jesus Question Revisited

> I dreamed that the gentiles crucified Mozart.
>
> —Jacob Glatstein, 1946

The works considered in this book represent a sea change in Jewish intellectuals' attitudes toward Jesus since the end of the eighteenth century, as reclaiming the figure of Jesus of Nazareth played an important part in the process of modernization of Jewish culture and thought. The cross and the image of Jesus allowed Jewish intellectuals to renegotiate their relationship to Western culture by reclaiming and Judaizing some of its most important foundations. The range and fluidity of Christian imagery made it compelling to Jewish intellectuals, especially to modernist writers and artists, whose preoccupation with Christian motifs became a distinctive feature of Yiddish modernism in the early 1920s. Yet, this world of Yiddish modernism lived a tragically curtailed existence, flourishing primarily in the 1920s and 1930s, and the works considered in this book represent a particular cultural moment, which ultimately proved to be short-lived.

As fascism, nationalism, anti-Semitism, and, finally, the Holocaust and Stalinism brought an end to this cultural moment, and to East European Jewish society in general, there was a marked turn back to the Jewish collective and away from the cosmopolitan, universalist impulses that had infused the cultural avant-garde. This in turn led many Jews to question whether they could still claim Jesus as their own. As mentioned above, writers like Uri Tsvi Grinberg, Itzik Manger, and Hey Leyvik turned away from their embrace of Jesus in the face of the Nazi genocide, implying that the outburst of rage and violence unleashed against the Jews in Europe once again tainted the figure of Jesus with the stain of Jewish blood as in earlier times. While Sholem Asch and Marc Chagall provide two remarkable examples of Jewish artists who continued to depict Jesus as an iconic image of Jewish martyrdom during and after World War II, the opposite trend of distancing Jews from Jesus became increasingly prevalent during those years.

In 1938, the same year that Chagall completed his *White Crucifixion*, the American Yiddish poet Jacob Glatstein (Yankev Glatshteyn) published his poetic rebuke and farewell to European civilization and culture: "A gute nakht, velt" ("Good Night, World"). Like Chagall in *White Crucifixion*, Glatstein was responding to the rising tide of fascism and anti-Semitism in Europe in the 1930s, but in a profoundly different way. His poem served as a bill of divorce, severing the relationship between the Jew and the European world that he had been living in for centuries. "A gute nakht, velt" proclaims the failure of the Enlightenment and modernity to make a home for Jews in Europe and advocates the return of the Jew to his hermetically sealed, insular culture, the medieval ghetto—an unknowingly ironic symbol of traditional Jewish culture given the Nazi ghettoization of European Jews that would take place in the subsequent war years):

> Good night, wide world,
> Big stinking world.
> Not you but I slam the gate.
> With a long gabardine,
> With a fiery yellow patch,
> With a proud stride,
> Because I want to,
> I'm going back to the ghetto.[1]

As part of Glatstein's symbolic retreat from European culture and society, he calls for a wholesale repudiation of all of the fruits of that culture, which modern Jews have enjoyed, from Marx to Wagner to Jesus.

> Good night. I'll make you, world, a gift of
> All my liberators.
> Take back your Jesus-Marxes, choke on their courage.
> Croak over a drop of our Christianized blood.[2]

For Glatstein, the ideological and cultural alternatives presented to modern Jews—Marxism and Christianity, secularism and assimilation—had proven false; the reclamation of Jesus had to be abandoned.

Glatstein's stinging critique of European culture and society and of the Jews' failed attempt to assimilate into that society ("our Christian- ized blood") is not unprecedented, and shares many of the polemical sentiments found in the poems of Grinberg, Markish, Halpern, and Shneour that have been addressed above. Fundamentally, Glatstein's poem represents a modernist's disillusionment with Western European culture, as he confronts the jarring reality that this culture can no lon- ger be his own, despite how much he previously embraced it. This helps explain the trend of Jewish modernists backing away from the figure of Jesus when they no longer felt that he could be fully extricated from European culture. Yet, this process was a complicated one, as most Jew- ish writers and artists were not willing to abandon Western culture al- together. Even in Glatstein's case, it was possible for him to incorporate Christian motifs from European culture while simultaneously attempt- ing to disentangle the Jews from that culture.

In his 1946 poem "Mozart," written in the immediate aftermath of the war, Glatstein again attacks the barbarism of Europe, while sub- versively depicting the Jews as the exclusive and authentic bearers of European culture, as embodied by Mozart.

> I dreamed that
> The gentiles crucified Mozart
> And buried him in a pauper's grave.
> But the Jews made him a man of God
> And blessed his memory.
> I, his apostle, ran all over the world,
> Converting everyone I met,
> And wherever I caught a Christian
> I made him a Mozartian.[3]

Writing against the backdrop of the Holocaust, Glatstein depicts a Eu- rope in which the forces of evil—the Christian Gentiles—crucify that which represents the true beauty of European culture—Mozart—while the Jews act as the champions of this cultural heritage, responsible for its transmission after the Christians have turned against it. Throughout the poem Glatstein ironically uses Christian imagery as he juxtaposes the crucified Mozart and Jesus— secular European culture and Chris- tianity— ultimately concluding: "How poor and stingy— / compared with Mozart's legacy— / is the Sermon on the Mount."[4] Christianity is morally bankrupt, and the Jews have become the apostles of the new religion of Mozart, the only praiseworthy legacy of European culture.

Despite his continued use of the crucifixion as a powerful symbol of persecution and martyrdom, Glatstein's denunciation of Christian Europe included seeing Jesus as on the side of the Christians, not the Jews. It is therefore not surprising that during the war Glatstein wrote many articles vociferously condemning the "Christian" writings of Sholem Asch, seeing him as a shameless and dangerous proselytizer.[5] While the reclamation of Jesus had almost always contained an anti-Christian polemical component, before the Holocaust most Jewish writers and artists had wielded the Jewish Jesus as their ultimate weapon against Christian anti-Semitism. However, with the war and the genocide of European Jews, Jesus again became associated more with the persecutors for many Jewish writers, and especially for their audiences. As we saw in the debates surrounding Asch's *The Nazarene* discussed in chapter 4, many in the Yiddish intelligentsia defended Asch, and still conceived of Jesus as a legitimate subject of Jewish art, if not as a fully Jewish figure himself. Yet, except for Asch, there were very few who depicted Jesus as he did; the fascination had faded and the climate was no longer deemed appropriate.

To be sure, as Ziva Amishai-Maisels has shown, the crucifixion and other Christian motifs still appealed to many Jewish visual artists, who attempted to confront the horrors of the Holocaust in their work, yet except for Chagall, none boldly depicted Jesus as a thoroughly Jewish figure.[6] The crucifixion might have been an appropriate visual symbol of Jewish suffering, but for many Jews—artists and audience alike— Jesus was now beyond the pale; his old status as the emblem of Christian anti-Semitism had resurfaced, and he was once again seen as *treyf*.

Philip Roth's short story "The Conversion of the Jews," which first appeared in 1958 in the *Paris Review*, exemplifies this new trend, especially for American Jews after the Holocaust. In Roth's story, the figure of Jesus serves Roth's troubled protagonist, the thirteen-year-old Ozzie Freedman, as a weapon in his battle against the hypocritical Jewish establishment. The rebellious Ozzie is able to vanquish his tyrannical rabbi by forcing him to profess his belief in Jesus Christ, while Ozzie rants on the synagogue rooftop, threatening to jump. Jesus is not presented as a Jewish martyr or prophet, or even a mythological archetype, but as the arch-villain of Jewish history and the emblem of all that is other; he is a symbol of the dominant Gentile culture in America in which Jews like Ozzie Freedman were struggling to find a place.[7]

There were realms of Jewish culture, however, in which the reclamation of Jesus never really ceased, such as Jewish scholarship and theology. From Martin Buber to Geza Vermes and Samuel Sandmel, there have been Jewish thinkers, scholars, and rabbis who have continued to view Jesus in a positive light, as a Jew and a brother, whose teachings originate in the Judaism of his times, and who is still relevant to the contemporary Jew in some way or other.[8] This scholarship tends to be less explicitly polemical against Christianity than the works of Geiger or Graetz in the nineteenth century, and is highly valued within both academic and liberal theological circles, Jewish and Christian. Since the 1970s there has been a marked increase in this renewed quest for the Jewish Jesus, and numerous Jewish scholars have attempted to demonstrate the inherent Jewishness of Jesus in their work.[9] This Jewish scholarly interest in Jesus is not as widespread as it was in the late nineteenth or early twentieth century, yet since the late 1990s, with the increase of Jewish-Christian dialogue, there is clearly a growing interest in the Jewish Jesus among Jews and Christians, scholars and laypeople alike.

However, at the same time, as the controversy surrounding the release of Mel Gibson's movie *The Passion of the Christ* in 2004 suggests, Jews still are afraid of Jesus, especially when Christians remind them that he is a key Christian figure. Unlike the modernist versions of the passion, in which the Jews are the Christ-like victims of a barbarous Christian world, the Christian passion play, as updated by Gibson, places Jesus outside of the Jewish camp and casts the Jews as Christ's persecutors. In a sense, the controversy over *The Passion of the Christ* is the latest manifestation of Jews' angst about Jesus and the role he plays in the public sphere, especially in the United States. After all, it is American Jews who are the most vociferous defenders of the separation of Church and state, because the day Jesus is hanging in American classrooms is the day that America is lost to Jews. Jews have always had to relate to Jesus, but if the Jewish intelligentsia of the early twentieth century wanted to reclaim him, the Jewish communal leadership of the twenty-first century wants him as far out of the public eye as possible.

Notes

Introduction. Jesus and the Jewish Question

1. I use the term West/Western here and throughout the book to refer to non-Jewish European culture and civilization. I also refer to the West as Christian, although this does not necessarily imply that modern Western values and ideals are based on Christianity, but that Christians who came from a Christian milieu generated them.

2. This term was coined by David Shneer and Caryn Aviv in their book *Queer Jews* (New York, 2002) to describe how queer Jews have appropriated heterosexual institutions and broadened their meanings.

3. For discussions of the treatment of Jesus in rabbinic literature see the following: Jacob Lauterbach, "Jesus in the Talmud," in *Rabbinic Essays* (Cincinnati, 1951), R. Travers Herford, *Christianity in Talmud and Midrash* (New York, 1975), Morris Goldstein, *Jesus in the Jewish Tradition* (New York, 1950), and Daniel Boyarin, *Dying for God* (Stanford, 1999). See also Avigdor Shinan, ed., *Oto ha-ish: Yehudim mesaprim al Yeshu* [That man: Jews talk about Jesus] (Tel Aviv, 1999), an anthology of Jewish primary sources dealing with Jesus from the Talmud to modern Hebrew literature.

4. For a discussion of the *Toldot Yeshu* see the following: Samuel Krauss, *Das Leben Jesu nach jüdischen Quellen* (Berlin, 1902), Hugh Schonfield, *According to the Hebrews* (London, 1937), Joseph Klausner, *Jesus of Nazareth* (New York, 1926), and Goldstein, *Jesus in the Jewish Tradition*.

5. See David Berger, ed., *The Jewish-Christian Debate in the High Middle Ages: A Critical Edition of the Nizzahon Vetus* (Philadelphia, 1979).

6. Amos Funkenstein coined this term in his discussion of Jewish-Christian polemics in his *Perceptions of Jewish History* (Berkeley, 1993), 171.

7. See Marc Shapiro, "Torah Study on Christmas Eve," *Journal of Jewish Thought and Philosophy* 8 (1999): 319–53, for a discussion of Jewish popular customs and beliefs about Jesus. One of the premodern superstitions Shapiro presents held that Jesus would roam the earth every Christmas Eve, going from latrine to latrine, which may partially explain the derivation of the title *Pandrek*.

8. Roger Chartier, *Cultural History: Between Practices and Representations* (Ithaca, 1988), 102.

9. Homi Bhabha, *The Location of Culture* (London, 1994), 1–2.

10. Ibid., 2.

Chapter 1. The Quest for the Jewish Jesus

1. Albert Schweitzer, *The Quest of the Historical Jesus* (New York, 1911), 4.

2. Ibid.

3. Arnold Eisen, "In the Wilderness: Reflections on American Jewish Culture," *Jewish Social Studies* 5, nos. 1 & 2 (Fall 1998–Winter 1999): 29.

4. Jonathan Brumberg-Kraus, "Jesus as Other People's Scripture," in *Jesus through Catholic and Jewish Eyes* (Harrisburg, 2000), 160.

5. Ibid., 160–161.

6. Pinchas Lapide, *Israelis, Jews, and Jesus* (New York, 1979), 108.

7. Brumberg-Kraus, "Other People's Scripture," 155. See Brumberg-Kraus, "A Jewish Ideological Perspective on the Study of Christian Scripture," *Jewish Social Studies* 4, no. 1 (1997): 121–52, for an analysis of this "ideological bias." See also Donald Hagner, *The Jewish Reclamation of Jesus: An Analysis and Critique of Modern Jewish Study of Jesus* (Grand Rapids, 1984), in which he critiques this ideological bias of Jewish scholarship. Hagner suggests that setting out to prove the Jewishness of Jesus stacks the results of Jewish scholarship in advance, in that "whatever does not coincide with modern Jewish estimates of first-century Judaism cannot be true of the Jesus of history" (82).

8. Harvey Cox, *Many Mansions* (Boston, 1988), 111.

9. Samuel Sandmel, *We Jews and Jesus* (New York, 1973), 51.

10. Paul Mendes-Flohr and Jehuda Reinhartz, eds., *The Jew in the Modern World* (New York, 1980), 184. *Maskilim* refers to followers of the Haskalah.

11. Ismar Schorsch, *From Text to Context* (Hanover, 1994), 154–55.

12. Ibid., 1.

13. The Russian *maskilim* I. B. Levinsohn (1787–1860) and A. B. Gottlober (1811–99) advanced these ideas in essays and verse in the latter half of the nineteenth century. Levinsohn avowed that Jesus was a law-abiding Jew, and "harshly attacked Christians who persecute the Jews rather than obeying Jesus' laws of humility and charity." Gottlober powerfully expressed similar sentiments in his poem "Hegeh va-Hi" of 1864, "in which Jesus disowns the Christians for their treatment of the Jews, reaffirming his blood kinship with the latter." See Ziva Amishai-Maisels, "The Jewish Jesus," *Journal of Jewish Art* 9 (1983): 95. Levinsohn makes these claims in his apologetic tract *Ahiya Shiloni ha-Hozeh* [Ahiya, the Seer of Shiloh], written in 1841 but not published until 1863.

14. Alexander Altman, *Moses Mendelssohn* (Tuscaloosa, 1973), 562.

15. Ibid., 261.

16. Ibid., 262. See also Jonathan Hess, *Germans, Jews, and the Claims of Modernity* (New Haven, 2002), 91–135, for a discussion of Mendelssohn's position on Jesus.

17. Moses Mendelssohn, *Jerusalem* (Hanover, 1983), 134.

18. Mendelssohn was not the first to make such claims. Jacob Emden (1696–1776), a leading figure of traditional Judaism in eighteenth-century Germany, also looked very favorably on Jesus, claiming that most Christians (and Jews) had misunderstood the true nature of his teachings. In a remarkable turnabout from traditional Jewish views, Emden argued that: (1) Both Jesus and Paul were observant Jews; (2) Jesus brought a "double kindness" to the world by strengthening the Torah and bringing religion and ethics to the Gentiles; (3) Paul did not negate the validity of the Law for Jews, only for Gentiles; and (4) Christianity was created as a religion for the Gentiles based on Noahide laws. Unlike Mendelssohn, though, Emden did not seek the integration of Jews into European society, and was more motivated by a desire to combat Christian persecutions of Jews. See Harvey Falk, "Rabbi Jacob Emden's View on Christianity," *Journal of Ecumenical Studies* 19, no. 1 (Winter, 1982): 105–11.

19. Mendelssohn, *Jerusalem*, 135.

20. Michael Meyer, *The Origins of the Modern Jew* (Detroit, 1967), 36. The letter can be found in Moses Mendelssohn, *Gesammelte Schriften, Jubiläumsausgabe*, ed. I. Elbogen, J. Guttman, and E. Mittwoch (Berlin, 1929–38), 7:300–305.

21. Schorsch, *From Text to Context*, 185.

22. Ibid. See Gershom Scholem, "The Science of Judaism—Then and Now," in *The Messianic Idea in Judaism* (New York, 1971), 304–13.

23. Ibid., 238.

24. Ibid., 239.

25. Susannah Heschel, *Abraham Geiger and the Jewish Jesus* (Chicago, 1998), 132.

26. Ibid., 133.

27. Walter Jacob, *Christianity through Jewish Eyes* (Cincinnati, 1974), 24.

28. Joseph Salvador, *Histoire des institutions de Moïse et du peuple hébreu* (Paris, 1822).

29. Paula Hyman, "Joseph Salvador: Proto-Zionist or Apologist for Assimilation?" *Jewish Social Studies* 34, no. 1 (January 1972): 4.

30. Jacob, *Christianity through Jewish Eyes*, 24.

31. Hyman, "Joseph Salvador," 3.

32. Ibid.

33. Ibid., 20.

34. Jacob, *Christianity through Jewish Eyes*, 26.

35. Hyman, "Joseph Salvador," 8.

36. Heschel, *Abraham Geiger and the Jewish Jesus*, 134.

37. Jacob, *Christianity through Jewish Eyes*, 28–29.

38. Ibid., 29–30.

39. Hyman, "Joseph Salvador," 9, citing Salvador, *Jésus-Christ et sa doctrine*, 2 vols. (Paris, 1838), 2:78–79.

40. Ibid., 12.

41. Ibid.

42. Ibid., 9.

43. Schorsch, *From Text to Context*, 291.

44. Michael Meyer, *Response to Modernity* (Detroit, 1988), 72.

45. Ibid.

46. Eliezer Schweid, *Toledot ha-hagut ha-yehudit ba-et ha-hadashah* [History of Jewish thought in modern times] (Jerusalem, 1977), 261, cited in Meyer, *Response to Modernity*, 411 n. 36.

47. Meyer, *Response to Modernity*, 72.

48. Schorsch, *From Text to Context*, 267.

49. Jacob, *Christianity through Jewish Eyes*, 52, citing Hirsch's *Das Judentum, der christliche Staat und die moderne wissenschaftliche Kritik* (Leipzig, 1843), 97ff.

50. Samuel Hirsch, *Die Religionsphilosophie der Juden* (Leipzig, 1842), 621.

51. Ibid., 622. See also David Catchpole, *The Trial of Jesus: A Study in the Gospels and Jewish Historiography from 1770 to the Present Day* (Leiden, 1971), 24–26.

52. Catchpole, *The Trial of Jesus*, 51.

53. Julius Guttmann, *Philosophies of Judaism* (New York, 1964), 317.

54. Jacob, *Christianity through Jewish Eyes*, 55. This notion echoes medieval Jewish thinkers such as Ha-Levy and Maimonides.

55. Hirsch, *Die Religionsphilosophie der Juden*, 728.

56. Heschel, *Abraham Geiger and the Jewish Jesus*, 135, citing Hirsch, *Die Religionsphilosophie der Juden*, 688.

57. Hirsch, *Die Religionsphilosophie der Juden*, 745.

58. Guttmann, *Philosophies of Judaism*, 319–20; see Hirsch, *Die Religionsphilosophie der Juden*, 646–90.

59. Hirsch, *Die Religionsphilosophie der Juden*, 728.

60. Ibid., 688.

61. Ibid.

62. Ibid., 672ff., 745ff.

63. Ibid., 689.

64. Schorsch, *From Text to Context*, 276, citing a criticism leveled by Zunz.

65. Ibid., 288.

66. Ibid., 279, from a letter written in 1869.

67. Heschel, *Abraham Geiger and the Jewish Jesus*, 2.

68. Ibid.

69. Ibid., 1.

70. Ibid., 4.

71. Schorsch, *From Text to Context*, 290.

72. See Heschel, *Abraham Geiger and the Jewish Jesus*, 197ff.

73. Geiger's doctoral dissertation, "Was hat Mohammed aus dem Judentum aufgenommen?" (1833), was a prime example of this.

74. Heinrich Graetz, *The Structure of Jewish History and Other Essays*, ed. and trans. Ismar Schorsch (New York, 1975), 93.

75. Abraham Geiger, *Judaism and Its History*, trans. Maurice Mayer (New York, 1866), vi. Subsequent citations from this book are given in the text.

76. Heschel, *Abraham Geiger and the Jewish Jesus*, 128.

77. Jacob, *Christianity through Jewish Eyes*, 43, citing Geiger's "Einleitung in das Studium der jüdischen Theologie," in *Nachgelassene Schriften*, ed. Ludwig Geiger, vol. 2 (Berlin, 1875), 116ff.

78. Geiger, "Ein Blick auf die neueren Bearbeitungen des Lebens Jesu," from the appendix to *Das Judenthum und seine Geschichte in zwölf Vorlesungen* (Breslau, 1864), 175ff.

79. Catchpole, *The Trial of Jesus*, 37.

80. Heschel, *Abraham Geiger and the Jewish Jesus*, 237.

81. Ismar Schorsch, "Ideology and History in the Age of Emancipation," in Graetz, *The Structure of Jewish History*, 56.

82. Moses Hess was a German Jewish socialist, highly assimilated and estranged from Judaism for much of his adult life, whose "return" to Judaism was marked by his proto-Zionist tract *Rome and Jerusalem* (1862).

83. Heschel, *Abraham Geiger and the Jewish Jesus*, 136.

84. Moses Hess, *The Revival of Israel: Rome and Jerusalem, the Last Nationalist Question,* tr. and ed. Meyer Waxman (Lincoln, 1995), 186.

85. Heinrich Graetz, *History of the Jews*, vol. 2 (Philadelphia, 1893), 150.

86. Ibid., 151.

87. Ibid., 149.

88. Ibid., 155.

89. Ibid., 155–56.

90. See Heschel, *Abraham Geiger and the Jewish Jesus*, 217–20.

91. Catchpole, *The Trial of Jesus*, 34. Derenbourg advanced this notion in his pivotal essay, *Essai sur l'histoire et la géographie de la Palestine d'après les Thalmuds et les autres sources rabbiniques* (Paris, 1867).

92. Isaac Mayer Wise, *Three Lectures on the Origins of Christianity* (Cincinnati, 1883), 7ff.

93. Heschel, *Abraham Geiger and the Jewish Jesus*, 217.

94. Elijah Benamozegh, *Jewish and Christian Morality* (Paris, 1867), 209, cited in Lapide, *Israelis, Jews, and Jesus*, 112.

95. Jacob, *Christianity through Jewish Eyes*, 36.

96. Jonathan D. Sarna, "The Cult of Synthesis in American Jewish Culture," *Jewish Social Studies* 5, nos. 1 and 2 (Fall 1998–Winter 1999): 52.

97. Ibid., 54.

98. George Berlin, *Defending the Faith: Nineteenth-Century American Jewish Writings on Christianity and Jesus* (New York, 1989), 45.

99. See ibid., 47–48.

100. C. G. Montefiore, *Some Elements of the Religious Teaching of Jesus* (London, 1910), 14ff.

101. Jacob, *Christianity through Jewish Eyes*, 103.

102. Daniel Langton, "Claude Montefiore and Christianity: Did the Founder of Anglo-Liberal Judaism Lean Too Far?" *Journal of Jewish Studies* 50, no. 1 (Spring 1999): 108.

103. Berlin, *Defending the Faith*, 166–67.

104. Hyman G. Enelow, *A Jewish View of Jesus* (New York, 1920), 176.

105. Sandmel, *We Jews and Jesus*, 114 n. 17.

106. Joseph Krauskopf, *A Rabbi's Impressions of the Oberammergau Passion Play* (Philadelphia, 1901), 20.

107. Ibid., 42 ff.

108. Berlin, *Defending the Faith*, 53–54, citing Kaufman Kohler in *Reform Advocate* 10 (December 21, 1895): 745.

109. Krauskopf, *A Rabbi's Impressions*, 152.

110. Emil Hirsch, *The Doctrine of Jesus* (Chicago, 1894), 5.

111. Ibid.

112. Emil Hirsch, *The Jews and Jesus* (Chicago, 1890), 22.

113. Bernhard Felsenthal, *Teacher in Israel*, ed. Emma Felsenthal (New York, 1924), 265.

114. Hirsch, *The Jews and Jesus*, 25.

115. Berlin, *Defending the Faith*, 168.

116. Wise, *The Martyrdom of Jesus of Nazareth* (Cincinnati, 1874), 134.

Chapter 2. The Crucifix Question

1. Chaim Zhitlovsky, "Sholem Asch's 'In a karnival nakht' un Lamed Shapiro's 'Der tseylem,'" *Dos naye lebn* 1 [New life] (June 1909): 413. Subsequent citations are given in the text, using the page number from the bound edition of all the 1909 issues of the journal.

2. The Second Aliya refers to the wave of Jewish migration to Palestine mostly from Eastern Europe, roughly spanning the years 1904–13.

3. A certain Herr Shmi excoriated Zhitlovsky's original *Dos naye lebn* article in the Russian-language Jewish journal *Evreiskii mir* [Jewish world] published in St. Petersburg, July 1909, 39–42. (Ansky was the literary editor of the journal.) Shmi criticized Zhitlovsky for what he felt was too strong a desire to see Jews enter the modern Western world "through Nazareth," an enthusiastic call for assimilating Christian culture to a dangerous extreme. Shmi went as far as equating Zhitlovsky with Christian missionaries!

4. Emanuel Goldsmith, *Modern Yiddish Culture* (New York, 1977), 176.

5. See Zhitlovsky's *Zikhroynes fun mayn lebn* [Memories of my life], 3 vols. (New York, 1935–40), 2:52.

6. David Weinberg, *Between Tradition and Modernity* (New York, 1996), 93.

7. When speaking of Christianity or Christian ideals, Zhitlovsky typically had in mind an enlightened liberal vision of Christianity as expressed by thinkers such as John Stuart Mill, Unitarian authors, and also the liberal Russian Orthodox theologian Vladimir Soloviev. Zhitlovsky, like Asch, also frequently conceived of an idealized ancient Christianity that was free of the later dogmas and prejudices that, he believed, plagued most Christian denominations, especially Eastern Orthodoxy and the Catholic Church.

8. S. Ansky, "Di tseylem frage," pts. 1 and 2, *Dos naye lebn* 1 (September 1909): 615ff., (October 1909): 665ff. Subsequent cites are given in the text.

9. Ansky does offer a brief, thoroughly scathing review of Asch's story, calling him a purveyor of *shund* (trash literature). He criticizes Asch's use of "cheap pathos" and "pseudoprophetic," flowery language in presenting Jesus' conversation with the Messiah at the gates of Rome. He takes issue with the fact that Asch refers to the Christ figure as a "man-god," implying that by stripping Jesus of his messianic status and converting him into some kind of "Jewish national man-god" Asch is actually destroying him (ibid., 616).

10. Ahad Ha-am offered similar criticism of Jesus' ethical doctrine in his 1910 essay "Al shete se'ifim" ("Between Two Options"), translated as "Judaism and the Gospels" in *Nationalism and the Jewish Ethic*, ed. H. Kohn (New York, 1962), 289–319.

11. See David Roskies, "S. Ansky and the Paradigm of Return," in *The Uses of Tradition*, ed. Jack Wertheimer (New York, 1992), 243–60; and his "Introduction" to S. Ansky, *The Dybbuk and Other Writings* (New York, 1992), xi–xxxvi, as well as Zhitlovsky's *Zikhroynes fun mayn lebn*, vol. 1.

12. See Roskies, "Introduction," xvi.

13. Ginsburg's article was published in *Dos naye lebn* (January 1910): 25–34, (February 1910): 31–39.

14. Ginsburg, "Tsu der tseylem frage," pt. 1, *Dos naye lebn* 2 (January 1910): 32.

15. Issur Ginsburg, *Di entshteyung fun kristntum* (New York, 1917).

16. "A briv fun a fraynd vegn der tseylem frage," whose author signed it "yours, Mendel" without including his full name, appeared after Ginsburg's first installment of his article in *Dos naye lebn* 2 (January 1910): 35.

17. Ibid., 36.

18. The article was entitled "The Christianity Question for Educated Jews" ("Di kristntum shayle far gebildete yidn") and appeared as the front-page feature in the October 1909 issue of *Dos naye lebn* (621–31), and continued in the November 1909 issue (728–45).

19. Zhitlovsky wrote on this topic in detail in an article entitled "Toyt un

vidergeburt fun getter un religiyonen" ("Death and Rebirth of Gods and Religions"), which he published in the first issue of *Dos naye lebn* (January 1909): 83–94. There he essentially endorses a secular (poetic) reinterpretation of religious myths and concepts that renders them useful for the modern civilized world.

20. See Marc Shapiro, "Torah Study on Christmas Eve," *Journal of Jewish Thought and Philosophy* 8 (1999): 319–53, for a discussion of Jewish popular customs pertaining to Christmas Eve.

21. Weinberg, *Between Tradition and Modernity* (New York, 1996), 92.

22. Ibid., 93.

23. Ibid.

24. Ibid.

25. Cited in Sophie Dubnov-Erlich, *The Life and Work of S. M. Dubnov* (Bloomington, 1991), 113–14.

26. Weinberg, *Between Tradition and Modernity*, 115.

27. Ibid., 116.

28. Ibid., 116–17.

29. Ibid., 117.

30. Ibid.

31. Like Ginsburg, Zhitlovsky, who settled in America in 1908, was certainly familiar with the historical writings of Graetz and Geiger, as well as of the Americans Wise, Hirsch, and Kohler, whose scholarly works were read beyond Reform circles.

32. See Todd Endelman, ed., *Jewish Apostasy in the Modern World* (New York, 1987), esp. chaps. 7 and 8.

33. Hurwitz was part of Ahad Ha-Am's circle of Cultural Zionists, who stood out as the gadflies of their generation, often embracing radical and subversive positions and challenging Ahad Ha-Am's views directly. He was one of the major theoreticians of the secular Zionist–influenced ideology known as Hebraism, and the editor of the journal *He-atid* (*The Future*, 1908–13) which served as a forum for Hebraism and the more radical wing of the Cultural Zionist intellectual world. His writings often stoked passionate opposition and he came under heavy criticism for his writings on Christianity.

34. The definitive book on the Brenner Affair is Nurith Govrin, *Meora Brener: Ha-maavak al hofesh ha-bitui* [The Brenner Affair: The fight for free speech] (Jerusalem, 1985). I have relied on Govrin for the basic contours and chronology of the affair, and for the primary articles, which she includes as well.

35. Ha-poel ha-tsair was a leading socialist Zionist labor organization active in Palestine from 1905 to 1930. It was founded by young Zionists who migrated to Palestine during the Second Aliya and it became a leading political and cultural force in the Yishuv. Its newspaper of the same name published work by major Hebrew writers and intellectuals, such as Brenner.

36. See Govrin, *Meora Brener*, 31–32.

37. See Steven J. Zipperstein, *Elusive Prophet: Ahad Ha'am and the Origins of Zionism* (Berkeley, 1993).

38. Menachem Brinker, "Brenner's Jewishness," in *Studies in Contemporary Jewry* 4, ed. Jonathan Frankel (New York, 1988), 239.

39. Govrin, *Meora Brener*, 32.

40. Ibid.

41. Ibid.

42. Brinker, "Brenner's Jewishness," 240.

43. The Hebrew article appeared as "Al shete se'ifim" ("Between Two Options") in the Cultural Zionist journal *Ha-Shiloach* 23, no. 2 (1910), and in English as "Judaism and the Gospels," published in *The Jewish Review* I (1910–11). I am using the version of "Judaism and the Gospels" found in Achad Ha-Am, *Ten Essays on Zionism and Judaism* (New York, 1973), 223–53.

44. See Ahad Ha-Am, "Judaism and the Gospels," 224–27.

45. See Weinberg, *Between Tradition and Modernity*, 268–70.

46. Stanley Nash, *In Search of Hebraism: Shai Hurwitz and his Polemics in the Hebrew Press* (Leiden, 1980), 255.

47. Brenner, "Ba-Ittonut u-va-sifrut," in Govrin, *Meora Brener*, 139.

48. Govrin, *Meora Brener*, 21.

49. Ibid., 136–37.

50. Ibid., 137.

51. Zipperstein, *Elusive Prophet*, 237.

52. Ibid., 237–38; see also Govrin, *Meora Brener*, 134–39, and Nash, *In Search of Hebraism*, 300.

53. See Govrin, *Meora Brener*, 33.

54. Ibid., 34–35.

55. Ibid., 72.

56. Ibid., 69.

57. Ibid., 70, citing B. Z. Katz, *Al itonim va-anashim* [Newspapers and people] (Tel Aviv, 1983), 83.

58. Govrin, *Meora Brener*, 91.

59. Ibid., 150ff.

60. December 14, 1910; see ibid., 32, 144–45.

61. Ibid., 144.

62. "Torah mi-tzion," cited in Brinker, "Brenner's Jewishness," 235, from *Kol kitve Ahad Ha-Am* [Collected writings of Ahad Ha-Am] (Tel Aviv, 1947), 406–9.

63. Govrin, *Meora Brener*, 31.

64. Ibid., 158–61.

65. November 4, 1911; Govrin, *Meora Brener*, 184–88.

66. Jacob Becker, *Yosef Klausner: Ha-ish u-poalo* [Joseph Klausner: The man and his works] (Tel Aviv, 1946), 137.

67. To Y. H. Ravnitsky, March 29, 1911; Govrin, *Meora Brener*, 49.

68. Ibid., 50ff.

69. See Nash, *In Search of Hebraism*, 298.

70. Becker, *Joseph Klausner*, 136.

71. Horodetsky, "Rabbi Yisrael Besht," *He-atid* I (1908): 123–25, cited in Nash, *In Search of Hebraism*, 255.

72. Nash, *In Search of Hebraism*, 259, citing Hurwitz, *Me-ayin u-le-ayin?* [Whence and whither?] (Berlin, 1914), 102.

73. Nash, *In Search of Hebraism*, 259.

74. Ibid., 273.

75. Ibid.

76. Ibid., 255.

77. Ibid., 206–7, citing Hurwitz, *Me-ayin u-le-ayin?* 279.

78. The phrase "Judaism and Humanity" served as the title for one of Klausner's early books, *Yehadut Ve-enoshiyut* (1910).

79. Nash, *In Search of Hebraism*, 273.

80. The Zionist historian Yehezkel Kaufmann (1889–1966) also claims in his *Golah ve-Nekhar* (*Exile and Alien Lands*, 1929–30) that the ultimate success of Christianity was on account of its "Jewish message" of monotheism taken to the pagan world. For Kaufmann, Christianity and, later, Islam are only successful in that they remove the burden of Jewish history, with its exile and dispersion, in offering the Jewish religious message to the wider Gentile world: ultimately "it is Judaism that conquered the world." David Berger, "Religion, Nationalism, and Historiography: Yehezkel Kaufmann's Account of Jesus and Early Christianity," in *Scholars and Scholarship: The Interaction Between Judaism and Other Cultures*, ed. Leo Landman (New York, 1990), 161.

81. Klausner, *Jesus of Nazareth: His Life, Times, and Teaching*, trans. Herbert Danby (New York, 1925). All cites appear in the text.

82. Berger, "Religion, Nationalism, and Historiography," 157.

83. Cited from *Ha-Toren* [The flagpole] (New York), May 1922, in Herbert Danby, *The Jew and Christianity* (New York, 1927), 103.

84. Danby, *The Jew and Christianity*, 104.

85. Nash, *In Search of Hebraism*, 211.

86. Danby, *The Jew and Christianity*, 96.

87. Ibid., 101.

88. See Montefiore's review of *Jesus of Nazareth* in the *Jewish Guardian* (London), November 13, 1925, cited in Danby, *The Jew and Christianity*, 108.

Chapter 3. Yiddish Modernism and the Landscape of the Cross

1. David Roskies, *Against the Apocalypse: Responses to Catastrophe in Modern Jewish Culture*, (Cambridge, Mass., 1984), 263–64.

2. While both Hebrew and Yiddish writers incorporated Jesus and Christian

imagery, I will be concentrating primarily on Yiddish modernist works in this chapter because of the widespread proliferation of such symbolism within these works. Hebrew writers from this period did not employ these images to such an extent, although there were some notable exceptions. Moreover, some of the writers I discuss here, such as Uri Tsvi Grinberg, wrote in both Yiddish and Hebrew, and poems of his in both languages are rife with Christ-figures and Christological motifs. See Hamutal Bar-Yosef, *Jewish-Christian Relations in Modern Hebrew and Yiddish Literature: A Preliminary Sketch* (Cambridge, UK, 2000), and Nahum M. Waldman, "Glimpses of Jesus in Yiddish and Hebrew Literature," in *Jewish Book Annual* 50 (1992–93): 223–39, for a fuller treatment of the theme of Jesus and Christianity in Hebrew literature.

3. Shmuel Niger, *Dertseylers un romanistn* [Storytellers and novelists] (New York, 1946), 498.

4. Ibid.

5. Shmuel Niger, *Sholem Asch: Zayn lebn un verk* [Sholem Asch: His life and work] (New York, 1960), 281.

6. Sholem Asch, however, though a leading figure of this generation, cannot be classified as truly modernist, and is much better characterized as neo-Romantic.

7. Curt Leviant, introduction to *The Jewish Government and Other Stories,* by Lamed Shapiro (New York, 1971), ix.

8. Ruth Wisse, *A Little Love in Big Manhattan* (Cambridge, Mass., 1988), 112.

9. Seth Wolitz, "Di Khalyastre, The Yiddish Modernist Movement in Poland: An Overview," *Yiddish* 4, no. 3 (1981): 10.

10. Ibid.

11. Ibid., 7.

12. See Shalom Ben-Chorin, "The Image of Jesus in Modern Judaism," *Journal for Ecumenical Studies* 11 (1974): 401–30.

13. See David Biale's essay "Shabbtai Zvi and the Seductions of Jewish Orientalism," *Jerusalem Studies in Jewish Thought*, 2 vols. (Jerusalem, 2000), 1:85–110, for a discussion of modern Jewish treatments of Shabbetai Tzvi, as well as Biale's "Names No Longer Blotted Out: Ambivalent Recuperations of Heretics in Modern Jewish Culture," in *The Margins of Modern Jewish History*, ed. Marc Raphael (Williamsburg, 2000), for an analysis of the larger phenomenon of reclaiming heretics.

14. See Aaron Abraham Kabak, *Ba-mishol ha-tsar* [The narrow path] (Tel Aviv, 1968).

15. Irving Howe, Khone Shmeruk, and Ruth Wisse, eds., *The Penguin Book of Modern Yiddish Verse* (New York, 1987), 488. I am using the Yiddish-derived spelling of the poet's name—Grinberg—rather than the more common Greenberg.

16. Uri Tsvi Grinberg, *Gezamelte verk* [Collected works], 2 vols. (Jerusalem, 1979), 2:514–16.

17. Ben Siegel, *The Controversial Sholem Asch* (Bowling Green, 1976), 30.

18. Cited in Itzik Turkov-Grodberg, *Sholem Asch's derekh in der yidisher eybikayt* [Sholem Asch's path in Yiddish eternity] (Bat Yam, 1967), 115.

19. In his discussion of Asch, Turkov-Grodberg mentions several other writers including Goldfaden, Pinsky, and especially Peretz, who incorporated the theme of Jewish martyrdom in their writing; see ibid., 114–15.

20. Eliezer Schweid, "The Justification of Religion in the Crisis of the Holocaust," *Holocaust and Genocide Studies* 3, no. 4 (1988): 403.

21. Alan Mintz, *Hurban: Responses to Catastrophe in Hebrew Literature* (New York, 1984), 6.

22. Ibid.

23. The assertion that Israel was the "suffering servant" referred to in Isaiah 53 was made by Rashi, the leading medieval rabbinic commentator.

24. Siegel, *Sholem Asch*, 8.

25. Ibid., 14. Asch said this in an interview in 1949.

26. Ibid., 41. Asch said this in an interview in 1955.

27. I am relying on the version of this story published in the collection of Asch's work, *Fun shtetl tsu der groyser velt* [From the shtetl to the great world], ed. Shmuel Rozshansky (Buenos Aires, 1972), 216–28; the translations are mine. All citations appear in the text. An English translation of this story appears under the title "The Carnival Legend" in a collection of Asch's short stories, *Children of Abraham* (New York, 1942).

28. Roskies, *Against the Apocalypse*, 265.

29. This image is itself a clear allusion to Jeremiah 31:15, in which Rachel is depicted "weeping for her children."

30. It should be pointed out that several other Yiddish writers also sympathetically depicted the figure of Mary, beginning with Der Nister's story "Miriam" (1907), and including Ber Horovitz's "Di legende fun der madona" ("The Legend of the Madonna," 1923) and Anna Margolins's cycle of seven poems about Mary (1921–25). Asch himself warmly depicted Mary in the third novel of his "Christian trilogy," *Mary* (1949).

31. In the short story "Dak" ("Doc"), included in Shapiro's 1931 collection *Nyu Yorkish un andere zakhen* ["New-Yorkish" and other stories] (New York, 1931), the protagonist, Izzi Fishler, laments the state of American Yiddish writers, including Shapiro himself, saying: "Lamed Shapiro lives off of the merit of his old story, 'The Cross,' which has always been a false, bombastic work, written in a falsetto" (179). Toward the end of his life, Shapiro even conceded about his famed story that his use of the cross as its central symbol was "forced and contrived" (Lamed Shapiro, *Der shrayber geyt in kheyder* [The writer goes to school] [Los Angeles, 1945], 26).

32. Avraham Nowersztern, "Di pogrom tematik in di verk fun Lamed Shapiro" [The pogrom theme in the work of Lamed Shapiro], *Di goldene keyt* 106 (1981): 128.

33. In the same year that he wrote "The Cross" (1909) Shapiro published a short idyllic sketch entitled "Children" whose epigraph is a passage from the New Testament: "Whoever is as small as a child, he is the greatest in the kingdom of heaven" (Shapiro, "Kinder," in *Ksuvim* [Writings] [Los Angeles, 1949], 85–88.) It seems that Shapiro paraphrased Jesus' saying (Matthew 18:4), as the Yiddish varies slightly from the standard New Testament translation. Nonetheless, for our purposes it further establishes that Shapiro felt free to incorporate Christian themes and motifs in some of his early writings.

34. Nowersztern, "Di pogrom tematik," 127.

35. Ibid., 125.

36. Roskies, *Against the Apocalypse*, 148.

37. Lamed Shapiro, "Der tseylem," in *Di yidishe melukhe un andere zakhen* (New York, 1929), 149–50. All translations from the Yiddish are mine; subsequent cites appear in the text. An English translation appears as "The Cross" in Lamed Shapiro, *The Jewish Government and Other Stories*, ed. Curt Leviant (New York, 1971), 114–30.

38. Nowersztern, "Di pogrom tematik," 132.

39. Roskies, *Against the Apocalypse*, 149.

40. Shmuel Niger, "Moderne mytos" [Modern myth], in his *Lezer, dikhter, kritiker* [Readers, writers, critics] (New York, 1928), 206.

41. Ibid., 207.

42. Ibid., 209.

43. See Malcolm Bradbury and James McFarlane, eds., *Modernism 1880–1930* (New York, 1976), 11–55.

44. Benjamin Harshav, "The Role of Language in Modern Art: On Texts and Subtexts in Chagall's Paintings" *Modernism/Modernity* 1, no. 2 (April 1994): 52; see also Harshav, *Language in Time of Revolution* (Berkeley, 1993), pt. 1.

45. Harshav, "The Role of Language in Modern Art," 66.

46. Benjamin Harshav, *The Meaning of Yiddish* (Berkeley, 1990), 146. Seth Wolitz also describes this phenomenon in an article on Yiddish modernism in Kiev immediately after World War I: "'Modernism' for Yiddish literature meant not only the incorporation of the 'advanced' sectors of contemporary European art and thought but the 'catching-up,' the inclusion of all the newly embraced accomplishments of Western culture. The discovery of the sentient individual, the romantic vision of self and nature, and even neo-classicism, all tumbled pell-mell into the Yiddish notion of 'Modernism.'" Seth Wolitz, "The Kiev-Grupe (1918–1920) Debate: The Function of Literature," *Yiddish* 3, no. 3 (1978): 101.

47. See Wolitz, "Di Khalyastre." See also Harshav's grouping of the major trends of modernist Yiddish poetry in America, *The Meaning of Yiddish*, 169–74.

48. Seth Wolitz, "Between Folk and Freedom: The Failure of the Yiddish Modernist Movement in Poland," *Yiddish* 8, no. 1 (1991): 30.

49. Bradbury and McFarlane, *Modernism 1880–1930*, 279.

50. Chana Kronfeld, *On the Margins of Modernism* (Berkeley, 1996), 179.

51. Max Erik, "Di shprakh funem yidishn ekspresyonizm" [The language of Yiddish expressionism], *Albatros* 2 (November 1922): 17.

52. Wolitz, "Di Khalyastre," 14; Markish's essay appears in the journal *Ringen* [Rings] 10 (1922).

53. Wolitz, "Di Khalyastre," 5. Markish chose this motto for the journal he edited—*Khalyastre*—which, like *Albatros*, first appeared in Warsaw in 1922.

54. Uri Tsvi Grinberg, "Proklamirung" [Proclamation], *Albatros* 1 (1922): 3, reprinted in Grinberg's *Gezamelte verk*, 2:421; all translations from the Yiddish are mine. See also David Roskies' translation of Grinberg's Proclamation in *Prooftexts* 15 (1995): 109–12.

55. Grinberg, "Proklamirung," 3.

56. Ibid., 422. It is important to note here that the Yiddish word *tseylem* stems from the Hebrew *tselem,* connoting "image," as in *tselem elohim* ("image of God"), as well as "idol." In Yiddish the word exclusively refers to the cross, in the pejorative sense, as a graven, idolatrous image, and does not have the same double meaning as the word "cross" in English with its geometric connotation of two lines intersecting. In Yiddish then, the word "crossroad" is not normally *tseylem-veg* as in Grinberg's proclamation, but *sheydveg.* So when Grinberg employs the term *tseylem-veg,* as he does quite often, he is creating a neologism, which actually conveys "path of the cross" in addition to "crossroads."

57. Ibid.

58. Ibid.

59. Ibid., 422–23.

60. A. Tilo Alt, "Ambivalence toward Modernism: The Yiddish Avant-Garde and Its Manifestoes," *Yiddish* 8, no. 1 (1991): 58.

61. Ravitsh had published a book of poems—*Nakete lider* [Naked songs] (Vienna, 1921)—which introduced his concept of "naked poetry."

62. Melekh Ravitsh, "Di naye, di nakete dikhtung: zibn tezisen" [The new, the naked poetry: Seven theses], *Albatros* 1 (1922): 15.

63. Ibid., 16.

64. Ibid.

65. Max Erik, "A briv tsu Uri Tsvi Grinberg" [A letter to Uri Tsvi Grinberg], *Albatros* 3–4 (1923): 5.

66. Wolitz, "Di Khalyastre," 10.

67. Grinberg, "Royte epel fun vey-beymer" [Red apples from pain trees], *Gezamelte verk* 2:437; the poem first appeared under the pseudonym Mustafa Zahib in *Albatros* 2 (1922): 8–12.

68. Chaim Nachman Bialik established this convention in modern Jewish literature in an early Yiddish poem, "Dos letzte vort" ("The Last Word," 1901), which opens with the speaker exclaiming "I have been sent to you by God" and goes on to unfold a calamitous vision of the end of the world: first published in *Der Yid* 3,

nos. 47–48 (December 1901): 6–10. See Avraham Nowersztern's discussion of this poem in his article "Tsvishn morgenzun un achris-hayomim: Tsu der apokaliptisher tematik in der yidisher literatur" [Between morning sun and the end of days: On the apocalyptic theme in Yiddish literature], *Di goldene keyt* 135 (1993): 112–16.

69. Melekh Ravitsh, *Dos mayse bukh fun mayn lebn* [The story of my life], vol. 2 (Tel Aviv, 1975), 90.

70. See ibid.

71. The fact that these Yiddish poets—typically born and educated in the shtetl—often drew motifs and images from the New Testament's Book of Revelation underscores the cultural cosmopolitanism of the modernist movement.

72. Eli Lederhendler, "Messianic Rhetoric in the Russian Haskalah and Early Zionism," in *Jews and Messianism in the Modern Era*, ed. Jonathan Frankel (New York, 1991), 17.

73. Ibid.

74. Ibid., 30.

75. Yisrael Chaim Pomerantz, *Moshiach-motiven in der amerikaner-yidisher poezia* [Messianic motifs in American-Yiddish poetry] (Haifa, 1966), 151–52.

76. In his poem "Di legende funm hoyve" ("The Legend of the Present," 1918), Grinberg explores this messianic theme for possibly the first time in his work. In the poem, Grinberg emphasizes the suffering nature of the Messiah, who is chained to the gates of Rome, describing him as a "wonderful tragic figure" with blood dripping from his wounds, and portraying the anguish he feels as he helplessly watches the world exist in its current state and is unable to usher in redemption. See Grinberg, *Gezamelte verk,* 1:189.

77. Menachem Boraisha and Moyshe Leyb Halpern, eds., *East Broadway: Zamlbukh* [East Broadway: A collection] (New York, 1916).

78. M. L. Halpern, *In Nu York* (New York, 1919), 74–77. Subsequent cites appear in the text.

79. Kronfeld, *On the Margins of Modernism,* 166.

80. Avraham Nowersztern, "Es veln di erd un di himel fargeyn: Vegen Moyshe Leyb Halpern's poema 'A nakht'" [Heaven and earth will pass away: On Moyshe Leyb Halpern's *poema* "A Nakht"], *Di goldene keyt* 138 (1994): 101–2.

81. See Nowersztern, "Es veln di erd un di himel fargeyn," 104, 117.

82. This passage bears a striking resemblance to the Polish Jewish artist Samuel Hirszenberg's painting *The Wandering Jew* (1899), which was widely known to European Jews in the first decade of the twentieth century, while Halpern was still living in Galicia. In the painting, a dazed, bearded older Jew, wearing nothing but a loincloth, is running wildly out of a forest divided by two rows of huge crosses, with dozens of Jewish corpses at his feet. See Richard Cohen, *Jewish Icons* (Berkeley, 1998), 217, 223–27.

83. Nowersztern, "Es veln di erd un di himel fargeyn," 118.

84. Grinberg, *Gezamelte verk,* 1:304.

85. Ibid., 304.

86. Ibid.

87. Ibid., 305.

88. Ibid.

89. Arthur Tilo Alt, "A Survey of Literary Contributions to the Post–World War I Yiddish Journals of Berlin," *Yiddish* 7, no. 1 (1987): 45.

90. Zalman Reisen, *Der leksikon fun der nayer yidisher literatur* [Lexicon of modern Yiddish literature] (Vilna, 1928), 644.

91. Grinberg, *Gezamelte verk*, 2:329. The poem invokes many of the world's religions besides Judaism and Christianity, including Islam, Buddhism, and Hinduism, as part of the cosmic portrait of the struggle of the spirit against the forces of darkness.

92. This refers to biblical passages (Leviticus 26, Deuteronomy 28) that detail God's punishment for Israel if they do not follow the commandments.

93. Grinberg, *Gezamelte verk*, 2:340. Subsequent cites appear in the text.

94. A similar image appears in Peretz Markish's epic poem published that same year, "Di kupe" ("The Heap," 1921), which he wrote in the wake of the Ukrainian pogroms of 1919–21.

95. See also Peretz Markish's *poema* "Veyland" [Woeland], *Albatros* 1 (1922): 7, which shares many of the same motifs as Grinberg's "Mephisto" and "Velt barg arop," including numerous allusions to Jesus and Christian symbolism in the context of the decline of European civilization.

96. Grinberg, *Gezamelte verk*, 2:438.

97. Yeshu was and is the most common name used for Jesus in Hebrew and Yiddish, and is basically a neutral term, unlike the more derisive Yoyzl, while Yezus is the European-Christian name Yiddish authors sometimes used in referring to Jesus. Therefore the choice of name in depicting Jesus often carries with it meaningful connotations.

98. The Polish censors banned this issue of *Albatros* (November 1922), which they deemed blasphemous, forcing Grinberg to relocate to Berlin, where he put out the last two volumes of the journal. Grinberg's poem "Uri Tsvi farn tseylem," typeset in the shape of a cross, was chiefly responsible for this decision.

99. This is a phrase used by the Hebrew prophets, e.g., Isaiah 2:2, Jeremiah 49:39, and Micah 4:1, as part of their prophecy of the end of days.

100. *Albatros* 2 (1922): 4. The full version of Horovitz's *poema* appears in his collection of poems: Ber Horovitz, *Reyakh fun erd* [Aroma of the earth] (Vilna, 1930).

101. There are many more works of Yiddish modernist poetry and prose from this period containing similar uses of Jesus-figures and Christian imagery; see, for example: Hey Leyvik's "Der goylem" [The golem] (1917–20) in *Ale verk* [Complete works], 2 vols., (New York, 1940), vol. 2; and Moyshe Kulbak's *Moshiach ben efraim* [The Messiah of the house of Ephraim] (Berlin, 1924), which also touch on many of these themes, and include Jesus-figures and abundant Christological

symbolism with apocalyptic and messianic themes.

102. Quoted in Theodore Ziolkowski, *Fictional Transfigurations of Jesus* (Princeton, 1972), 27.

103. Leyvik, *Ale verk*, 1:32.

104. Charles Madison, *Yiddish Literature: Its Scope and Major Writers* (New York, 1968), 360.

105. The poem originally appeared in the Communist Yiddish paper *Frayhayt* [Freedom] (January 23, 1927) and was reprinted in Halpern's posthumous collection of poetry, *Moyshe Leyb Halpern* (New York, 1934), 92–94. One of Halpern's contemporaries, the Introspectivist poet A. Leyeles, wrote a poem entitled "Gott's harts" (God's Heart, 1922), in which the poetic speaker visits St. Patrick's Cathedral and laments the pain of "God's wounded, red heart" as he gazes at the figure of Jesus on the wall of the church. Leyeles depicts Jesus weeping on his cross, with the tears streaming down onto his red heart. A. Glants-Leyeles, *Lider, poemas, drames* [Songs, long poems, dramas] (New York, 1968), 16–18.

106. Wisse, *A Little Love*, 93–94.

107. The title of the poem is a play on the traditional Jewish aversion to mentioning Jesus' name; in rabbinic Hebrew he was often referred to as *oto ha-ish* ("that man"), loosely rendered here in Yiddish as *er*.

108. Leyvik, *Ale verk*, 1:156.

109. Ibid., 152–55.

110. Itzik Manger, *Shtern afn dakh* (Bucharest, 1929), 15–16.

111. Ibid., 17.

112. Janet Hadda, "Christian Imagery and Dramatic Impulse in the Poetry of Itzik Manger," *Michigan Germanic Studies* 3, no. 2 (1977): 3.

113. Interestingly, the poem Manger cites as illustrative of this new trend is Leyvik's "Er."

114. Manger, "Driter briv tsu X. Y." [Third letter to X. Y.], *Getseylte verter* 1, no. 4 (September 1929): 1.

115. See: Grinberg, *Gezamelte verk*, 1:67, 72, 91, 102, 174.

116. Manger, "Pascha-Nakht," in *Kultur: A zhurnal far literatur, kunst, un pedagogik* [Culture: Journal of literature, art, and pedagogy] (Czernowitz, 1921): 34.

117. Rikudah Potash, *Vint af klavishn* [Wind on piano keys] (Lodz, 1934), 20. Thanks to Yael Chaver for calling my attention to this poem.

118. Manger, "Ershter briv tsu X. Y." [First letter to X. Y.], *Getseylte verter* 1, no. 1 (August 1929): 2. It is interesting to note that in the last paragraph of this essay Manger makes an oblique reference to the *Khalyastre* poets when he states that "the blaspheming gang [*lesterer Khalyastre*] . . . with its historical jumble of images has passed away. The next chapter is open." He implies that the *Khalyastre* poets' time has passed and that he and his generation must step in and claim their mantle.

119. Manger, "In memoriam: Hugo von Hofmannsthal," *Getseylte verter* 1, no. 2 (August, 1929): 1.

120. Manger, *Shtern afn dakh*, 61.
121. Hadda, "Christian Imagery and Dramatic Impulse," 2.
122. Manger, *Shtern afn dakh*, 107.
123. Ibid., 68–69.
124. Ibid., 69.

Chapter 4. The Passion of Jewish History

1. Joseph Bonsirven, *Les juifs et Jésus—Attitudes nouvelles* (Paris, 1937).
2. Ibid., 170–72, quoted in Ziva Amishai-Maisels, *Depiction and Interpretation: The Influence of the Holocaust on the Visual Arts* (Oxford, 1993), 183.
3. Bonsirven, *Les juifs et Jésus*, 199, quoted in Amishai-Maisels, *Depiction and Interpretation*, 183.
4. Francois Mauriac, foreword to Eli Wiesel, *Night* (New York, 1960), x.
5. Franklin Littell, *The Crucifixion of the Jews* (New York, 1975), 6.
6. Ibid., 16. This allusion to the suffering servant of Isaiah 53 picks up on a thread of Jewish theology that understands the Jews as a whole to embody the suffering servant as opposed to the Christian interpretation of Isaiah 53 as referring to Jesus.
7. Ibid., 131.
8. See above, chap. 1 n. 39.
9. See above, chap. 1 n. 108.
10. Glenda Abramson, "The Reinterpretation of the Akedah in Modern Hebrew Poetry," *Journal of Jewish Studies* 4, no. 1 (1990): 103; see also Alan Mintz, *Hurban: Responses to Catastrophe in Hebrew Literature* (New York, 1984), 90ff.
11. See Shalom Spiegel, *The Last Trial* (New York, 1967).
12. Abramson, "The Reinterpretation of the Akedah," 112.
13. See Amishai-Maisels, *Depiction and Interpretation*, 167–72. She discusses Holocaust-related works by Chagall, Mordechai Ardon, Pinchas Burstein (alias Maryan), Leonard Baskin, and others that utilize the Akedah motif.
14. Emma Lazarus, *Poems of Emma Lazarus*, 2 vols. (New York, 1899), 2:58.
15. Ibid., 9.
16. Ibid., 3.
17. Shira Wolosky, "An American Jewish Typology: Emma Lazarus and the Figure of Christ," *Prooftexts* 16, no. 2 (May 1996): 119.
18. Lazarus, *Poems*, 2:120.
19. See Ziva Amishai-Maisels, "The Origins of the Jewish Jesus," in *Complex Identities: Jewish Consciousness and Modern Art*, ed. Matthew Baigell and Milly Heyd (New Brunswick, 2001), 71ff.
20. Ibid.
21. Ibid., 71–72.
22. For a thorough treatment of the Wandering Jew legend in European folk-

lore see Galit Hasan-Rokem and Alan Dundes, eds., *The Wandering Jew: Essays in the Interpretation of a Christian Legend* (Bloomington, 1986).

23. See George Anderson, *The Legend of the Wandering Jew* (Providence, 1965).

24. See, for example, Manger's poem "Ahasver" in *Shtern afn dakh* [Stars on the roof] (Bucharest, 1929), 152. In this poem the cross embodies the endless exile of Ahasver, the Wandering Jew.

25. See Amishai-Maisels, *Depiction and Interpretation*, 19–25. Amishai-Maisels particularly focuses on Chagall's obsession with this image, calling him the "originator" of the modern version of the Wandering Jew, who is depicted in countless Chagall paintings as an elderly Jew with a sack on his back. See also Samuel Hirszenberg's painting *The Wandering Jew* (1899), chap. 3 n. 82.

26. Moyshe Leyb Halpern and Moyshe Nadir, *Unter der last fun tseylem* [Under the burden of the cross] (1920), 29. The play was never published, and the only copy—as far as I know—is a 139-page typed manuscript with handwritten corrections in the margins, located in the uncatalogued Moyshe Nadir papers at the National and Hebrew University Archive in Jerusalem.

27. See Arthur Tilo Alt, "A Survey of Literary Contributions to the Post–World War I Yiddish Journals of Berlin," *Yiddish* 7, no. 1 (1987): 42–52, for an overview of Yiddish modernism in Berlin in the 1920s.

28. Jonathan Skolnik remarks that in the period from 1750 to 1850, "Ahasuerus appears in many works as a chronicler, a narrator of history"; "Writing Jewish History between Gutzkow and Goethe: Auerbach's Spinoza and the Birth of Modern Jewish Historical Fiction," *Prooftexts* 19, no. 2 (May 1999): 102. See also Anderson, *The Legend of the Wandering Jew*, 141–60.

29. Zalman Shneour, "Di verter fun Don Henriquez," in *Fertsik yor lider un poemen* [Forty years of songs and poems] (New York, 1945), 277. Subsequent cites appear in the text. I am relying on the Yiddish version of the poem because it contains additional passages not in the original Hebrew that are thematically relevant to our discussion. I have examined both the Hebrew and Yiddish closely, as well as translations of both, finding out surprisingly that the translation from the Yiddish appears to follow the Hebrew version more closely, not including the verses that were added in the longer Yiddish version.

30. See Yosef Haim Yerushalmi, *From Spanish Court to Italian Ghetto: Isaac Cardoso: A Study in Seventeenth-Century Marranism and Jewish Apologetics* (New York, 1971). In this, as well as in other works of his treating the theme of Marranos, Yerushalmi posited that Marranos could be seen as prototypical of modern Jewish identity.

31. Cited in Amishai-Maisels, *Depiction and Interpretation*, 182. It should be pointed out that Fleg's book was published in Paris only two years after the Yiddish version of Shneour's poem.

32. Emil Hirsch, *My Religion* (New York, 1925), 46. This essay is published in a posthumous collection without a date, but based on the reference Hirsch makes to

Jews dying in Ukraine, Poland, and Hungary it seems likely that the essay was written sometime between the years 1919 and 1921. During this period pogroms claimed thousands of Jewish lives in Ukraine, and riots and acts of violence against the Jews in Hungary—"The White Terror"—claimed about three thousand lives. If this is the case, then Hirsch and Shneour were writing in response to the same historical events even though they were almost certainly not aware of each other's work.

33. Noah Rosenbloom, "Ha-antitetyot ha-teologit-ha-historit she'ba-notsrut ba-shirat Uri Tsvi Grinberg" [Theological-historical conflicts with Christianity in Uri Zvi Greenberg's poetry], *Perakim* 4 (1966): 280.

34. Uri Tsvi Grinberg, *Gezamelte verk*, vol. 2 (Jerusalem, 1979), 431.

35. Ibid.

36. Ibid., 433.

37. Ibid.

38. Leyb Kvitko, *1919* (Berlin, 1923), 116–17.

39. Amishai-Maisels, *Depiction and Interpretation*, 179.

40. Wachtel (1892–1971) lived in Vienna, and Kvitko in Berlin during these years, which makes it possible that Kvitko might have been familiar with Wachtel's painting.

41. Kvitko, *1919*, 117.

42. Ibid., 118.

43. Berel Lang, *Writing and the Holocaust* (New York, 1988), 179.

44. Hilda Schiff, *Holocaust Poetry* (New York, 1995), xxi.

45. David Roskies, *Against the Apocalypse: Responses to Catastrophe in Modern Jewish Culture* (Cambridge, Mass., 1984), 273. See also Janet Hadda, "Christian Imagery and Dramatic Impulse in the Poetry of Itzik Manger," *Michigan Germanic Studies* 3, no. 2 (1977): 8–9, for a discussion of Manger's omission of Christian images from his later works.

46. See Goldie Morgentaler, "The Foreskin of the Heart: Ecumenism in Sholem Asch's Christian Trilogy," *Prooftexts* 8 (1988): 219–44.

47. Maurice Samuel's English translation of Asch's Yiddish novel—*Der man fun Notseres*—was published before the Yiddish original because Asch's usual publishers—the *Forverts*—refused to serialize the Yiddish version, which was not published until 1943.

48. See Hannah Berliner Fischtal's Ph.D. dissertation, "Sholem Asch and the Shift in His Reputation: *The Nazarene* as Culprit or Victim?" (City University of New York, 1994), for a detailed analysis of *The Nazarene*. See also her forthcoming book on Sholem Asch.

49. It should also be mentioned that much of the objection to Asch's novel had to do with personal conflicts between Asch and leading figures in the Yiddish press, especially the editor of the *Forverts*, Abe Cahan. See Fischtal, "Sholem Asch and the Shift in His Reputation," 89–120.

50. Cited in Hannah Berliner Fischtal, "Reactions of the Yiddish Press to *The*

Nazarene by Sholem Asch," in *Sholem Asch Reconsidered*, ed. Nanette Stahl (New Haven, 2004), 269ff. See also Anita Norich, "Sholem Asch and the Christian Question," ibid., 251–65, for a trenchant discussion of the reaction to Asch's Christian novels in the Yiddish press.

51. Fischtal, "Reactions of the Yiddish Press," 270–71.

52. Besides becoming one of Asch's most bitter detractors after the publication of *The Nazarene*, Lieberman was at the time a frequent polemicist against radical secularists in the Yiddish intellectual community, especially Zhitlovsky, who also became the subject of Lieberman's blistering attacks. See Chaim Lieberman, *Sheydim in Moskve* [Devils in Moscow] (New York, 1937); *Yidn un yidishkayt in di shriftn fun dr. Chaim Zhitlovsky* [Jews and Jewishness in the writings of Dr. Chaim Zhitlovsky] (Washington D. C., 1944); and *Dr. Chaim Zhitlovsky un zayne fartaydiker* [Dr. Chaim Zhitlovsky and his defenders] (New York, 1944).

53. Fischtal, "Reactions of the Yiddish Press," 269.

54. Ibid.

55. Ibid., 269–70.

56. Melekh Ravitsh, *Eseyin* [Essays] (Jerusalem, 1992), 123–24.

57. Shmuel Niger, *Sholem Asch: Zayn lebn un verk* [Sholem Asch: His life and work] (New York, 1960), 275.

58. Ibid., 276.

59. *Fraye arbeter shtime* [Free voice of labor], the anarchist weekly, January 5, 1940, 3.

60. Ibid., 6.

61. See Norich, "Sholem Asch and the Christian Question."

62. The story was initially published in Yiddish and English in 1943 before it appeared in book form in Asch's *Der brenendiker dorn* [The burning bush] (New York, 1946), 53–73. All cites appear in the text, and are to the anthology *Fun shtetl tsu der groyser velt* [From the shtetl to the great world] (Buenos Aires, 1972), 229–48.

63. Asch and other Yiddish writers such as Markish and Leyvik, along with Chagall, were some of the first artists, Jewish or otherwise, to address the Holocaust experience in their work.

64. As early as 1938, Marc Chagall began to paint Jesus-figures with distinctive Jewish features amid tableaux of Jewish suffering, as well as portraying stereotypical shtetl Jews being crucified, e.g., *White Crucifixion* (1938), *The Martyr* (1940), and *The Crucified* (1944), all of which will be discussed in the following chapter.

65. Sholem Asch, *One Destiny: An Epistle to the Christians* (New York, 1945), 23.

66. Ibid., 26.

67. See, for example, Markish's *poema* "Veyland" [Woeland], *Albatros* 1 (1922).

68. Nakhman Mayzel, introduction to Peretz Markish, *Milkhome*, vol. 1 (New York, 1956), 5.

69. Markish, *Milkhome*, 1:112. The contemporary Jewish scholar Byron Sherwin, who experienced World War II as a young boy in Poland, envisions Jesus as

being a Gur Aryeh–type figure; in an article outlining his own theological conception of Jesus, Sherwin states: "I picture Jesus as a tortured, wandering, wounded Polish Jew crawling in pain into the doorway of a Polish Catholic home during the Nazi occupation and asking for refuge." Byron Sherwin, "Who Do You Say that I Am?: A New Jewish View of Jesus," *Journal of Ecumenical Studies* 31, nos. 3–4 (1994): 267.

70. Quotations from Markish, *Milkhome*, 1:112.

71. Ibid., 113.

72. Ibid.

73. Ibid.

Chapter 5. The Artist Crucified

1. Ziva Amishai-Maisels, "Chagall's *Dedicated to Christ*: Sources and Meanings," *Journal of Jewish Art* 21–22 (1995–96): 72–73.

2. Ibid., 74.

3. Chagall also expressed such a personal identification with the figure of Jesus in some of his Russian poetry from those same years. In a poem from his 1909–10 collection, Chagall speaks of his intimate relationship with Jesus: "I am his high pupil / [Hanging] in tandem, we are lonely / Forever. / From the morning I was assigned / My early destiny on the Cross." Cited in Benjamin Harshav, *Marc Chagall and His Times* (Stanford, 2004), 191–92.

4. Vitebsk was also the birthplace of Ansky and Zhitlovsky, who were both a generation older than Chagall.

5. Avram Kampf, *Chagall to Kitaj: Jewish Experience in 20th Century Art* (New York, 1990), 21.

6. Chagall himself collaborated frequently with leading Yiddish modernists—especially in Russia in the early 1920s, but also throughout later stages of his career—often contributing illustrations to Yiddish periodicals and books.

7. Seth Wolitz, "Between Folk and Freedom: The Failure of the Yiddish Modernist Movement in Poland," *Yiddish* 8, no. 1 (1991): 31.

8. Ibid., 32.

9. Kampf, *Chagall to Kitaj*, 13.

10. Ibid.

11. Ibid., 12.

12. Letter to Alfred Barr, 11 October 1949, quoted in Amishai-Maisels, "Chagall's *Dedicated to Christ*," 77.

13. The question of pictorial representation by Jews is a complicated one, and beyond the scope of this book. For in-depth treatments of the visual arts and Jewish culture see the following: Kalman Bland, *The Artless Jew: Medieval and Modern Affirmations and Denials of the Visual* (Princeton, 2000), Richard I. Cohen, *Jewish Icons: Art and Society in Modern Europe* (Berkeley, 1998), Ezra Mendelsohn, ed.,

Art and Its Uses: The Visual Image and Modern Jewish Society (New York, 1990), and Ruth Apter-Gabriel, ed., *Tradition and Revolution: The Jewish Renaissance in Russian Avant-Garde Art, 1912–1928* (Jerusalem, 1988).

14. There were, of course, exceptions to this, such as Marc Chagall himself, who studied art as a young man in the school of the Jewish artist Yehuda Pen.

15. Gabrielle Sed-Rajna, *Jewish Art* (Paris, 1997), 326.

16. Antokolsky was considered a pioneering Jewish artist by his younger contemporaries and was a source of inspiration and influence for many later Russian Jewish artists, including Chagall.

17. These biographical details are taken from Hillel Kazovsky, "Jewish Artists in Russia at the Turn of the Century," *Journal of Jewish Art* 21–22 (1995–96): 20–39.

18. Ibid., 21.

19. See Ziva Amishai-Maisels, "The Jewish Jesus," *Journal of Jewish Art* 9 (1982): 85–104.

20. Ibid., 93–94. He based much of his depiction on contemporaneous historical writings such as Heinrich Graetz's *History of the Jews*, which also envisioned Jesus in first-century Palestinian Jewish garb.

21. Ibid., 94.

22. Ibid. These are Antokolsky's own words.

23. Norman Kleeblatt, "Master Narratives/Minority Artists," in *Complex Identities: Jewish Consciousness and Modern Art*, ed. Matthew Baigell and Milly Heyd (New Brunswick, 2001), 2.

24. See above, Introduction n. 9.

25. For a more in-depth discussion of Gottlieb and his Jesus paintings see Ezra Mendelsohn, "Amanut ve-ha-historiyah yahudit: 'Yeshu doresh Ba-kfar Nahum' le-Moritsy Gotlib" [Art and Jewish history: Maurycy Gottlieb's *Christ Preaching at Capernaum*], *Zion* 2 (1997): 173–91.

26. Amishai-Maisels, "The Jewish Jesus," 97.

27. Ibid., 98.

28. A contemporary of Gottlieb's, the German Jewish Impressionist painter Max Liebermann (1847–1935), elicited controversy among his non-Jewish critics with his *Twelve-Year-Old Jesus in the Temple* (1878–79), in which he depicts the young Jesus, as well as his audience, as markedly Jewish. See Amishai-Maisels, "The Jewish Jesus," 98, and Sed-Rajna, *Jewish Art*, 331.

29. See Ziva Amishai-Maisels, "The Origins of the Jewish Jesus," in Baigell and Heyd, *Complex Identities*, 52.

30. Ibid., 73.

31. See ibid., 73–75.

32. Ibid., 75. *Ost und West* was a German Jewish monthly, which first appeared in Berlin in 1901.

33. Ezekial's sculpture from 1903 shares many of the same themes as Israel Davidson's poem "Eli, Eli, Lama Sabachtani?" (discussed in the previous chapter),

from the same year; both bring together Jesus and the Wandering Jew and shift the Christological focus from Jesus to the Wandering Jew, or Israel.

34. David Roskies, *Against the Apocalypse: Responses to Catastrophe in Modern Jewish Culture* (Cambridge, Mass., 1984), 280–81.

35. For a more in-depth discussion of Lilien's work, especially his cultural eclecticism, see Milly Heyd, "Lilien and Beardsley: 'To the Pure All Things Are Pure,'" *Journal of Jewish Art* 7 (1980): 58–69.

36. Susan Compton, *Chagall* (New York, 1985), 19.

37. Seth Wolitz, "The Kiev-Grupe (1918–1920) Debate: The Function of Literature," *Yiddish* 3, no. 3 (1978): 103.

38. Ibid.

39. See Seth Wolitz, "Chagall's Last Soviet Performance: The Graphics for *Troyer*, 1922," *Journal of Jewish Art* 21–22 (1995–96): 95–115, for a discussion of Chagall's collaboration with the Yiddish poet Dovid Hofshteyn, on the Yiddish art book *Troyer* [Sorrow]. Wolitz sees Chagall's graphics for the book as "fusing Yiddish particularism in theme and image with modernist techniques he was continuously absorbing" (96). Moreover, Hofshteyn incorporated Christological motifs into much of his poetry, including poems in that collection.

40. Ingo F. Walther and Rainer Metzger, *Marc Chagall: Painting as Poetry* (Cologne, 1987), 73–74. Chagall painted two versions of *Falling Angel* (1923 and 1933) without any Christian motifs; he then updated it in a sketch of 1934 with the addition of two small crosses, before completing the final version in 1947 with additional Christian images included. See Amishai-Maisels, *Depiction and Interpretation: The Influence of the Holocaust on the Visual Arts* (Oxford, 1993), figs. 61–62.

41. Walther and Metzger, *Marc Chagall*, 74.

42. Franz Meyer, *Marc Chagall: Life and Work* (New York, 1963), 135.

43. See Mark Duris, "The Crucifixion of Christ in Marc Chagall's Art and Life" (M.A. thesis, Trinity Evangelical Divinity School, Deerfield, Ill., 1977), 38.

44. January 22, 1977, interview in the Paris Yiddish daily, *Unzer vort* [Our word], quoted in Amishai-Maisels, "Chagall's *Dedicated to Christ*," 79.

45. S. L. Schneiderman, "Chagall Torn?" *Midstream* 23, no. 6 (1977): 52–53.

46. Amishai-Maisels, "The Jewish Jesus," 100.

47. Sidney Alexander, *Marc Chagall: A Biography* (New York, 1978), 476.

48. Charlie Sorlier, ed., *Chagall by Chagall* (New York, 1979), 219.

49. Compton, *Chagall*, 175.

50. Meyer, *Chagall*, 173–74.

51. Benjamin Harshav argues that Chagall's Christ imagery and identification with the Christ figure were influenced directly by the Russian poet Aleksandr Blok, especially his poem "Autumn Love" (October 1907), and he claims that Chagall's *Golgotha* is "almost an illustration of Blok's poem." See Harshav, *Marc Chagall*, 192–93.

52. *Museum of Modern Art Bulletin* (17), cited in Jane Dillenberger, *Secular Art with Sacred Themes* (New York, 1969), 35.

53. Marc Chagall, *My Life* (New York, 1960), 1.

54. Duris, "The Crucifixion of Christ," 37.

55. Chagall's sketch from 1930, *Vision of Christ on the Cross*, in which Jesus is depicted through an open window on his cross, wearing a *tallis* for a loincloth, with a calm, pastoral backdrop, is one exception to this; see Amishai-Maisels, *Depiction and Interpretation*, fig. 393.

56. Marc Chagall, "Mayne trern," in *Di goldene keyt* 60 (1967): 95.

57. Ibid., 96.

58. Meyer, *Chagall*, 435.

59. See the following paintings in the classified catalog in Meyer, *Chagall*: *Mexican Crucifixion* (1943), cc 711; *Resurrection at the River* (1947), cc 780; *Christ Against Blue Sky* (1950), cc 827; and *The Crucifixion* (1950–53), cc 845, to name only a few. This type of Christ-face resembles the Jesus of Byzantine and Orthodox icons, which Chagall would have been familiar with from Russian church art.

60. Titian's *Entombment* of the 1520s, which hangs in the Louvre, may have been the model for the Entombment painting within this painting.

61. Chagall was by no means the first modern artist to depict the artist himself on the cross. For example, the painter James Ensor (1860–1949) identified his artistic self with the figure of Christ from an early point in his career. He painted *Ensor's Crucifixion* in 1886 in which a classical crucifixion scene of Jesus hanging between the two thieves is distinguished by the tablet at the top of his cross reading "ENSOR." The face of the crucified is also Ensor's. In an 1891 painting, *Ecce Homo or Christ and the Critics*, Ensor portrays the artist as Christ, with a crown of thorns on his head, surrounded by two formidable-looking critics wearing black ties, one with a top hat. See Horst Schwebel, *Das Christusbild in der bildenden Kunst der Gegenwart* (Marburg, 1980), 59–67.

62. Meyer, *Chagall*, 438. The descent from the cross was a traditional motif in Christian art, which Rembrandt, for example, depicted in 1651, showing a mourning Nicodemus receiving Jesus at the foot of the cross, with Joseph of Arimathea and several men on the ladder helping to bring down his body. A pale and swooning Mary is in the background, supported by two women at her side.

63. Thanks to Yael Chaver for pointing out this allusion to me. It is especially plausible considering the fact that Chagall linked the figures of Jesus and Isaac in some of his many paintings of the binding of Isaac, such as *Sacrifice of Isaac* (ca. 1960–65), in which the figure of Jesus carrying his cross occupies the upper right corner, while the image of Abraham holding Isaac in one hand and the knife in the other dominates the foreground.

64. Meyer, *Chagall*, 470.

65. Amishai-Maisels, "The Jewish Jesus," 103.

66. These works are: *White Crucifixion* (1938), *White Crucifixion* (second version, 1940), *The Martyr* (1940–41), *The Way to Calvary* (sketches, 1941), *Yellow Christ* (1941), *Descent from the Cross* (1941), *Persecution* (1941), *Crucifixion and Candles* (1941), *Yellow Crucifixion* (1943), *Obsession* (1943), *The Crucified* (1944). See Meyer, *Chagall*, cc 696–702; Chagall also produced five other works from this period that contain the crucifixion motif, albeit in a more personal or general context, see, for example, ibid., cc 711–12.

67. Chagall produced another version of *White Crucifixion* in 1940 in which he further emphasized the Jewishness of Jesus by placing a skullcap on his head and replacing the INRI tablet altogether with the Ten Commandments. See Monica Bohm-Duchen, *Chagall* (London, 1998), 232.

68. Several of Chagall's paintings from this period (1940–43) contain scenes of war and the destruction of the shtetl without including the crucifixion motif; see, for example: *Flames in the Snow, War, The Burning Village, War* (1943), and *Fire*, in Meyer, *Chagall*, cc 690–93, 695. Chagall also produced numerous paintings during the war years with various other themes, including many circus motifs.

69. See Amishai-Maisels, "The Jewish Jesus," 101–2.

70. Compton, *Chagall*, 214.

71. Alfred Werner, "Epstein, Chagall, and the Image of Jesus," *Judaism* 8 (Winter 1959): 47.

72. Interview in *Unzer Vort*, January 22, 1977, quoted in Amishai-Maisels, "The Jewish Jesus," 104.

73. It is interesting to note that Chagall felt the need to distance his own crucifixion works, such as *White Crucifixion*, from Sholem Asch's so-called "Christian" novel, *The Nazarene*. In a letter to his friend, the Yiddish writer Joseph Opatoshu, from April 1940, he refers to his Paris exhibition, "where I exhibited Christ (but, I believe, not such as in Asch's work)." Cited in Harshav, *Marc Chagall*, 479.

74. Sorlier, *Chagall by Chagall*, 219.

75. Jose Maria Faerna, ed., *Chagall* (New York, 1985), 50.

76. Walther and Metzger, *Marc Chagall*, 62.

77. Ibid., 65.

78. H. M. Rotermund concludes that in *Yellow Crucifixion* as well as in other crucifixion scenes of Chagall's from that period, the eschatology expressed is purely "Old Testament Jewish" and not "Christian-oriented redemptive longing"; "Der Gekreuzigte im Werk Chagalls," in *Mouseion: Studien aus Kunst und Geschichte für Otto H. Förster*, ed. Heinz Ladendorf and Horst Vey (Cologne, 1960), 272–73.

79. See Amishai-Maisels, *Depiction and Interpretation*, fig. 376.

80. Isaiah Avrekh, "Funem heft: Di Shagal bletlekh" [From the notebook: The Chagall pages], *Di goldene keyt* 60 (1967): 60.

81. Rotermund, "Der Gekreuzigte im Werk Chagalls," 270.

82. See Amishai-Maisels, "The Jewish Jesus," 86–88, and *Depiction and Interpretation*, 184–94.

83. Amishai-Maisels, *Depiction and Interpretation*, 179–82.

84. See ibid., plates 41–42, figs. 386, 397, 399.

Epilogue. The Jesus Question Revisited

1. Jacob Glatstein, "Good Night, World," in *An Anthology of Modern Yiddish Poetry*, ed. and trans. Ruth Whitman (Detroit, 1994), 36–39. The poem originally appeared in Glatstein's journal, *Inzikh* [Introspection] 8, no. 3 (April 1938): 66–67.

2. Glatstein, "Good Night, World," 39.

3. Jacob Glatstein, "Mozart," in Whitman, *An Anthology of Modern Yiddish Poetry*, 45.

4. Ibid.

5. See Jacob Glatstein, *Prost un poshet* [Plain and simple] (New York, 1978), 145–57.

6. See Ziva Amishai-Maisels, "The Jewish Jesus," *Journal of Jewish Art* 9 (1982): 85–104, and *Depiction and Interpretation: The Influence of the Holocaust on the Visual Arts* (Oxford, 1993).

7. Philip Roth, "The Conversion of the Jews," in *Paris Review*, no. 18 (Spring, 1958), reprinted in Roth's *Goodbye, Columbus* (Boston, 1959).

8. See, for example: Martin Buber, *Two Types of Faith* (London, 1951), Geza Vermes, *Jesus the Jew: An Historian's Reading of the Gospels* (New York, 1973), and Samuel Sandmel, *We Jews and Jesus* (New York, 1973).

9. See Beatrice Bruteau, ed., *Jesus through Jewish Eyes: Rabbis and Scholars Engage an Ancient Brother in a New Conversation* (New York, 2001), for a recent example of this phenomenon.

Index

285